Short-Selling with the O'Neil Disciples

Founded in 1807, John Wiley & Sons is the oldest independent publishing company in the United States. With offices in North America, Europe, Australia and Asia, Wiley is globally committed to developing and marketing print and electronic products and services for our customers' professional and personal knowledge and understanding.

The Wiley Trading series features books by traders who have survived the market's ever changing temperament and have prospered—some by reinventing systems, others by getting back to basics. Whether a novice trader, professional or somewhere in-between, these books will provide the advice and strategies needed to prosper today and well into the future.

For more on this series, visit our web site at www.WileyTrading.com.

SHORT-SELLING WITH THE O'NEIL DISCIPLES

Turn to the Dark Side of Trading

Gil Morales
Chris Kacher

WILEY

Published by John Wiley & Sons, Inc., Hoboken, New Jersey.
Published simultaneously in Canada.

For general information on our other products and services or for technical support, please contact our
Customer Care Department within the United States at (800) 762-2974, outside the United States at
(317) 572-3993 or fax (317) 572-4002.

Wiley publishes in a variety of print and electronic formats and by print-on-demand. Some material included
with standard print versions of this book may not be included in e-books or in print-on-demand. If this book
refers to media such as a CD or DVD that is not included in the version you purchased, you may download this
material at http://booksupport.wiley.com. For more information about Wiley products, visit
www.wiley.com.

Library of Congress Cataloging-in-Publication Data:

Morales, Gil, 1959–
    [How to make money selling stocks short]
    Short-selling with the O'Neil disciples : turn to the dark side of trading / Gil Morales, Dr. Chris Kacher.
        pages cm. – (Wiley trading series)
    Includes index.
    ISBN 978-1-118-97097-3 (paperback)
    1. Short-selling. 2. Stocks. 3. Speculation. I. Kacher, Chris. II. O'Neil, William J. How to make money
selling stocks short. III. Title.
    HG6041.O64 2015
    332.63'228–dc23

                                                                        2014047580

Printed in the United States of America

10 9 8 7 6 5 4 3 2 1

As the old aphorism says, "When life gives you lemons, make lemonade." When the stock market gives you lemons, one should make lemonade by selling short. This book is dedicated to all those who seek to improve and transform themselves by taking the lemons that life throws at them and turning them into lemonade.

CONTENTS

viii

CONTENTS

This book is intended as a follow-up and updated "second edition" of the book I originally ghost-wrote in 2004, *How to Make Money Selling Stocks Short* by William J. O'Neil with Gil Morales (John Wiley & Sons, October 2004). While that book has been a strong seller and does a reasonable job of outlining the basic concepts behind the art of short-selling, it is woefully inadequate in terms of its coverage of the basic mechanics of short-selling at the granular level. In that book, we relied entirely on weekly charts, and while weekly charts most certainly have their purpose in helping to identify the macro-patterns that develop in short-sale candidate stocks, it is on the daily chart that we determine the precise point within a stock's pattern at which to sell it short. Thus, the fact that the 2004 short-selling book did not contain any daily charts meant that it essentially ignored the most important aspects of short-selling. What is radically different about this book is that it relies mostly on daily charts and gives readers a much more detailed and realistic view of just how the short-selling process can play out. This is the essential difference between this book and the last, and one which I believe makes a huge difference in terms of conveying a true sense and understanding of how short-selling works at the point of impact (e.g., the precise point or points at which the short-sale trade can be executed). This can only be seen on the daily chart.

In this book, we update and modify what I see as a fluid, evolving set of short-selling principles rather than a static, dogmatic one. In the process, some of the old short-selling "golden rules" described in both *How to Make Money Selling Stocks Short* and Chapter 6 of the first book that I wrote with my friend and colleague Chris Kacher, *Trade Like an O'Neil Disciple: How We Made 18,000% in the Stock Market* (John Wiley & Sons, 2010), have been exposed as myths. One major myth about short-selling is that one can only short stocks during a bear market. That is simply not true, and the objective material in this book more than blows that premise out of the water. So it is that as I continue to trade on the short side of the market and gain more experience, my objective research and post-analysis of my own short-sale trading as a matter of course reveals more sides to the multifaceted diamond that short-selling, when done right, can be.

One of the major new developments in my work and research on the short side is the use of "fractal" short-selling patterns. My colleague Chris Kacher has frequently brought up the idea of the stock market's technical action as being of a highly fractal nature, with each observable pattern breaking down into and containing within its structure smaller patterns and sub-patterns. I must give credit to Chris in helping to inspire my clarification of what I was seeing on my charts, and his concept of a *fractal market* is shown to be quite valid on the short side. Fractal technicals can be thought of in simple terms by taking a basic cup-with-handle base formation on a weekly chart and then seeing that the handle of this pattern in turn consists of another, smaller or fractal cup-with-handle formation. If we then look at a 60-minute chart of the same pattern, we might notice that the handle of the fractal cup-with-handle in turn consists of an even smaller cup-with-handle formation. This is a basic illustration of what we mean when we talk about fractal chart patterns.

Sometimes, however, the fractal nature of a pattern can also be observed on a single time-frame, such as the example of a smaller head-and-shoulders formation forming within the head of a larger head-and-shoulders formation. In this case, the fractal components can all be seen in one time-frame on the weekly chart. In any case, the use of fractal chart formations can be very useful in helping one exploit a top in a stock long before the large head-and-shoulders formation becomes obvious on the weekly chart. This also underscores why the sole use of weekly charts in short-selling, and in particular in trying to teach short-selling, is highly deficient. This book corrects all of that.

The short-selling model book section in Chapter 10 of this book is also vastly different from the one in the 2004 book. This new model book section shows both weekly and daily charts, and both time-frames are annotated in detail. Each short-selling example also includes relevant notes, as well as space for readers to make their own notes as they engage in more detailed study. I highly recommend HGS Investor Software (www.highgrowthstock.com) as an excellent analytic and charting tool for use in studying the short side of the market. The great advantage of this particular product is that it allows one to easily scroll backward in time and therefore facilitates the study of a stock's historical price/volume action. This particular feature is also useful for studying the historical long side of the market as well.

The final difference between this book and the 2004 short-selling book is that this time around I have the luxury of being backed up by Chris Kacher with respect to the research that went into this book. Because I am the only one between the two of us who actually sells short, I was the only one who could write and produce this book. That is why the book is written in first person by me, while the research backup and editing assistance of Chris Kacher keeps things tight.

Finally, I think the material in this book is not only quite useful for would-be short-sellers, but also for investors and traders who stick to the long side of the market. The truth is that understanding short-selling is also all about understanding how leading stocks top. That sort of understanding not only helps short-sellers make money when "good stocks go bad," but also helps those playing a leading stock on the upside and milking a strong uptrend optimize their long-only process by being able to recognize when their good stock has gone bad and the time to sell has finally arrived. When considering whether this book is right for you, this is an important factor to take into account.

To me, short-selling encompasses all of the common sense methodology and wisdom that runs through the works of William J. O'Neil, Richard D. Wyckoff, and Jesse Livermore, or the OWL, as we refer to them. While the roots of my investment methodologies and philosophy lie in my tenure at William O'Neil + Company, Inc. from 1997–2005 as a vice president, internal portfolio manager, and head of O'Neil's institutional advisory business, my current work as a short-seller (and as a buyer of stocks on the long side) makes me more of an "OWL Disciple" than an O'Neil Disciple. Short-selling is a complicated game to play, and as I already noted, is much like a diamond with many, many facets. Thus it becomes a fascinating process that most certainly contributes to the element of self-discovery that every trader and investor experiences over time as they expand and refine their skills.

As Chris Kacher and I wrote in our first book:

> *Like athletes and thrill-seekers who engage in activities that seem extremely dangerous, almost to the point of the unthinkable, to those who live more normal lives, we as traders seek the "rush" that comes not from a successful trade, but from the experience of being entirely in the present as we operate "in the zone," and a certain fluidity and calmness pervades our actions as we engage the markets in real-time. Ocean wave surfers experience this as the intensity of riding a powerful wave-form that forces them to focus on the matter at hand as a matter of sheer survival. Focusing on the matter at hand forces one to operate entirely in the present—there is no worrying about yesterday's problems, or tomorrow's challenges, there is only the "now."*

Nowhere does this concept hold true more than when one is selling short and doing it well. Given the inherent risk and danger of short-selling, it might be considered the stock market equivalent of big-wave surfing. Certainly, as a trader, there is no greater satisfaction to be had than being "in the zone" on the short side and making big money during a period where the vast majority of investors on the long side of the market are losing their shirts. Good luck!

GIL MORALES
Playa del Rey, California
November 2014

ACKNOWLEDGMENTS

The term "O'Neil Disciple" was first coined by our colleague Kevin Marder, who co-founded MarketWatch.com in the 1990s. In the book *The Best: Conversations with Top Traders* by Marc Dupee and Kevin N. Marder (M. Gordon Publishing Group, September 15, 2000), we are both interviewed in Chapter 1, titled "The Disciples." When we wrote our first book in 2010, the use of the term "disciples" came up as something of an inside joke, and we eventually settled on calling ourselves "The O'Neil Disciples." Ultimately, it is a very succinct and accurate description of what we are. Our methods are steeped in the literature and methods of Jesse Livermore, Richard D. Wyckoff, and William J. O'Neil, and it was O'Neil who was our real-life, real-time mentor back in the days when we worked for his organization as internal portfolio managers. As disciples, we have taken what we have learned from these masters and synthesized it into what we believe are far more concrete and precise methods on both the long and short sides of the market. We teach and discuss these methods in our books, media and tradeshow appearances, and our website, www.virtueofselfishinvesting.com. Thus, we feel that this is the right time to acknowledge the fact that Kevin Marder was the originator of the "disciple" moniker, and we thank him for providing this seed for what we later expanded to The O'Neil Disciples.

We should also acknowledge that this work, as with all our works, was produced without the aid, cooperation, approval, or endorsement of the O'Neil organization.

We gratefully acknowledge the role that our followers and subscribers have played with their questions and feedback in helping us to improve how we teach our methods as disciples of O'Neil, Wyckoff, and Livermore (the OWL). This book is no different in this regard.

We would also like to acknowledge the help and support we have received from HGSI Investment Software, LLC (www.highgrowthstock.com) and its three main principals, George Roberts, Ron Brown, and the Big Kahuna himself, Ian Woodward. HGS Investment Software has become our "weapon of choice" when it comes to an equity analytics, screening, and charting software program, and the product includes many templates, screens, and chart views that are directly based on and related to our work and methods as discussed in our books and on our website. Their enthusiastic support in providing us the full use of their charts throughout our books, including this one, is a welcome endorsement of the validity and effectiveness of our methods and techniques, and for this we are deeply grateful.

Finally, we would like to send a shout-out to the great staff at John Wiley & Sons who helped us with this project: Judy Howarth, Tula Batanchiev, Evan Burton, Kumudhavalli Narasimhan, Darice Moore, and Pamela Van Giessen. When you are working with the top publisher of financial books in the world, not much needs to be said. These individuals set the standard for the rest of the industry!

Dr. Chris Kacher
Gil Morales
Playa del Rey, California
November 2014

CHAPTER 1

Introduction to Short-Selling

Reduced to its mechanics, short-selling is simply the act of identifying a change of trend in a stock from up to down and then seeking to profit from that change of trend as one rides the stock to the downside. To do this, the investor or trader sells the stock in question while not actually owning it, e.g., being "short" the stock, and pockets the proceeds of the sale with the idea of buying the stock back later at a lower price as the downtrend takes hold and extends to the downside. To go short, the seller must first borrow the stock from her broker and may have to pay a very small fee to do so. If and when the stock drops in price, the seller then repurchases the shares, "covering" her short position for less than she sold them, returning the borrowed securities and pocketing the difference. This is, of course, not a risk-free proposition, as the short-seller may also end up owing the difference if the stock rises in price and the cost of buying back those shares exceeds the proceeds they pocketed at the time of the initial short-sale. Because stocks can theoretically rise to infinity, while their decline is finite given that a stock price cannot go below zero, or 100 percent of its current value, then the potential losses a short-seller faces are unlimited. Of course, this assumes that a short-seller is operating without a stop-loss that provides a clear point at which the short-sale would be covered and the trade closed out at a loss, hopefully a small one.

To some, short-selling represents the "dark side" of the market, and history has often characterized the art of selling short as an evil enterprise, embodying a conspiratorial or pessimistic frame of mind that fixates on the negative. Consider that during the Great Crash of 1929, Jesse Livermore made $100 million in 1929 dollars, an astronomical sum at that time, by short-selling stocks during this severe market downturn. When this was later disclosed to the public, Livermore was the subject of extreme public outrage, even to the point where his short-selling activities were blamed as part of the cause of the great crash. In reality, Livermore merely observed and acted upon the market facts as they became apparent. The true cause of the Crash of 1929 was the fact that everyone had piled into the market and there was nobody left to buy stocks at that point. As well, paltry 10 percent margin requirements allowed investors to buy $100 worth of stock with only $10 in their pocket, creating a massive asset bubble and the optimal conditions for a rapid and destructive popping of that bubble.

Thus stocks find their value given the circumstances, and short-sellers can act as a catalyst to help stocks reach their true value faster than they might without any short-sellers. Supply–demand mechanics have shown time and time again that even when short-sellers pile onto stocks as they did the dot.coms, such as Amazon.com (AMZN) in the early 2000s, their short-selling has no long-term effect on depressing price if the perceived value of the stock continues to be higher than where the stock is currently trading.

Nevertheless, during the earlier existence of the United States, short-selling was in fact banned because of the inherent instability of the then very young country's fragile markets, mostly thanks to speculation surrounding the outcome of the War of 1812. It was not until 1850 that the short-selling ban was repealed. More recently, in 2008, government officials banned the short-selling of certain financial stocks that had come under pressure as a result of severe, even deadly, liquidity issues related to having swarms of bad mortgages held on their books. Excesses in the mortgage industry, fostered by government subsidies and policies that forced and/or allowed banks to lower their lending standards in order make home loans to low-income consumer borrowers who had no means of paying back the loans, created a housing bubble as demand for homes was artificially spiked, sending real estate prices soaring. These low-quality mortgages were in turn repackaged into bundles known as *mortgage-backed securities* (MBS), and the structure of these MBSs magically enabled them to be rated Triple-A by the credit-rating agencies such as Standard & Poor's and Moody's. With Triple-A ratings, such mortgage-backed securities were eagerly purchased by investors, ending up en masse on the books of a large number of financial institutions as well as in the portfolios of many institutional and retail investors. When the real estate bubble finally popped in 2008, these loans went bad, sending the institutions that had many of these mortgages on their books into insolvency.

In keeping with the fact that history often rhymes with the present, government officials attempted to deflect part of the blame for the financial crisis of 2008 onto short-sellers who were accused of the predatory practice of "naked" short-selling as they swarmed vulnerable financial stocks on the short side and helped to drive their prices lower. Forget the fact that short-sellers were doing little more than what smart speculators do in the first place, which is to identify a potential or emerging trend and to then capitalize on it by investing in the direction of that trend. The excesses of the mortgage and housing industries by 2008 deserved to be exposed for the frauds that they were, and short-sellers were simply part of that process of exposure and "cleansing." As well, investors who were foolish enough to buy the stocks of financial companies on the way down did not heed what the trend was telling them. Obviously, anyone who understood what was going on knew that the only logical endpoint for the excesses of the housing and mortgage industry and the resulting insolvencies that it produced once the bubble popped was bankruptcy. And that is precisely what happened to venerable financial institutions like Lehman Brothers, Merrill Lynch, and Bear Stearns, which went belly-up or were absorbed by other financial companies.

Aggressive short-selling was alleged by regulators to have played a role in the demise of both Lehman Brothers and Bear Stearns, but the fact is that the insolvency of the financial system in 2008 was real, and true insolvency leads to bankruptcy, whether the stock is a favorite target of short-sellers or not. Without the Fed stepping in to flood the system with unprecedented amounts of liquidity using unprecedented systemic schemes collectively known as *quantitative easing*, or QE for short, more such financial institutions would have suffered the same fate as Lehman Brothers and Bear Stearns. Ultimately, the Financial Accounting Standards Board (FASB) would also step in to aid the Fed's QE propping by changing Rule 157, otherwise known as the "mark-to-market rule," which required financial institutions to value their assets at fair market value. By allowing banks and other financial institutions to value their bad mortgages at whatever they wanted to rather than what they were in fact worth, further insolvencies in the system were avoided, at least temporarily and on paper.

What is interesting to observe is that the government's creation of an entirely artificial force to prop up and stimulate a reversal in the deleterious downtrend of the financial sector stocks is accepted as a legitimate way to influence stock prices, but the actions of short-sellers are seen as an unnatural and evil influence. We would argue that short-selling is a natural part of the process that defines the life-cycles of all stocks as they benefit from growth and the ensuing speculative excess on the upside, but at some point must go through a process of correction and downside price movement that clears the decks, so to speak, and either helps to build a foundation for a new uptrend and cycle of growth or results in a final and complete demise of a company that is no longer able to compete in its core industry. In a sense, the demise of older companies also helps to foster new growth cycles in that the way is cleared for newer, more innovative companies to supplant the older, slower, and larger companies that have lost their innovative and, hence, competitive edge. Short-selling, at its core, is nothing less than the investment manifestation of the virtuous cycle of creation and destruction, as well as the periodic need to cleanse excesses from the system that is the hallmark of an entrepreneurial economy.

As a very instructive and current example, one need look no further than the financial crisis of 2008 and the market events that led up to it. The reality is that the financial crisis of 2008 and the severe bear market that accompanied it actually began well before it reached full-blown crisis proportions between September 2008 and April 2009. It began quietly with the topping of home-building stocks in July of 2005. Recall that the financial crisis was a function of a mortgage crisis based on the promotion and writing of ridiculously risky home loans by banks and other home-lending institutions. The lowering of lending standards in turn fueled what was really a ballooning artificial demand for houses, and this heroin-induced rush of home buying drove home prices higher, spurring a homebuilding boom that manifested in the stock market as a strong uptrend in the prices of homebuilding and building-related stocks from 2000–2005. While the demand for housing reached a crescendo in 2006–2007, homebuilding stocks had already begun to top, as the charts of two separate homebuilding stocks, Toll Brothers (TOL) and Pulte Group (PHM) (Figures 1.1 and 1.2) show.

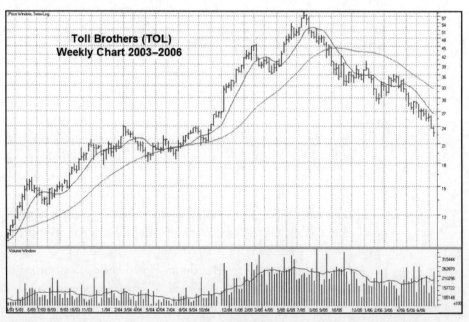

FIGURE 1.1 Toll Brothers (TOL) weekly chart, 2003–2006. Luxury homebuilder TOL topped in July of 2005 with the rest of the homebuilding stocks, presaging the coming housing and mortgage crisis that would shake the financial market three years later.

Source: Chart courtesy of HGSI Investment Software, LLC (www.highgrowthstock.com), ©2014.

FIGURE 1.2 Pulte Group (PHM) weekly chart, 2003–2007. This builder of single-family homes, townhouses, condominiums, and duplexes in 28 states had a nearly tenfold price move from 2000 to midsummer 2005.

Source: Chart courtesy of HGSI Investment Software, LLC (www.highgrowthstock.com), ©2014.

Homebuilding stocks to a large extent represented the point at which the rubber meets the road for the financial crisis as the consumer "end-product" of the housing stimulus, provided by an extremely low interest rate environment and lax lending standards both mandated and promoted by government policies that were readily embraced by the home-loan industry. As more and more consumers purchased homes they could not afford, eventually the chickens began to come home to roost as the reality of making loan payments took hold. The stock market, in its inimitable ability to foresee and begin discounting the future, saw this coming, and when the homebuilding stocks topped, they represented the first warning shot across the bow for the homebuilding industry at large, including the financiers and suppliers that both fed it and fed off of it. In this manner, the top in homebuilding stocks represented stage one of the impending financial crisis.

The great bear market of 2007–2009 officially started when the major market indexes topped in October 2007. Figure 1.3 shows the NASDAQ Composite Index topping in late October 2007 and then moving sideways for six weeks before breaking down further in January of 2008. The observant reader might also note that around this time the NASDAQ Composite had formed something of a "head and shoulders" top formation, a pattern that we will examine in detail later on in this book.

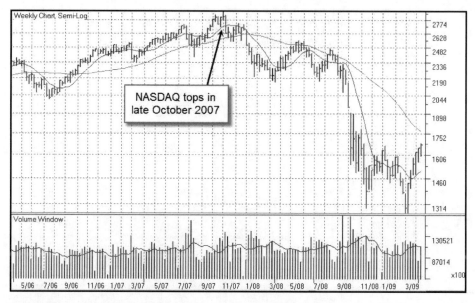

FIGURE 1.3 NASDAQ Composite Index, weekly chart 2006–2009. The general stock market, as represented by the NASDAQ Composite Index, tops in late October 2007.

Source: Chart courtesy of HGSI Investment Software, LLC (www.highgrowthstock.com), ©2014.

While the general market did not top until October of 2007, we have already observed that the homebuilding stocks topped in July of 2005, more than two years prior to the general market top in 2007. That was the first warning shot across the bow, but the second warning shot took place in the financial stocks themselves when they began to top in May of 2007, preceding the general market top by exactly five months. The chart of the Financial Select Sector SPDR (XLF), shown on a weekly chart in Figure 1.4, shows a classic head and shoulders topping formation around the peak in May 2007.

The breakdown in the peak off the top in the financial sector constituting the first down leg in the XLF took place from May to August, at which point the XLF rallied twice back up to its 40-week moving average. As financials led the downturn off the peak in May 2007, the period from August to October produced volatile reaction rallies and bounces in the group as a number of other leading groups, including solar energy stocks like First Solar (FSLR), shown in Figure 1.5, and Sunpower Corp. (SPWR), and technology stocks like Apple (AAPL), shown in Figure 1.6, and Baidu (BIDU) continued to rally well past the general market top in October 2007 and into late December 2007 and early January 2008.

So as the general market was continuing to move higher from May to October, the financials were trying to bounce and rally with the market, but this action only served to create a right shoulder in an overall head and shoulders top in the XLF, which then broke down in synchrony with the actual general market top in

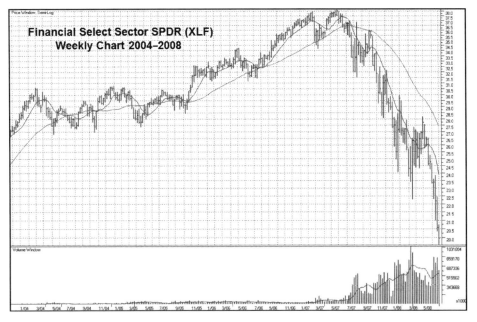

FIGURE 1.4 The financial sector, as measured by the Financial Select Sector SPDR (XLF) ETF, tops in May of 2007, well before the general market indexes and long before the actual financial crisis took hold in the fall of 2008.

Source: Chart courtesy of HGSI Investment Software, LLC (www.highgrowthstock.com), ©2014.

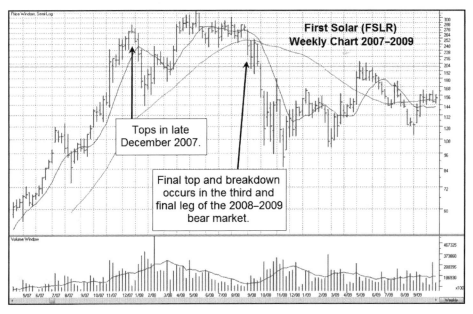

FIGURE 1.5 First Solar (FSLR) weekly chart, 2007–2008. Notice that FSLR initially tops out in late December 2007, and is then able to rally back to new highs when the general market stages a reaction rally and puts in a final top later in 2008, as the third and final leg of the 2008–2009 bear market takes hold.

Source: Chart courtesy of HGSI Investment Software, LLC (www.highgrowthstock.com), ©2014.

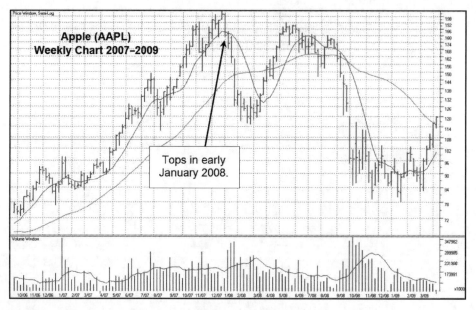

FIGURE 1.6 Apple (AAPL) weekly chart, 2007–2008. Notice that AAPL does not top out until early January 2008, over two months after the general market tops.

Source: Chart courtesy of HGSI Investment Software, LLC (www.highgrowthstock.com), ©2014.

October 2007, as illustrated by the weekly chart of the XLF in Figure 1.4. Once the general market topped in October 2007, the other areas of leadership during the bull phase started to top over the next few months as a final wave of topping leaders took hold in early 2008, resulting in the second leg down off the peak in the NASDAQ Composite Index in January 2008, as can be seen in Figure 1.3.

The lesson here is that bear markets and the short-selling opportunities they present are thematic, unfolding events that reflect what is going on in the general economy—essentially, the "underlying conditions" that the great trader Jesse Livermore described as the backdrop of any market trend, whether bull or bear. Before the bear market becomes obvious to everyone, including government officials, stocks are already starting to top in waves, as money that had moved in during the uptrend now seeks to exit the market and leading stocks. This is a natural process and is in no way, shape, or form something that is artificially created by short-sellers.

Very real excesses build up in any bull market phase, which is often propelled by underlying growth in specific areas of the economy. In the early- to mid-1990s we saw a strong bull phase that was generated by strong growth in the technology area, specifically semiconductors and related computer technology, as the PC boom took root. In the late 1990s it was growth in the potential and profitability of the Internet that drove the wild dot.com boom, which in turn drove a parabolic bull market. In the mid-2000s, the bull market that ended in October 2007 was helped along by a housing bubble that resulted from excesses in easy money policies. Easy money policies by the Fed also served to sharply devalue the U.S. dollar, leading to huge growth in the prices of "stuff" stocks—companies that mined or produced basic materials such as steel, precious metals, fertilizers, coal, and building materials.

The ensuing bear markets are nothing more than the natural clearing out of excesses that were built up in the prior bull phases as winners and losers are sorted out and the foundation is laid for the next growth phase. Short-sellers are merely smart investors who can recognize a change in trend in the general market and leading stocks and profit thereby. If the stock market is accepted by all as a way to build wealth, why shouldn't investors also be able to take action to protect that wealth during a bear market, and even seek to further build that wealth by profiting on the short side? In our view, short-selling is as American as baseball, Mom, and apple pie.

■ How Not to Sell Stocks Short

This book will explain in detail how we sell stocks short, and before we get started, it might be worthwhile to discuss how we DO NOT sell stocks short.

Often times we hear of a prominent hedge fund manager who goes on financial cable TV and declares a certain high-flying stock to be the beneficiary of nothing more than irrational, speculative fever on the part of mindless, lemming-like investors. Generally this hedge fund manager is a graduate of what we like to refer to as the University of "I-Am-Smarter-than-the-Market." As such, he or she is one who is "smarter" than the mass of investors who get carried away with the "hype" surrounding a given "hot stock" and thereby sees fit to declare that the fundamentals of the company in question "do not justify" its often-high and going-higher stock price.

High-flying stocks that have attracted more than their fair share of naysayers who consider the stocks' ever-rising prices as representative of a sort of moral infirmity among investors have in recent years included great companies like Netflix (NFLX), Tesla Motors (TSLA), and 3D Systems (DDD), for example. Getting up on financial cable TV and declaring investors in such stocks to be misguided doesn't win one a lot of fans, and because most of these hedge fund managers try to short these stocks on the way up, they generally end up looking stupid before they start looking smart, as the basic axiom of investing, essentially that the trend is your friend, often persists, even when it comes to allegedly overvalued stocks. Trying to short a stock based on the fact that it is overvalued ignores basic stock market reality when it comes to P/E ratios in leading stocks and seems to stand in the way of the dominant upside technical trend. Countless numbers of high-flying stocks over the years have been downgraded by analysts on the basis of being overvalued. This was especially true in the late 1990s with so many dot.com stocks reaching dizzying heights in price despite being downgraded a number of times by analysts.

Netflix (NFLX) is a more recent example of such a phenomenon, as it endured the wrath of a couple of very vocal "valuation" short-sellers all the way up during the incredible price run it had from early 2009 to mid-2011. Valuation short-sellers are those who believe a stock's price is going to go down because its price-to-earnings ratio, or P/E, is far too high. In December of 2010, a hedge fund manager we will simply refer to as "W" wrote an article in a prominent investment blog discussing the reasons why he was selling NFLX short. The day that article appeared, NFLX closed at a price of $181.65 a share. Within seven months the stock price hit an all-time high of $304.79, not too long after "W" had revealed that his fund had covered its short-sale position, unable to withstand the pain of the losses its NFLX short position generated as the stock ground its way higher, as can be seen in Figure 1.7.

W's primary reason, his only reason in fact, for shorting NFLX was that its P/E was "too high" and that the company's business model could not possibly generate the revenues and profits such a valuation implies. This, of course, ignores the fact that a P/E ratio is less a measure of static value and more a measure of the marketplace's current assessment of a company's forward earnings stream. If one objectively studies the price/volume action of leading stocks that have huge price moves, one quickly realizes that during these massive upside price runs the P/Es

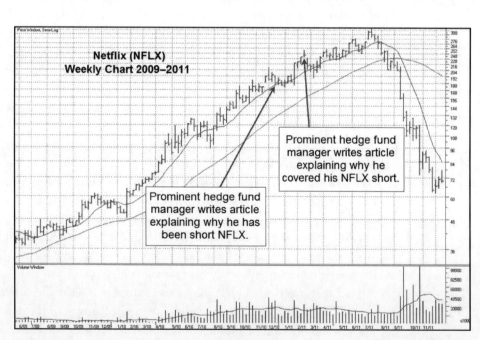

FIGURE 1.7 Netflix (NFLX) weekly chart, 2009–2011. There was a time to be long NFLX and a time to be short NFLX. Self-proclaimed graduates of the University of "I-Am-Smarter-than-the-Market" had trouble identifying either.

Source: Chart courtesy of HGSI Investment Software, LLC (www.highgrowthstock.com), ©2014.

of these stocks actually *expand*, often to 100 or more times the current earnings. Price strength often begets further price strength, thus stocks and even markets themselves often go far higher than most analysts expect.

Individuals like these are seen as "negative nellies" who fail to understand the dynamic nature of the U.S. stock market and the essential direction of money flows into and out of leading stocks during their life cycles. It's one thing to walk into a clothing store and declare a pair of jeans with holes in the knees to be grossly defective and hence not worth the price tag; it's quite another to recognize the contextual fact that sometimes jeans with holes in them represent the hottest, cutting-edge fashion statement that every style-minded consumer must make at any price. And so it is with stocks.

In our view, these valuation short-sellers give short-selling a bad name. They want to think negatively about a situation that is being viewed positively by investors who see the stock market as a realm of opportunity and possibilities. As well, valuation short-sellers ignore the psychological nature of the markets, and the inherently dynamic potential, often unknowable in precise terms before the fact, of an emerging-industry business model that can only be sorted out in advance by the "mass mind" of the stock market, e.g., millions of investors making real-time decisions with real money based on their best real-time knowledge and forward assessments.

To illustrate this idea, take the example of Apple (AAPL) in 2004 after it had come out with the iPod, ostensibly, as some argued at the time, an mp3 player "in drag" and nothing more. But the iPod product, fathered along by the genius of one Steve Jobs, would provide the platform for even more massive-selling products like the iPhone, which truly revolutionized the smartphone, and the iPad, which turned the PC on its head, over the next several years. The point is that stock market opportunities are dynamic and evolve as more and more investors begin to see the potential of a company's product platform and its role within a potentially huge emerging market for those products. Such was the case with Apple.

Eventually, however, there came a time to sell Apple short, but only when the stock's strong uptrend had finally reversed itself as everybody who was going to be in the stock eventually was. This left only one direction for money flows in the stock to begin moving, and that was out. "Pile in, pile out" was a critical phenomenon that was readily observed in the institutional fund ownership data for Apple as it finally topped and rolled over.

Another entirely underestimated company and investment opportunity that serves as an added example is the highly innovative electric car maker Tesla Motors (TSLA), shown on a weekly chart in Figure 1.8. In May of 2012, we notified our subscribers of a "buyable gap-up" in the stock in the mid-60 price range at what was roughly the start of a robust upside price run that eventually carried above 290 by the summer of 2014. At the time we also saw Tesla Motors as being similar to General Motors (GM) in 1915 when the stock of that future "big three" U.S. automaker began its

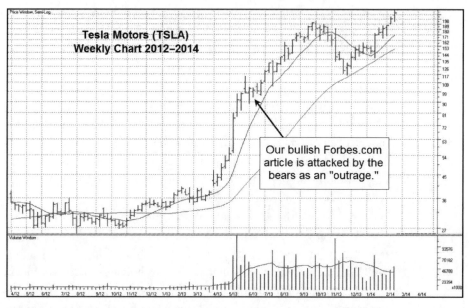

FIGURE 1.8 Tesla Motors (TSLA) weekly chart, 2012–2014. The emotional rants of the "Tesla bears" only seemed to propel the stock higher as short interest in the stock remained high all the way up through the $200 price level.

Source: Chart courtesy of HGSI Investment Software, LLC (www.highgrowthstock.com), ©2014.

own significant post-IPO price move. In the same manner that Tesla was bringing style and power to the otherwise mundane and utilitarian-oriented electric vehicle market in 2013, General Motors had introduced a mass-produced V-8 combustion engine that enabled the fledgling auto concern to bring style and power to the mainstream and help to accelerate the popularization of the automobile. Like Tesla in 2013, General Motors in 1915 was a recent IPO, having come public in 1911. Also like Tesla in 2013, General Motors in 1915 had been moving in a big, sideways consolidation for about 2.5 years before breaking out and initiating a massive upside price move. Thus we saw a historical "precedent" for what was going on with Tesla Motors based on the theme of a new company pushing the envelope of an emerging industry, in this case electric vehicles in 2013 as compared to what General Motors was doing with the combustion engine as it was pushing the envelope of the auto industry in 1915.

Despite the fact that Tesla was selling at 100 times forward earnings estimates at the time, it was still able to generate a huge upside price move that began at the point where we first bought the stock, essentially in the mid-60 price area, in early May of 2013. Considering that it is not uncommon for such a "ridiculously high P/E" to attract short-sellers who consider themselves to be smarter than the market, Tesla quickly became a popular target of short-sellers hell-bent on seeing "foolish" buyers of the stock punished. In the end it was the short-sellers who were foolish and who suffered a brutal but still self-inflicted punishment. After all, a basic reality of the stock market is that a young, new, dynamic company with game-changing technology and a cutting-edge approach can often sell at 100 times forward estimates or more at the very point where it begins a huge upside price run. This has been seen time and time again with stocks like eBay (EBAY) and Amazon.com (AMZN) in 1998, Salesforce.com (CRM) from 2009–2010, or even Taser International (TASR) in 2003 when it had no earnings to speak of and hence an "infinite" P/E yet still was at the cusp of a nearly twenty-seven-fold price move over the next nine months! Such was the case with Tesla Motors in 2013. As we wrote in an article for Forbes.com in early June 2013, "What the GM example tells us is that maybe there will be more to this price move in TSLA than currently meets the eye, and investors should remain open to whatever the stock's future price/volume action tells us and not rely on simple-minded valuation analysis that can often cause investors to miss huge stock market opportunities."

One reader commented in the article's blog section (remember that TSLA stock was around $90 at the time), "What about us who are short above $100? How dare you compare TSLA to GM in 1915!!! Now I know the longs are like cult members." This sort of comment is typical of valuation short-sellers who, as a result of their graduate degrees from the University of "I-Am-Smarter-Than-the-Market," believe they possess superior abilities and knowledge that they express by denigrating those who buy and profit from strongly trending stocks as "cult members."

The mind-set of short-sellers like these is fraught with emotion, and at times it appears that their investment methodology in such a situation is born more of indignation than of any intelligent assessment of the trend and the stock's potential. Tesla Motors (TSLA) eventually moved higher than $290 a share as of the time of this writing, and so our answer to the individual who commented "What about us who are short above $100?" is that we hope they were smart enough to cover their positions once the stock rallied well past the $100 price level. In our experience, however, such individuals simply become even more indignant and continue to short the stock on the way up as they go bust.

When you argue against stocks like Apple, Netflix, Tesla, or 3-D Systems, you are arguing against the virtuous system of entrepreneurial capitalism that embraces the freedom, nobility, humanity, and shining promise of new ideas, new ways of thinking, positive change, and new products and services that enable people of all socioeconomic stages to improve their productivity, their leisure enjoyment, and ultimately their standard of living, and that is, well, downright un-American! Thus one facet of the dark side of short-selling is revealed, but in fact we see it more as the *dumb side* of short-selling by those who consider themselves as graduates of the University of "I-Am-Smarter-Than-the-Market."

In our view, short-selling is nothing more than a method of investing and trading that recognizes the life-cycle paradigm arising from an economic system that thrives on creative destruction. A major component of that creative destruction is the process of cleaning out prior excesses and forcing the redeployment of capital to more productive areas of the economy. The quicker that process is able to cycle through the system, the better. Stocks, like people, have life spans. Unlike people, however, they can have more than one life span, providing opportunities on both the long and short sides depending on which side of the creation/destruction cycle they are in. Great companies like Apple can experience periods of tremendous growth that fuel a higher stock price, followed by periods of contraction as they become obsolescent and lose their competitive edge. During such a period, the price of the company's stock shares declines as it should. But great companies like Apple also adapt and respond by coming up with new ideas and new products to regain that edge and generate a new cycle of tremendous sales and earnings growth, which in turn fuels a higher stock price once again. In such a manner, a strong, adaptive, and innovative company can be born and reborn many times.

Investing and trading is about making money by profiting on the price movement of stocks and other securities. Short-selling is simply one component of smart investment and money management. Preserving gains is crucial in optimizing the performance of one's investments over the long term, and short-selling serves as a way to either profit outright or to help offset declines in other stocks that make up the positions in a portfolio with more of an intermediate- to long-term investment horizon during a bear market. The study and practice of short-selling not only provides investors with a useful arrow to keep in their quiver of investment skills, but it also aids in developing one's skill and understanding with respect to when to sell long positions in leading stocks when they have finally reached the end of their upside life cycle.

CHAPTER 2

Short-Selling Essentials

Thursday, May 6, 2010 began pretty much like any other trading day at our offices in the Southern California beach town of Playa del Rey. Our office resides in a red brick two-story building that was built in 1906 as the First Bank of Playa del Rey at the foot of Mount Ballona in what is basically downtown PDR, as the locals refer to it. Playa del Rey itself, which translates into "King's Beach," lies at roughly the mid-point of the so-called Queen's Necklace, a semicircle of smaller beach cities that line the shores of the Santa Monica Bay from Malibu in the north to Palos Verdes in the south. The nickname was inspired by the view one has at night from just about any reasonable vantage point along the bay as the chain of lights from Malibu to Palos Verdes twinkles and sparkles like a string of radiant jewels.

Playa del Rey is in a sense a beach town lost in time, as it has somehow managed to escape the attention of developers who have otherwise "modernized" and built up every other beach town in the Queen's Necklace. Toes Beach, which was once an "epic" surf break at the mouth of Ballona Creek before the City of Los Angeles decided to build the small boat harbor that became Playa del Rey's neighbor to the north and was named Marina del Rey, lies some 100 yards to the west. To the east, downtown Playa del Rey is buffered from the urban/suburban sprawl of west Los Angeles by the Ballona Wetlands, a smaller remnant of the vast wetland that once covered this part of west Los Angeles but which today still provides a resting spot for migratory birds that include among their numbers geese, herons, egrets, and brown pelicans. These wetlands "bird digs" are nice enough for great blue herons and snowy egrets to stop and make use of this prime piece of West Los Angeles real estate as a rookery where they mate and bring their young into the world.

If there is such a thing as a bucolic setting amidst the tony but congested suburbs of West Los Angeles, PDR was probably it. As far as I could, tell the day was just another one of those "s----y days in paradise," as they say: a mellow, clear, warm, sunny Southern California beach day like any other, with a nice ocean breeze blowing across the sands of Toes Beach and in through our office windows. The market had been acting weak over the prior several days, something that I had been making note of in my twice-weekly market missives that were published on the web at the time as The Gilmo Report, a website I had founded back in early 2008 before we founded VirtueofSelfishInvesting.com in August of 2010. I was already operating aggressively on the short side with short positions in stocks like Research in Motion (RIMM) and U.S. Steel (X). Unrest in Greece was cited as the cause of the initial breakdown that began at the tail end of February, but news of a European Union credit lifeline to the beleaguered Mediterranean nation over the weekend did little more than spark a one-day "wonder rally," the markets rolled over again.

The day before, on Wednesday, May 5, I had written in the report, "As I've discussed in the last two reports, risk for the long side of this market has been growing and in the past two days has grown exponentially, as I see it ... I began operating on [the basis of] a sell signal as of last Wednesday, and the short side has worked well enough in the past few days to make significant progress if one is aggressive enough. Sellers have come out of the woodwork, hitting everything in sight."

On Thursday the indexes briefly blipped to the upside at the open before quickly turning red and starting a shallow descent. The indexes continued moving lower until sometime just after 8:30~AM (11:30~AM New York), when an intra-day bounce suddenly set in. Watching my short positions bounce with the market, I began to lean into my computer monitors as I studied the action closely, alert for any sign that I needed to cover my short positions. A few minutes later, the movement was revealed as a head fake when the indexes began to roll over again. Over the next couple of hours the descent began to accelerate, and by a little after 11:15~AM (2:15~PM New York) things were starting to get funky. The otherwise laidback atmosphere of my Playa del Rey beach office was about to contrast sharply with the impending chaos that was starting to show up on my trading monitors. At around that time, the NASDAQ Exchange began to issue alerts regarding unusual price movements. While May 1 is traditionally known as May Day, that day, May 6, was about to become "Mayday! Mayday!"

The prices on my quote monitors were beginning to flash with rapidly increasing frequency, and I told my trader, Bill Griffith, "Something's not right here." Suddenly, the indexes began to plummet in a steep decline that defied anything else I had ever witnessed in my career up until that point. The Dow was now moving below minus-300. It was if someone were pouring the indexes out of some giant pitcher and steadily increasing the pouring angle at an accelerating rate as the indexes gushed lower. As the Dow passed below minus-500 points, I made the decision to take advantage of this "crush" of liquidity to cover my short positions. I began furiously clicking and tapping away on my PC mouse and keyboard as I entered "buy to cover" orders for each of my positions, one after the other. On a normal trading day I would receive my "fills," basically real-time reports that my trade had been executed at a particular price, very quickly with the confirming trade showing up on my monitors almost instantaneously. But this was not a normal trading day. The Dow was spiraling downward, passing downside century marks very rapidly as it moved below minus-600, minus-700, minus-800, and then minus-900 points down on the day! I'd only seen something like this once before during my rookie broker days at Merrill Lynch in Beverly Hills. It was known as a *fast market*, where a delay in order reporting was occurring whenever a deluge of trading activity flooded the system. But back then there was no electronic order entry, and we were writing orders to buy and sell stocks down on green and pink order forms with carbon copies attached. Once all the required fields on the form were filled out, we would get out of our chair, roll the order form up, and place it inside a cylindrical container that we would then fire off through a pneumatic tube to the wire order operator in the back office. The wire operator would receive the order form on the other end of the pneumatic tube system that snaked through the office and then wire out the details of our trade to the firm's main trading desk. In those days, it didn't take much for the system to back up using such antiquated and relatively time-intensive methods. But this was 2010, and the markets were all electronic, where everything moved at the speed of light, or at least at the speed of electrons, providing instant access and reporting for all. With no reports coming back, it was like sending my trades into a black hole.

This was a fast market of epic proportions, allegedly exacerbated by high frequency trading programs not unlike what was blamed as the cause of the massive market dive seen on Black Monday in October 1987, and I waited a good 20 minutes before I began to get execution reports back for my trades. During this time I watched the Dow break down to a point where it was not quite down 1,000 points before bouncing back to around -300. Six hundred Dow points had disappeared and reappeared within a matter of minutes and I had no idea if and where my buy-to-cover orders were being filled. As the system worked through the delay and my fills began to come in, I could see exactly where I had covered my short-sale positions. To my astonishment, they were all covered very near the lows of the day. With the market springing back so suddenly, the fact that I had started entering my orders just as the market was beginning to break sharply to the downside had enabled me to "catch" stock as it was being thrown out the window. By taking advantage of this crush of liquidity and looking to cover my shorts into the selling rather than waiting for a low and a subsequent turn back to the upside to set in, I was able to optimize the execution prices on my buy-to-cover orders, getting filled very near the intraday lows in each case. Figure 2.1 shows the

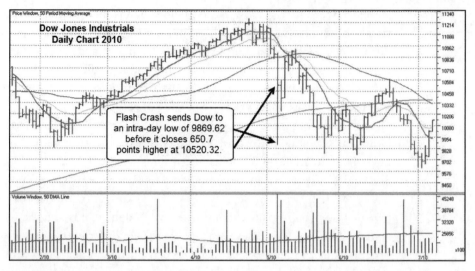

FIGURE 2.1 Dow Jones Industrials daily chart, 2010. The Dow closed well off of the lows after plummeting nearly 1,000 points to the downside earlier on May 6, 2010, the day of the infamous Flash Crash.

Source: Chart courtesy of HGSI Investment Software, LLC (www.highgrowthstock.com), ©2014.

huge daily range of the Dow on that day as well as the close well off of the lows and in the upper half of the day's trading range.

May 2010 ended up as a proving ground of sorts for my short-selling methods, which I had corrected, refined, and expanded in response to getting kicked in the teeth by staying too short for too long back in April 2009, an event that I discuss in detail in Chapter 6 of our first book, *Trade Like an O'Neil Disciple*. Using that negative experience to identify the weak links in my short-selling method and come up with drastic and effective improvements in my technique was what enabled me to achieve a rather stunning result on the short side in May 2010. To give you an idea of just how successful my short-sale operations were during the merry month of May 2010, consider one of the personal accounts I was trading on the short side at the time. The value of that particular account on May 1 was $1,228,540.89. Accounting for $275,000 that I withdrew for taxes in the middle of the month, the value on May 31 was $2,083,808.73. I'll leave it up to the reader to calculate the percentage return for the month.

We can be frank and recognize that this type of short-selling success was aided by a very unusual start to the month in the form of the now infamous Flash Crash of May 2010. But a fortuitous event like the Flash Crash, what we might consider the "luck" component, can only be taken advantage of on the short side by being in the right place at the right time. You can't get lucky if you don't first put yourself in the position of being able to get lucky by knowing when and where to begin selling stocks short. The fact is that I was already reacting to the market and individual stock weakness by selling short several days before the Flash Crash, so the signals were there; I merely had to act on them. I didn't need to know that there was going to be a Flash Crash in the next few days. No clairvoyance was necessary; my short-selling rules had put me into position naturally and normally before the fact.

The second and probably most important component to taking advantage of a sharp market drop is also knowing when to cover. Had I hesitated in covering my positions on that fateful day instead of understanding that one must take advantage of the crush of liquidity that occurs as sellers capitulate and send the market into a rapid, deep nosedive, my results would have without a doubt been quite a bit less spectacular.

To get an idea of just how well the short side of the market played out in May of 2010, we can take a look at one of my big short positions at the time, Research in Motion (BBRY), which up until 2014 traded under the symbol RIMM. We can see in Figure 2.2 how this played out during the month of May 2010. By the end of February, BBRY was just finishing off the formation of a right shoulder in a head-and-shoulders (H&S) pattern where the left shoulder was slightly above the left shoulder. The most optimal H&S formations generally have the right shoulder forming below the left shoulder, but in this case BBRY was a notable exception, of which I have seen a few over the years. Suffice it to say that BBRY was starting to "roll over" in the right shoulder of a fairly symmetrical three-month H&S pattern. The huge gap-down in late January that occurred on massive selling volume was

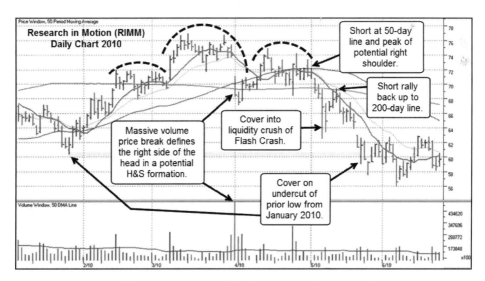

FIGURE 2.2 Research in Motion (BBRY) daily chart, 2010. The action of BBRY (RIMM at that time) leading up to and immediately following the Flash Crash of May 2010 made it a very identifiable short-sale target that cooperated nicely on the downside during May.

Source: Chart courtesy of HGSI Investment Software, LLC (www.highgrowthstock.com), ©2014.

your first clue that institutions were selling the stock in force and served to form the right side of the head in the H&S formation.

Referring to Figure 2.2, the gap-down through the 50-day moving average at around the 71–72 price within the first few days of May confirmed the formation of the right shoulder. From there the stock broke sharply through the 200-day moving average, and on the day of the Flash Crash it undercut the 63 price level as the massive selling pressure slammed the stock about 10 percent lower. Having reacted to the sudden liquidity crush of selling that occurred as a result of the Flash Crash, I ended up covering near the lows of the day. From there the stock cooperated very nicely as it rallied back up into 200-day moving average, where it became quite shortable again. The stock hung around the 200-day moving average for another day before it began moving to the downside again over the next five days. Another gap-down move on the sixth day gave the stock enough downside momentum to send it all the way down to the 56 price level, where it undercut a major low in the pattern from January 2010. At that point the stock was covered again for a tidy profit. This concluded the "fat" part of BBRY's breakdown, and the stock then spent the next few weeks chopping sideways.

By understanding where to cover most if not all of my short position in BBRY on the downside breaks as well as where to re-enter the short side of the stock on the rallies into logical resistance, in this case the rally back up into the 200-day moving average following the Flash Crash washout, I was able to optimize my short-sale profits in the stock. One could have also taken the route of shorting the stock on the breakdown through the 50-day moving average and then sitting with it until it achieved a roughly 20-percent profit once it had undercut the January 2010 low. But by making use of my understanding of how to actively trade the stock as it broke down sharply and then rallied sharply in rapid succession as it zig-zagged its way down to the 56 price level, I was able to "milk" the position for even more.

While the short-selling process in May of 2010 looks relatively simple, the reality is that most of the time short-selling is very difficult, and one should probably have a higher risk-tolerance in terms of dealing with the volatility. Also, a little courage doesn't hurt! While stocks can break down very fast, they are also subject to frequent, sharp upside bounces and rallies on the way down. This tends to be characteristic of the short-side as stocks sell off and become "cheaper." Optimism reigns supreme in the stock market, and the collective mentality of buying "bargains" that exists among stock market participants can result in short but furious bouts of bottom-fishing when stocks are oversold in the very short-term. These reaction rallies, however, can provide optimal re-entry points on the short side, and my strategy takes this into account.

Looking back over my career as a trader since 1998, when I first started practicing the art of short-selling, I can safely say that outside of the last two months of 1999, I have made more money faster on the short side than the long side when I have made it, but I have also experienced sharper losses on the short side. In fact, all of my significant drawdowns since 1997 have been a result of short-selling. This, of course, speaks to the need to develop a much more robust risk management system when it comes to short-selling. I should emphasize that as it relates to short-selling, risk management is not just about having stop-loss rules; another major and critical component is knowing when to take profits and how to "work" the short side of a stock as it breaks and rallies, breaks and rallies, several times during a longer-term price breakdown. This is what puts the *robust* in robust risk management!

Now that your appetite for short-selling has no doubt been whetted, it's time to get down to the basic concepts and sober realities of short-selling as Bill O'Neil taught me and as I practice it. In Chapter 6 of our first book, *Trade Like an O'Neil Disciple*, we discussed six basic rules for short-selling that we titled "The Golden Rules of Short-Selling." At the time the discussion was quite brief, and as well, the rules have evolved somewhat since that book was written in late 2009. This chapter will serve to clarify and expand upon these six basic rules in greater detail.

Rule #1: Know where you are in the cycle.

In the past we stipulated that short-selling should only be undertaken during a bear market, and as close to the start of the bear market as possible. In hindsight and after gaining much more experience as a short-seller, I can safely say that this is not so much wrong as it is woefully simplistic. Today I would refine this to a more essential and slightly broader concept of understanding where one is in the bear cycle as well as understanding whether one is in fact sitting at the precipice of a longer-term bear market or just a less severe and normal market correction during an overall bull market. Having a basic grasp of how bear markets unfold and applying that to the timing of one's short-sale operations can help one to more effectively exploit the most optimal points during the bear market at which to sell short and remain short. Obviously, one does not want to start shorting stocks after the market has been in a bear phase for a while and the selling has become obvious to just about everyone, since the risk of a major new rally starting increases as the bear market wears on.

Bear markets, however, do not come in a handy-dandy one-size-fits-all form. They can vary greatly with respect to duration, downside velocity, and total percentage decline. In addition, the way they unfold is dependent to a reasonable degree on the context of the current economic and political backdrops. Sometimes they aren't even bear markets at all. Normal market corrections of 7–12 percent during an overall bull market cycle can offer decent opportunities on the short side. We also observe that some of the leaders in each cycle top and fall by the wayside as part of the normal rotation that occurs in a longer-term bull cycle; new groups rise up to carry the bull market banner as old ones correct or outright top. In Chapter 1, we saw that during the bull market cycle of 2003–2007, housing stocks and financials, both leaders during that cycle, topped well before the final top in October 2007. Often these tops will coincide with shorter-term market corrections of 7–12 percent. When leaders initially top during such a short-term correction, they can often continue lower even as the market turns back to the upside, as some of the model short-sale stocks we will look at later in the book will show.

We can get a sense of how things play out by looking at historical bear markets and sifting through the stocks, the chart patterns, and the underlying conditions of those market periods. For the purposes of keeping things short, we will cover more recent bear markets, starting with the great financial crisis bear market of 2007–2009, which we show in a weekly chart of the NASDAQ Composite Index in Figure 2.3. The first thing that is readily observable is the fact that this particular bear market had three major downside movements or *down legs* as they are referred to in the market vernacular. I also use the term *wave* instead of *leg*, and for the purposes of this book the two terms mean the same thing and are interchangeable. The first down leg occurred after the top in late 2007 as the NASDAQ broke down and successfully tested its 200-day moving average. This was followed by a five-week period of sideways movement with the index twice rallying up into its 10-week moving average, which corresponds to the 50-day moving average on the daily chart, which we do not show here. The NASDAQ then broke through support at the lows of this five-week range in a four-week-long down leg that greeted the New Year in

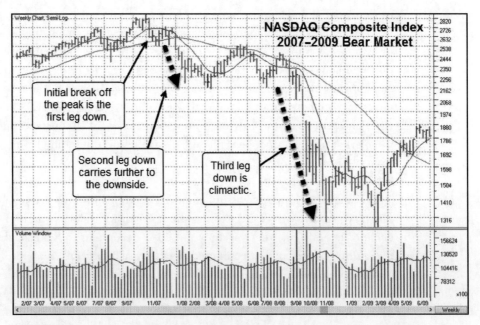

FIGURE 2.3 The bear market of 2007–2009 had three major downside selling legs or waves, with the third wave being the most severe.

Source: Chart courtesy of HGSI Investment Software, LLC (www.highgrowthstock.com), ©2014.

2008 with a −21.2 percent decline. This four-week down leg represented the "fat" part of the move, since once a low was put in at the end of January, the market rallied and then moved sideways throughout February of 2008 before rolling over and undercutting the January low.

This obvious breach of "support" at the late January low faked out short-sellers, and the market then turned back to the upside as it set off on a nine-week rally that carried all the way up to the 40-week moving average, corresponding to the 200-day moving average on the daily chart. If you were suddenly convinced that shorting stocks was the thing to do in March of 2008, you were quickly run in. It is exactly this type of undercut and rally action that short-sellers need to watch for very carefully. Often, after a sharp break to the downside, the market will find a low and then bounce, only to roll over after a few weeks or less and head back for that original low. Since the crowd sees that low as a "critical" support level, when the index undercuts that low in the manner that the March 2008 low undercut the January 2008 low, it sucks in short-sellers and forces remaining longs to capitulate. This washes out the short-term selling momentum in the market and fakes everyone out as the indexes then turn higher.

It is important to know that at that March low, Bear Stearns, a major financial brokerage and an institutional investor, went belly up. This sent a shockwave through the financial markets, but once the event was known and J.P. Morgan agreed to buy out Bear Stearns at a whopping $2 a share (yes, we're being facetious) a handful of days later, the initial panic reaction was out of the way and the market rallied. Of course it was a terrible event, with broad implications for the global financial system (as we would learn later in the year), but the market had *already been selling off for the past five months.* The NASDAQ Composite dipped below the late January 2008 low, the crowd saw the break of support, everyone leaned to the downside, and the market set off in the opposite direction, back to the upside, as we see in Figure 2.5, below. The Bear Stearns "event," as I call it now, was a climactic event within the context of the prior selling that began at the time of the October 2007 top. If one understood what was happening, one would have used the crush of liquidity that occurred as sellers panicked and cut stock loose to cover short positions.

The nine-week rally off the March lows was decent enough that it was actually playable on the long side, as I recall, with interesting recent IPOs like Visa (V), breaking out of beautiful chart bases and making new highs. So there were fresh "new merchandise" plays in the market on the long side at the time. As well, financial stocks like Goldman Sachs (GS) had significant rallies off of their lows, and GS was able to bounce off a low of 140.27 up to a peak of 203.39 in about seven weeks. This well serves to illustrate how much pain late short-sellers experienced during those nine weeks of bear market rally. It also shows how that even during what turns out to be a major, long-term bear market, there are periods where it does not pay to be short, and in fact the smart trade, if one

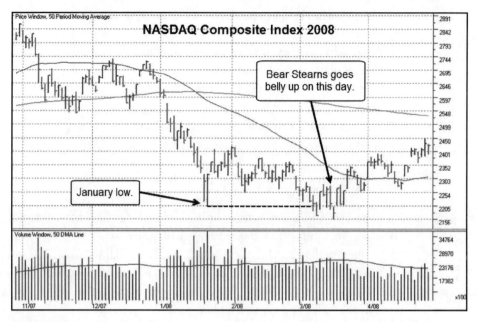

FIGURE 2.4 NASDAQ Composite Index daily chart, early 2008. The bankruptcy of Bear Stearns causes the index to undercut its January low, as once Bear Stearns is swallowed up by J.P. Morgan at $2 a share, the market breathes a sigh of relief.

Source: Chart courtesy of HGSI Investment Software, LLC (www.highgrowthstock.com), ©2014.

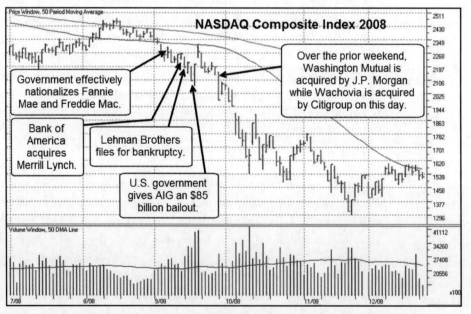

FIGURE 2.5 NASDAQ Composite Index daily chart. A confluence of events relating to broad insolvency issues in the financial sector set off a huge −47.6 percent downside break in the NASDAQ Composite Index in September 2008.

Source: Chart courtesy of HGSI Investment Software, LLC (www.highgrowthstock.com), ©2014.

can execute it, exists in understanding how to play the reaction rallies on the long side.

After that nine-week rally following the rescue of Bear Stearns by J.P. Morgan, the NASDAQ rolled over again and declined for six weeks before successfully testing the March lows. This led to one more rally up into the 40-week moving average at the end of the summer of 2008 before the index broke sharply to the downside, as the liquidity issues that characterized the 2008 financial crisis forced financial institutions to liquidate assets as quickly as possible and at whatever prices the market would bear. The deluge of forced selling led to a massive meltdown in the markets. If one was positioned on the short side at the right time in early September 2008, the potential for making huge profits on the short side was quite substantial.

That massive −47.6 percent leg to the downside was given a nice downhill "shove" in September 2008, when a confluence of news events hit the market. First, the federal government was forced to take over Fannie Mae and Freddie Mac, effectively nationalizing the two huge private (but government-backed) mortgage entities, which at that point owned or guaranteed about half of the United States' $12 trillion mortgage market. On September 9, the stock of Lehman Brothers plunged 45 percent, sending shock waves through the market. After several days of hand-wringing, the venerable old brokerage firm filed for bankruptcy on September 15. Like Bear Stearns, Lehman Brothers was suffering from massive insolvency as a result of severe balance-sheet indigestion caused by the overconsumption of toxic mortgage paper. This time around, however, the Lehman insolvency was not an isolated event like the Bear Stearns news in March of 2008. On September 14, Merrill Lynch, at one time considered one of the most solid brokerages on the Street and the firm where I got my start in the business as a stockbroker in 1991, agreed to be bought out by Bank of America (BAC). "Mother Merrill," as we used to refer to it in the Beverly Hills branch where I worked, had $41 billion of exposure to "toxic" subprime mortgage paper, more than its entire shareholders' equity of $38 billion at the time. Multinational insurance behemoth American International Group (AIG) was also on the verge of bankruptcy, and on September 17 the U.S. government threw AIG an $85 billion lifeline to keep it from going under. On September 25, Washington Mutual was seized by the Federal Deposit Insurance Corporation (FDIC), and its assets were sold to J.P. Morgan Chase (JPM) for $1.9 billion in what was essentially a rescue operation. Four days later, on September 29, the FDIC announced that the banking operations of another financial institution with heavy exposure to toxic subprime mortgage paper, Wachovia, would be acquired by Citigroup in another rescue operation.

What is interesting to note is that while the news of Bear Stearns going under in March served as a climactic news event that led to a springtime rally once the crisis was "solved" by the acquisition of Bear Stearns by J.P. Morgan, the chain of events in September 2008 effectively laid bare the underlying insolvency crisis that was now sweeping over the financial sector. If you see one cockroach, chances are there are a lot more, and by September 2008 the rest of the cockroaches were now scurrying about in the open as the Fed and government officials scrambled to control the situation.

As this news was unfolding, former leading stocks were just finishing off the right shoulders in overall H&S formations they had been forming since the prior January 2008 and October 2007 market down legs. The reader can refer to Chapter 10, "Templates of Doom," to see examples of stocks that broke down from short-sale chart set-ups in synchrony with the indexes at that time. That downside break of −47.6 percent in the NASDAQ Composite was in fact created by a huge number of very actionable and profitable short-sale set-ups. The NASDAQ bottomed out in October of 2008 and rallied for six to seven weeks before rolling over and undercutting that same October low in March of 2009. This undercut of the October low marked the end of the bear market, as the Fed began flooding the financial system with their creative new monetary policy tool known as *quantitative easing*.

The 2009 market low is very instructive from the standpoint that as a short-seller, one must work hard to remain unaffected by the emotions of the moment; otherwise, the low of 2009 was not apparent. At the time, most thought the end of the world was surely at hand, and after all the market carnage of the prior year and a half, one easily could have become locked into a doomsday mentality. Furthermore, the 2009 low was unique because it represented the culmination of a market period where the existence of the financial system itself was in jeopardy. But after three major legs to the downside, with each selling wave more amplified (e.g., far steeper and deeper) than the prior one, from a technical perspective the market was washed out. With panicked sellers out of the way, stocks were essentially "sold out," and a number of sentiment indicators such as the Investors Intelligence survey of investment advisors and the American Association of Individual Investors were showing extreme bearish sentiment among both professionals and individual investors. Mix in the tsunami of liquidity barreling into the financial system and you have the necessary fuel to ignite enough reverse thrust to ensure the low. The ensuing rally sparked a new bull cycle that persists at the time of this writing in 2014.

The key takeaways from the 2007–2009 experience are that once bear markets get into their third or fourth wave to the downside, the risk that a major low is approaching increases sharply, and short-sellers need to be aware of this. Once you got to the third or fourth wave down, the profits were immense. At the same time, one has to also keep in mind that the third down leg in that bear market, which was characterized by the extremely brutal downside break that began in September 2008, was the most profitable time to be short during the overall bear market. If there was ever a time to be short during the 2007–2009 bear market, late August to early September of 2008 was the time. While daily and weekly charts give one

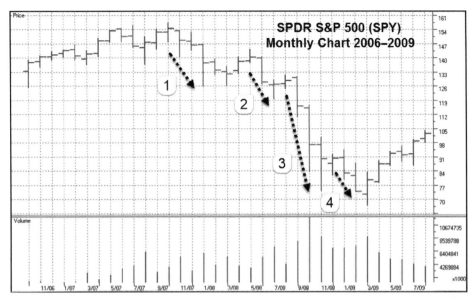

FIGURE 2.6 SPDR S&P 500 ETF (SPY) monthly chart, 2006–2009. Four distinct down legs or selling waves characterized the 2007–2009 bear market.

Source: Chart courtesy of HGSI Investment Software, LLC (www.highgrowthstock.com), ©2014.

a reasonable idea of how many down legs or downside waves, including what we might call *sub-waves* within each down wave, it is also useful to refer to monthly charts as I have done with the chart of the SPDR S&P 500 ETF (SPY), shown in Figure 2.6. If we use a simple definition of counting each succession of downside bars in the chart as one down leg/wave, we can see that there were four downside selling waves. Referring back to the weekly chart of the NASDAQ Composite in Figure 2.3, we can see that the NASDAQ had three primary selling waves off the top and one additional but smaller wave that occurred in February 2008, for a total of four waves. A monthly chart of the NASDAQ, which I don't show here, also confirms this. While it was possible to make money on that final downside wave, the risk of a market bottom was very high, and indeed if one lingered too long on the short side after February 2008, the consequences were severe.

One investor's story from that period will always stand out in my mind. In late July of 2008, I gave a presentation on the current state of the market to an *Investor's Business Daily* Meet-Up group of about 100–150 people at the Microsoft Building in midtown Manhattan, New York. The main topic of that presentation was my thesis that we were in a bear market at the time, and that it was about to get worse. I discussed several short-sale set-ups, including First Solar (FSLR), which I pointed out was likely setting up to break down from a "punchbowl of death" short-sale formation. In my studies of short-sale set-ups, I noticed that often, after a long upside price run of many weeks or months, a leading stock would sometimes build a huge "cup" or more accurately "punchbowl" on its weekly chart that was somewhat out of character with its behavior during the prior uptrend. This late-stage, wide, loose, and deep punchbowl formation often preceded a top in the stock. In FSLR's case I noticed that it was acting much like Broadcom (BRCM) was back in the 2000–2003 bear market and that the patterns were quite similar. FSLR blew apart at the very start of September 2008, plummeting from a price of 271.48 at the time to a low of 85.28 by the end of November 2008. That was a −68.6 percent decline in a mere 12 weeks.

A few months later I received an e-mail from an investor who had attended that July 2008 presentation. He told me that he had purchased about $40,000 worth of FSLR put options on the basis of my presentation and discussion of the stock, and that the puts were now worth $1.44 million. He asked me what he should do. My advice was obvious: take your profits, pay the taxes due, and be very, very happy! When you get a doozy of a bear market as we did in 2007–2009, the use of options instead of the underlying stocks is certainly a viable way to play the short side of the market, and the huge leverage that they enable while limiting your risk to the cost of the options can be advantageous. Catch the right wave and you can enjoy a very nice ride. The key with FSLR, however, was being short the stock at the right time, and being cognizant of the fact that it was setting up to break down in synchrony with the general market at the outset of September 2008. Having a clear target stock, in this case FSLR, and understanding its technical action in conjunction with where you might be in the bear cycle is how you make big money on the short side.

Moving on to a bear market where I was relatively successful on the short side, the period of 2000–2002 represented one of the most severe bear markets in market history. The weekly chart of the NASDAQ Composite Index from that period, shown in Figure 2.7, illustrates a bear market that consisted of four major downside legs or selling waves. Notice how in contrast to the 2007–2008 bear market, the second wave down was the steepest one, accounting for a total decline from peak to trough of −62.2 percent. This third-wave decline was larger than the first wave of −40.7 percent, the third wave of −40.4 percent, and the fourth wave of −47.2 percent. From a macro perspective, the bear market appears to decelerate as the angle of descent slows going into 2002.

It is said that bear markets serve the purpose of clearing out the excesses of the prior bull period, helping to clear the decks and till the soil for the next bull cycle. If there were ever excesses in need of a good clearing out, those produced by the dot.com bubble bull market that ended climactically in March of 2000 certainly fit the bill. Most investors either remember or have learned of that glorious market period when the indiscriminate buying of any Internet-related stock, regardless of whether its business model had any realistic hope of ever generating a profit, resulted in huge, instantaneous profits. Mediocre investors became investment geniuses overnight (even I made over 1,000 percent in my personal account in 1999!). Not realizing

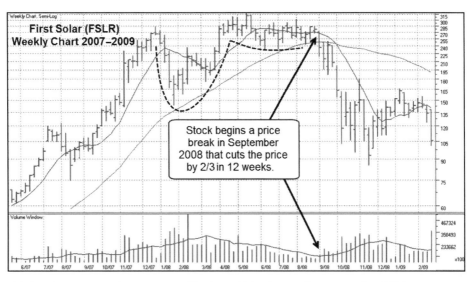

FIGURE 2.7 First Solar (FSLR) weekly chart, 2007–2009. Like an Acapulco cliff diver, FSLR plummeted −68.6 percent in 12 weeks.

Source: Chart courtesy of HGSI Investment Software, LLC (www.highgrowthstock.com), ©2014.

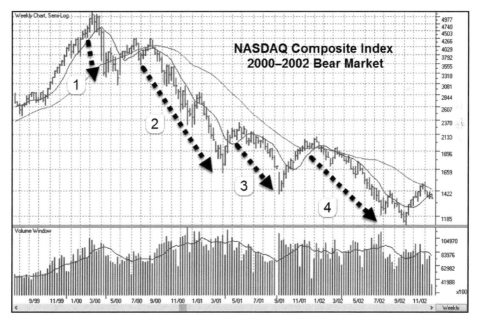

FIGURE 2.8 NASDAQ Composite Index weekly chart, 1999–2002. The bear market of 2000–2002 consisted of four primary downside selling waves in the NASDAQ.

Source: Chart courtesy of HGSI Investment Software, LLC (www.highgrowthstock.com), ©2014.

that the ride they were getting was more a function of the size of the market wave they were riding rather than their stunningly brilliant investment prowess, many investors quit their day jobs and made trading their full-time occupation in the belief that they could extract perpetual profits from the stock market. Eventually the bubble market and all its excesses came to an end, and the severe bear market of 2000–2002 turned once investment geniuses into punch-drunk market refugees.

Out of fairness, I should point out that not everything was a dot.com mirage. There were, in fact a number of technology stocks, such as Qualcomm (QCOM), that fully participated on the upside while at the same time showing strong fundamentals with huge earnings and sales growth. But in a bubble market like that seen in 1999, everything is priced to heavenly perfection, and when the party ends it ends for everyone. QCOM in fact ended its huge price run with a climactic top going right into March 2000, and the NASDAQ Composite Index formed a little double-top after going parabolic through 1999 and early 2000 before getting body-slammed to the downside. The break off the peak was a six-day decline of −16.4 percent on an intra-day basis that bounced very hard on the sixth day, as can be seen in Figure 2.9. That decline started on March 24 and ended on April 4, at which point a prominent and well-respected market technician (for whom some widely-used market indicators are named) declared that the market decline was over in a "classic v-bottom." The alleged v-bottom lasted three days before the index took another five-day cliff dive.

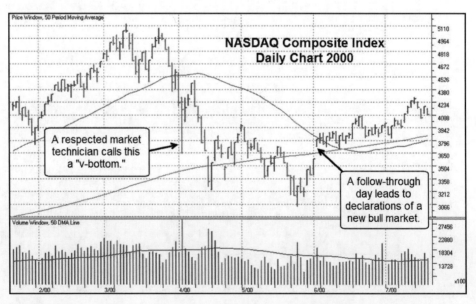

FIGURE 2.9 NASDAQ Composite Index daily chart. The break off of the March 2000 peak was not obvious as the start of what would become a brutal 2-1/2-year-long bear market.

Source: Chart courtesy of HGSI Investment Software, LLC (www.highgrowthstock.com), ©2014.

The fact that we were about to enter one of the most brutal bear markets was not obvious at the time. And this is something that short-sellers have to contend with. While you supposedly want to be shorting during a bear market, it's not so easy, at least at the start, to determine whether you are actually starting a bear market or just another shorter-term market correction. By the time the market put in a short-term low at the end of May 2000, as Figure 2.9 shows, the total decline off the peak in the NASDAQ Composite was 40.7 percent. By any standard, that was enough of a correction to qualify as a bear market, given that the financial TV definition of a bear market is a decline of 20 percent or more in the major market indexes. Surely, that was enough to clean out the excesses of the dot.com bubble bull market, was it not?

As we know now, it was not. And the reality is that nobody really knew what we were headed for, not even William J. O'Neil, the guy that we objectively consider to be the greatest stock market investor of all time and for whom we worked and managed money at that time. Bill thought we were in a new bull market after a follow-through day that occurred on Friday, June 2, a follow-through that incidentally is the only follow-through day I have witnessed while actually being on floor of the New York Stock Exchange. At that time, the NYSE floor was still the chaotic, at times circus-like, place made famous by stock market lore. Today, of course, electronic trading has turned the place into a ghost town, and the roar that I heard on the floor that day as the deluge of buy orders hit the floor right at the opening bell is something I will never forget. It sure sounded like a roaring bull market had just come out of the gate, and even Bill O'Neil considered it similar to the bull market that started right after the steep, brutal correction that occurred during the Cuban Missile Crisis and its ultimate resolution in October 1962. I was the head of the Institutional Services Group at William O'Neil + Co., Inc., and we were running around telling all of our clients that we were in a new bull market based on the "precedent" of the October 1962 market bottom and start of a fresh, new bull market.

Little did anyone know, but this "new bull market" was really just a bear market rally within an overall bear market. It would top out by mid-July, barely a few weeks later. The second major selling wave of the 2000–2002 bear market began right at the beginning of September 2000. That vicious down leg, numbered "2" in Figure 2.8, was the worst of the 2000–2002 bear market and measured 62.2 percent from September 2000 to the short-term low that took hold in April 2001.

Another bear market rally that lasted all of seven weeks ended in May and the market rolled over as another wave of selling took hold, and this third down leg in the 2000–2002 bear market took its place in the record books as a 40.4-percent break from the May peak to the low that occurred two weeks after the terrorist attacks of September 11, 2001.

The tragic events of 9/11 triggered a climactic low, as sellers panicked even as the Fed came in and decisively cut interest rates by a full percentage point. One could have easily assumed that the rally that rose up from the ashes of 9/11 was

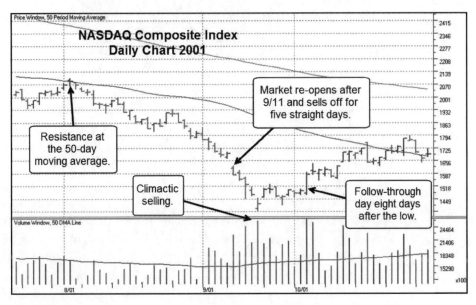

FIGURE 2.10 NASDAQ Composite Index daily chart, 2001. The events of 9/11 served to create a climactic, intermediate low during the 2000–2002 bear market.

Source: Chart courtesy of HGSI Investment Software, LLC (www.highgrowthstock.com), ©2014.

the start of a new bull market. I know I did. I had been fairly short stocks going into 9/11 based on the market's final rally up into its 50-day moving average before it began its sharp descent right into 9/11, as we can see in the daily chart of the NASDAQ Composite Index in Figure 2.10. At the time, on August 5, 2001, Bill O'Neil questioned my short positions, asking me "Just how much more do you think you can make?" To some extent, it was a fair question based on how far down the market already was at that point. I answered, "A lot more." While perhaps a bit cocky at the time, that answer turned out to be correct.

When the market started to roll off the 10-week moving average on the weekly chart in Figure 2.8 and the 50-day moving average on the daily chart in Figure 2.10, it looked to me like the third leg of the 2000–[Year Unknown] bear market was possibly starting. On the other hand, we had been in a bear market for nearly 18 months, and the NASDAQ had fallen from a peak of 5,132 in March of 2000 to 2,066.30 on August 3, 2001, a decline of not quite 60 percent. Surely, this was enough to clean out all the excesses of the great dot.com bubble market, was it not? As it turned out, it wasn't, and there was still plenty of downside left in that bear market, as we shall see.

If you go back and look at the tail end of the third down leg on the weekly chart of the NASDAQ Composite shown in Figure 2.8, you will notice that the downside break from early August to September 11 was a mere seven weeks in duration. But it carried the NASDAQ from a weekly close of 2,066.30 on August 3 to a weekly close of 1,423.10 on September 21, a week after the markets had reopened following 9/11. That was more than 31 percent of downside in the indexes in seven weeks, certainly enough to qualify as a bear market in any financial cable TV commentator's investment vocabulary and definitely enough to make some serious money on the short side.

The point is that even in the tail end of the third wave of one of the most brutal bear markets in history, it was possible to make some very fast short-side profits. And if you understood where you were in the cycle and were able to objectively observe and understand that the conditions for at least a short-term low and "liquidity crush" to develop were unfolding around the events of 9/11, you kept a good deal of those profits. *This is a critical concept for any short-seller to understand.*

I spent the next week covering my shorts into the final break and then turned and went long big-stock defense names Lockheed-Martin (LMT), which had just had a buyable gap-up move. The trade in LMT was very profitable, and the stock continued higher well into May 2002. Unfortunately, the market didn't make it that far, and what was merely another bear market rally ended in January 2002. The fourth and final selling wave, at least as measured on the weekly chart of the NASDAQ in Figure 2.8, was about to come crashing down on the market's already damaged shores, which would have to endure another 47.2 percent to the downside from there.

While the NASDAQ weekly chart shows four clear downside waves or down legs in the 2000–2002 bear market, the monthly chart of the SPDR S&P 500 (SPY) ETF shown in Figure 2.11 reveals roughly three selling waves, and by the time you get to the lows of the third wave around the middle of 2002, you can get a sense that the bear market is fairly long in the tooth. What I find useful is keeping an eye on the weekly and monthly charts of the NASDAQ Composite and the S&P 500, which in this case the SPY serves as a suitable proxy. In general, real bear markets have three to four downside waves, and this might differ between the indexes, as was the case between the NASDAQ and the S&P 500 during the 2000–2002 bear market. On a monthly chart, the NASDAQ's four waves are confirmed, while the S&P 500 had the more "standard" three waves down. If we consider that it was the NASDAQ that served as the epicenter for the speculative frenzy that ended in 2000, then the fact that it formed four downside waves during the 2000–2002 bear market as the extreme dot.com excesses were sandblasted away probably serves as testament to that.

The concept of bear markets having three waves down was given an interesting twist in the quick and dirty bear market of late 1998, which is illustrated on a daily chart of the NASDAQ Composite Index in Figure 2.12. At the time, Long-Term Capital Management, L.P., a hedge fund that boasted two Nobel Prize–winning economists on its board of directors, Myron S. Scholes and Robert C. Merton, collapsed. Both men shared the 1997 Nobel Memorial Prize in Economic Sciences for a "new method to determine the value of derivatives." After several highly

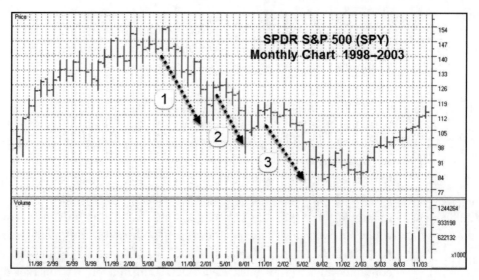

FIGURE 2.11 SPDR S&P 500 (SPY) ETF monthly chart, 1998–2003. As measured by the movement in the S&P 5000 Index, three major downside legs or selling waves characterized the 2000–2003 bear market.

Source: Chart courtesy of HGSI Investment Software, LLC (www.highgrowthstock.com), ©2014.

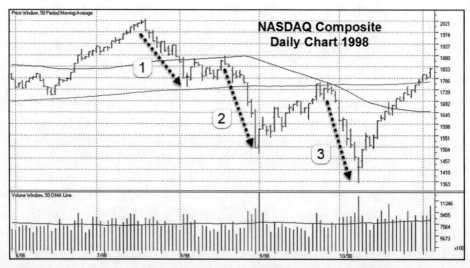

FIGURE 2.12 NASDAQ Composite Index daily chart. A short three-month bear market that has three distinct downside selling waves was centered on what became known as the Long-Term Capital crisis.

Source: Chart courtesy of HGSI Investment Software, LLC (www.highgrowthstock.com), ©2014.

leveraged bets went bad, the fund collapsed and 14 financial institutions had to come together to engineer a $3.6 billion bailout on September 23, 1998. This spooked the market, as many feared that the collapse of Long-Term Capital Management would bring down the financial system.

In hindsight, this "crisis" doesn't look like much of a crisis compared to the 2008 financial meltdown in terms of the threat it posed to the overall financial system, but it was enough to scare investors into a selling panic that generated a 33-percent decline in the NASDAQ. Since the definition of a bear market is a decline of 20 percent or more, which any financial cable TV talking head will tell you is "bear market territory," the August–October 1998 decline qualified as a bear market. There were some short opportunities, but most were just short, sharp breakdowns in stocks that were acting reasonably well up until the time the Long-Term Capital crisis hit.

Relying on the bromide of only shorting during a bear market, the brevity of this particular bear market in 1998 made it difficult to make any serious money on the short side in a sustained manner. In fact, I recall being short right at the bottom when the Fed came in and lowered interest rates on October 15, triggering a follow-through day and a new bull market rally. When the news hit, I was meeting with an institutional client of William O'Neil + Co., Inc. in my office and immediately interrupted the meeting to pick up the phone to call our in-house trading desk, which was right down the hall, cover all my short positions, and immediately go long stocks like Charles Schwab & Corp. (SCHW). Quick thinking and a quick reaction to the news given the position of the indexes and the action of the Fed helped me turn a −32-percent return up to that point in October 1998 to a 68-percent gain by year-end.

The period of 2003–2007 could have been considered an overall bull cycle with three decent market corrections occurring within the overall choppy upside trend. The weekly chart of the NASDAQ Composite Index in Figure 2.13 shows a correction in the NASDAQ of 18.7 percent that began in late December 2003 and lasted for about six months before bottoming in August of 2004. A second four-month correction of 13.8 percent occurred from early January through the end of April 2005, and a third intermediate correction of 15.3 percent hit the market in May of 2006 and lasted until about mid-July for a total duration of about two and a half months. While none of these would have qualified as true bear markets, it was possible to make money on the short side.

The overall recovery that has characterized the uptrend from April 2009 to the time of this writing has also had its share of intermediate corrections, one of which was just barely deep enough to meet the so-called −20-percent downside minimum move required for a bear market. The weekly chart of the NASDAQ Composite Index in Figure 2.14 shows a very sharp correction that began in May 2010 with the Flash Crash and lasted four months before bottoming at the end of August 2010.

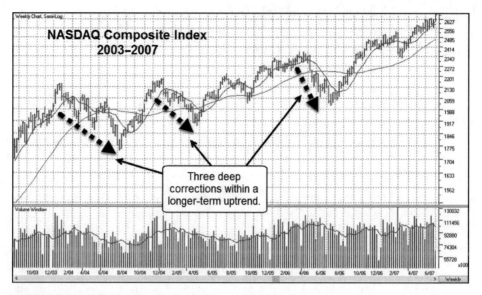

FIGURE 2.13 NASDAQ Composite Index weekly chart, 2003–2007.

Source: Chart courtesy of HGSI Investment Software, LLC (www.highgrowthstock.com), ©2014.

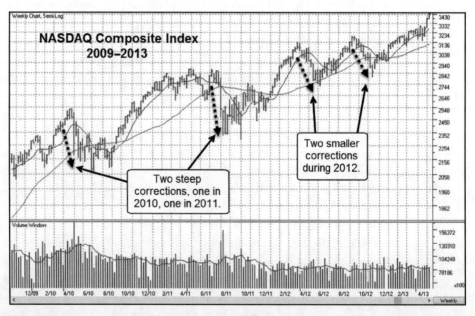

FIGURE 2.14 The 2009–2013 bull market cycle had four sharp intermediate corrections, with the second of these corrections meeting the definition of a bear market by dropping more than −20 percent.

Source: Chart courtesy of HGSI Investment Software, LLC (www.highgrowthstock.com), ©2014.

As we already know from my discussion at the beginning of this chapter, that was a very profitable downside break to play on the short side. The second correction in 2011 was another sharp break off the peak where most of the "juice" on the short side came in just a handful of weeks or less. By the time the market finished retesting and undercutting its May low in the first week of October 2011, the NASDAQ had corrected −20.4 percent, enough to earn the label of "bear market." Unfortunately, as soon as it fit the so-called definition of a bear market by dropping more than the required −20 percent, it was over. This gives us some idea of just how useless trying to apply quantitative labels to determine whether the market is or isn't in a bear market can be in the pursuit of short-selling success. Here we see a situation where if one had adhered to a rule of "short stocks only during a bear market" and waited for the market to meet the required −20-percent drop that supposedly marks the point at which a market correction becomes a bear market, one would have been shorting at the end of the market's downtrend. The rule is again exposed as being far too simplistic and, more importantly, impractical when it comes to making money on the short side—and keeping it.

The two smaller corrections in 2012 were less severe on the downside, both coming in at roughly equal magnitudes of 13 percent and 12.1 percent, respectively. It is instructive to note that one of the biggest big-stock technology leaders at the time, Apple (APPL), topped at the exact time the market topped in late September 2012. While the NASDAQ ultimately corrected all of 12.1 percent in that intermediate correction, AAPL continued lower even after the market had turned back to the upside. While the market trended to higher highs throughout the first several months of 2013, AAPL moved the other way, eventually bottoming out in April after declining a total of 45.4 percent off of its peak price of 705.07, achieved in September 2012.

The example of AAPL, which we will discuss in greater detail later in this book, shows how a major leading stock will often top in synchrony with the general market. However, while the stock's top leads to a sustained downside move that can cut the price in half or more, the general market will come out of its intermediate correction and continue higher. This is typical of the rotational action that characterizes all bull cycles, as certain stocks lead the market at the beginning and middle portions of the cycle but eventually fall by the wayside as new leaders rise up to take their place and keep the bull cycle going. AAPL shows why one can do quite well shorting the right stock when it tops during an intermediate-term market correction. In the case of the intermediate correction of late September to late December 2012, AAPL was a leader that topped and made for a very profitable short-sale target at that time and even after the market turned back to the upside in January 2013.

This is a key concept in our understanding of when one needs to be vigilant and aware of which leading stocks might be topping at the time and thereby making prime short-sale targets. The natural and normal rotation during a bull cycle—in which leading stocks carry the market for a period of time but eventually begin to become over-owned, at which point they must give way to newer, fresher leadership that takes over the task of perpetuating the bull cycle—means that short-sale opportunities don't just show up during bear markets.

While this has been something of a long-winded discussion of our first "golden rule" of short-selling, it is intended to comprehensively illustrate some basic realities about when to sell short. First of all, you don't have to confine your short-selling operations to "bear markets." Many short-selling opportunities arise during short- to intermediate-term market corrections. After all, the reality is that when the market indexes and leading stocks first roll over from their peaks, you have absolutely no idea whether you are starting a short-term or intermediate-term market correction or a more substantial bear market. As well, you have no idea how deep or how long the bear market or correction will carry. We've seen how even the most seasoned and experienced investors cannot gauge with exact precision where one is in the bear cycle, much less when the actual and final bottom is firmly in place.

But using a contextual understanding of where you *might be* within the overall bear cycle can at least provide some practical methods for knowing when and where to go short, as well as when and where to cover those shorts and take profits. Hopefully, as we move further through this book, the reader will begin to gain a feel for this in terms of some basic rules and conditions relating to the actual mechanics of short-selling, which we will cover in more detail as we move through the book.

In summary, the old first golden rule of "Short stocks only during bear markets" is now updated to "know where you are in the cycle." This means knowing where you are in the bear cycle as well as the bull cycle, because even intermediate corrections in the market indexes during a longer-term, overall bull cycle can also lead to major tops in leading stocks that in and of themselves make for "juicy" short-sale targets.

Rule #2: Focus on those "big-stock" leaders that had huge upside price moves in the immediately preceding bull market phase and that are showing significant signs of topping.

For the most part rule #2 hasn't changed much. But what exactly is a "big stock"? On page 9 of our first book, *Trade Like an O'Neil Disciple: How We Made 18,000% in the Stock Market*, we described the Big Stock Principle and its implementation in the following passage:

> Knowing which stocks represented the cutting edge of developments driving any particular economic, and hence market, cycle means knowing where institutional investors "have to be" with respect to positioning their portfolios. When institutional investors start shoveling money into stocks that they "have to be" invested in, this fuels tremendous upside price moves in those stocks, and it is what makes them "big stocks."

In Jesse Livermore's day, he referred to them as "the leading issues of the day."

The Big Stock Principle is as important on the long side of the market when the bulls are running as it is on the short side when it comes to short-sale stock selection. Big, leading stocks run up in price over many weeks, months, or years as institutions pile in and push them up with their enormous buying power. But eventually, every institution and every investor that can buy the stock already has, and the *accumulation* phase is over. At that point, the only direction for the money to start flowing is out of the stock as the *distribution* phase begins. This is when leading stocks top, and when they begin to break down the magnitude of the downside trends can be very profitable for the short-seller. To some extent, we apply the old adage that "what goes up must come down." Since leading stocks go up the most and the fastest, they are the most vulnerable to coming down fast and hard.

One way to assess when a big-stock leader might be moving into a distribution phase is to track institutional sponsorship in the stock. From my experience advising institutional investors, most begin accumulating a position in a stock with the idea of holding it for three to five years. Sometimes certain institutional investors become the "axe" in a particular big stock, as they continuously buy the stock, making it an ever larger position in their portfolio as the stock continues to rise. A good example of this is how Fidelity Contra Fund, one of the smarter mutual funds at the time, handled their position in Apple (AAPL). Starting with an initial position at around the time AAPL started its big price move in 2004, Fidelity Contra Fund built up a position in AAPL that at one point exceeded a 10 percent position size. For any mutual fund, this is a very aggressive position, but the smarter mutual funds do their homework and thereby gain the conviction to build such a large position over time. In 2012, mutual fund tracking data revealed that Contra Fund began selling their position in AAPL as it was topping in 2012. Their selling, along with other institutional investors who were now distributing the stock after a long period of accumulation, is what drove AAPL down after its peak in September 2012.

Another aspect of big, leading stocks is that during their uptrends they tend to benefit from very large price-to-earnings or P/E ratio expansions. Leading stocks can sell for 30–40 times earnings or more at the time that they begin their price runs, and their P/E ratios can expand to more than double or triple that (sometimes even more!) through the course of their upside trends. When the stock finally tops, the P/E ratio can deflate very quickly, particularly in an all-out bear market, and this can drive the stock down in a consistent and sometimes accelerating rate. Remember that P/E ratios are not really a measure of static value but rather reflect investors' demand for a particularly company's future or "forward" earnings stream. Stocks whose already-high P/E ratios expand even higher are doing so because investors have a high and increasing demand for that company's future earnings. In a competitive world, a company's future prospects are of course subject to difficulties and setbacks, and if investors begin to perceive a flaw in the company's future, then their demand for that company's future earnings stream can disappear quickly. P/E contractions are the reason why when stocks top and decline after a big prior upside price run they may initially look "cheap," only to get a lot cheaper.

Examples of big-stock leaders from recent history would include Qualcomm (QCOM) in 1999; Lockheed Martin (LMT) in late 2001; eBay (EBAY) in 2002–2004; Taser International and Netease (NTES) in 2003; Hansen's Beverage (HANS), now known as Monster Beverage (MNST), in 2003–2006; Intuitive Surgical (ISRG) from 2002–2007; coal names Peabody Energy (BTU), Consolidated Energy (CNX), and Arch Coal (ACI) in 2003–2008; oil and gas concern Southwestern Energy from 2006–2008; First Solar (FSLR) 2007–2008; Sunpower Corp. (SPWR) in 2007; Crocs (CROX) in 2007; Apple (AAPL) in 2004–2007 and 2009–2012 (see Figure 2.15); Google in 2004–2005; Baidu (BIDU) in 2006–2007; Research in Motion (RIMM), now known as Blackberry Ltd. (BBRY), in 2006–2007; Fertilizer stocks like Potash Corp. Saskatchewan (POT), Mosaic Company (MOS), and Agrium (AGU) in 2006–2008; MasterCard (MA) in 2006–2008 and again in 2011–2014; Netflix (NFLX) in 2009–2011; Keurig Green Mountain (GMCR) in 2011; Mellanox Technologies (MLNX) in 2011–2012; Ocwen Financial (OCN) and Nationstar Mortgage Holdings (NSM) in 2012–2013; Amazon.com (AMZN) in 2009–2014; Priceline.com (PCLN) in 2009–2014; Chipotle Mexican Grill (CMG) in 2010–2014; LinkedIn (LNKD) in 2013; Facebook (FB) in 2013–2014; Qihoo 360 Technology (QIHU) in 2013–2014; and Tesla Motors (TSLA) in 2013–2014.

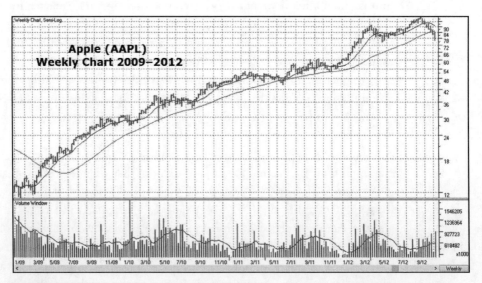

FIGURE 2.15 Apple (AAPL) weekly chart 2004–2013. Apple was the quintessential big-cap big-stock leader that became a viable short-sale candidate twice during its meteoric rise from 2003–2012.

Source: Chart courtesy of HGSI Investment Software, LLC (www.highgrowthstock.com), ©2014

This is just a slice of all the big-stock leaders over the past decade-plus, but it gives you a good idea of what a big stock is.

One major point: Do not confuse the term *big-stock* for *big-cap*. While some big-stock leaders can have very large market capitalizations, such as, for example, Apple (AAPL), Priceline.com (PCLN), and Facebook (FB), that is merely incidental to their big stock status. Small-cap and mid-cap stocks can also be big stocks if they meet the definition as dictated by the Big Stock Principle. While a stock like Facebook (FB), for example, might have a market capitalization of $50 billion when it starts its price move, a stock like Tesla Motors (TSLA) might only have a market cap of $10 billion when it gets going to the upside. In Figure 2.16, we see the weekly chart of Taser International (TASR) during the period 2003–2005. At the time of its big price move, institutions were coming into the stock based on the idea that Tasers would be increasingly used by law enforcement, particularly after the terrorist attacks of September 11, 2001. Its market cap was barely a few hundred million, however, so it most certainly was not a big-cap or even mid-cap stock. But it qualified as a big-stock leader in 2003, and once it topped from a late-stage failed-base set-up within a larger POD formation, the downside move was tremendously profitable on the short side.

Focusing on the big-stock leaders from the prior bull cycle also simplifies the process of building a short-sale watch list. If stocks on your buy watch list and starts showing heavy-volume selling off the peak after a long price run, you can move

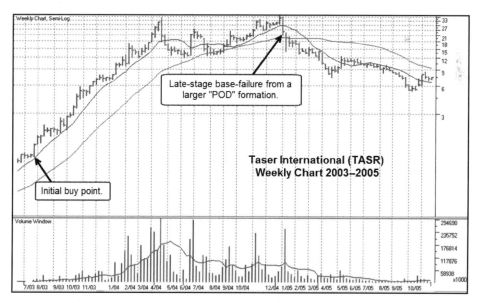

FIGURE 2.16 Taser International (TASR) weekly chart 2003–2005. TASR was a smaller big-stock leader during its big price run in 2003–2004.

Source: Chart courtesy of HGSI Investment Software, LLC (www.highgrowthstock.com), ©2014

them to a short-selling watch list. All of the short-selling chart pattern set-ups that we use rely on a high-volume break off of the peak, and this is often the first sign of institutional money exiting a stock en masse as they begin "distributing" stock. Often this high-volume price break will define the right side of the head in an H&S topping formation or a new base breakout that fails as the stock reverses back into its prior base on heavy selling volume, as we will see when we discuss short-selling set-ups in Chapter 3. Once a big-stock leader breaks sharply off of its peak on heavy volume, the stock is then monitored to determine whether it is in fact in the process of shaping and then completing an overall topping pattern.

To summarize, Short-Selling Golden Rule #2 really just makes use of the Big Stock Principle in reverse. Those same big stocks that led the market during a bull phase become the same stocks we seek to sell short when the market trend turns bearish. In this manner, we can exploit the trends that develop in former big-stock leaders when the flow of institutional money into a stock reverses and the same big buyers that drove the stock higher become the big sellers that drive it lower.

Rule #3: Seek to short former big-stock leaders eight to twelve weeks after their peak price following a major upside price run.

As we will see in Chapter 5, major topping formations such as an H&S top can take eight to twelve weeks or more from the absolute peak to finish developing and fully forming out before resulting in a sharp downside "breakout" that takes the stock much lower. Some big-stock leaders will top and break down faster than others. Sometimes we see a situation where it takes months after the top before a stock completely comes unglued on the downside, as in the example of Lululemon Athletica (LULU), shown on a weekly chart in Figure 2.17. After breaking down hard from its peak price of $82.50 in June of 2013, LULU took exactly six months before it finally split wide open.

In some cases, the opposite is true. The stock can sometimes take only a few weeks before it literally appears to "blow out of the sky" and rapidly plummets to the downside. For example, Crocs (CROX) was a smaller big-stock leader in 2007 that blew up after earnings in October 2007. This is represented by the huge downside price bar off the peak on massive selling volume on the weekly chart of the stock shown in Figure 2.18. After two weeks of moving to the downside, CROX then attempted to rally. The rally lasted only four weeks before the stock rolled over again and broke out through the neckline of a fully formed H&S topping formation.

In general, smaller "heater" stocks like CROX will break down faster than larger cap names, although this is not always the case. The exact point at which to short CROX occurred exactly six weeks from the peak, as the stock rallied up into its 40-week moving average and the top of what turned out to be a right shoulder within an overall H&S topping formation. The critical factor here is to simply watch to see how the pattern plays out. In the CROX example, one could easily figure out

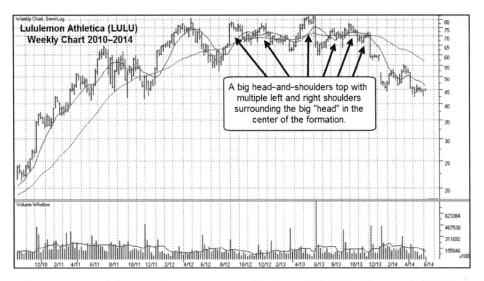

FIGURE 2.17 Lululemon Athletica (LULU) weekly chart, 2010–2014. The extended H&S "complex" that LULU formed at its top took a full six months from the peak to finally break down in earnest.

Source: Chart courtesy of HGSI Investment Software, LLC (www.highgrowthstock.com), ©2014

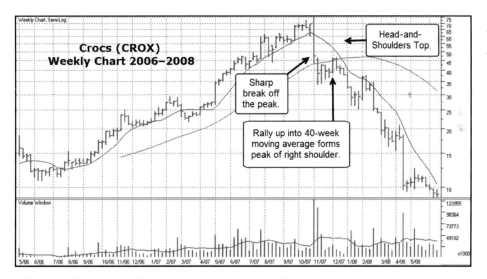

FIGURE 2.18 Crocs (CROX) weekly chart, 2006–2008.

Source: Chart courtesy of HGSI Investment Software, LLC (www.highgrowthstock.com), ©2014.

that the rally into the 40-week moving average was a possible right shoulder peak regardless of the fact that you were only six weeks from the absolute peak in the stock. The essence of Rule #3 is that we rarely, if ever, short a stock at the exact peak, instead waiting for the stock to set-up in a bona fide topping pattern.

In almost all of the examples that we study in this book, we will see that the sharp breakdowns generally occur eight to twelve weeks after the peak. The primary reason for this is that bullish sentiment in a big-stock leader will remain persistent for a period of time after the peak. Those who missed the big price run will initially see the break off the peak as a "buying opportunity," and this perception by late bulls may persist for a period of time until all of the bullish sentiment is literally wrung out of the stock.

In summary, Rule #3 can be revised to understanding that most big-stock leaders will take eight to twelve weeks after an absolute peak is put in before breaking down from their topping patterns, but some may take more time to break down and others less time. Therefore, while we do not seek to short stocks right after the peak, we let the price/volume action of the stock in real-time within the context of the overall topping pattern's formation guide us as to the potential proper short-sale entry point.

Rule #4: Only sell short stocks that trade a minimum of 1–2 million shares a day, and preferably more. In general, avoid thinly traded stocks as short-sale candidates, as risk can correlate inversely to a stock's trading liquidity.

In most cases, big-stock leaders will be highly liquid traders with average daily volume well in excess of 1–2 million shares. I prefer to short stocks that trade more than 2–5 million shares or more a day on average. The more liquid they are, the better, for some very simple reasons. The first is that the bigger any big-stock leader is, the more volume it will trade; the second is that the more liquid the stock is, the easier it is to move in and out of quickly. I use a "mouse-click" standard: the fewer mouse-clicks it takes me to get my short position in place or to cover an existing short position, the less the potential price slippage in either direction. Stocks that trade only a few hundred thousand shares a day should be avoided, unless an investor intends to deal in a much smaller position size relative to one's overall account equity. But getting into and out of a short position quickly is just half of the problem. While one can operate with the idea of taking a much smaller position, say a couple of thousand shares at most, when dealing with a thinner stock that trades maybe 200,000 to 300,000 shares a day, the fact remains that the thinner the stock, the greater and faster the potential movement in the stock if it suddenly begins to push higher in a classic *short squeeze*.

Summarizing Rule #4, the basic idea is that in your short-selling operations you should seek to traffic in stocks where you will be able to enter and exit your short-sale positions quickly. Trying to put on big short positions in thinly traded stocks is a recipe for disaster. However, if one is shorting small positions, say 1,000 to 2,000 shares and/or much less than 1 percent of the average daily trading volume, even in thinly traded stocks, then this can be feasible. But there is still some price velocity risk with thinner stocks, since in general the thinner the stock, the faster it can theoretically start moving against you given a specific change in demand for that stock. The basic equation can simply be thought of in strictly mathematical terms such that given the size of your short position in any stock, then the further below 1 percent of the stock's average daily volume that your position size represents, the better.

Rule #5: Set stop-losses at an average of 3–5 percent, using the tighter 3-percent stop if the stock begins to rally against you on strong, above-average volume. A layering technique can also be used by peeling off and covering portions of the position as the stock rallies against you a series of specified percentage thresholds, such as covering one-third at 3 percent, another third at 5 percent, and the final third at 7 percent, or any other permutations. Stops are dependent upon personal psychological preference and risk tolerance, so short-sellers should try to determine what works best for them in real-time.

Stop-losses on short positions should range around 3–5 percent. If you are down 3 percent on a position and the stock is trading above average volume as it rallies from your short-sale point, it is best to implement the 3 percent threshold for your stop-loss, with the idea that the stock can always be re-shorted if the rally suddenly fizzles out. One key general rule to keep in mind at all times, regardless of where you set your stop for a short position, is that if a stock you are short generates a pocket pivot type of upside buy signal, it is generally wise to cover the stock right there. The example of Netflix (NFLX) in May 2014, shown in Figure 2.19, illustrates why one should heed these types of upside buy signals and get out of the way quickly. In May 2014, NFLX looked to be forming another right shoulder within an overall H&S topping formation that was nearly six months in duration, but out of nowhere the stock flashed a pocket pivot buy point as it moved up through its 50-day moving average. For anyone short the stock at that point, that was a strong signal to cover the short position and get out of the stock's way. NFLX moved much higher from that point in a classic short squeeze.

Authors' note: A pocket pivot *buy point occurs when a stock moves up through or off of the 10-day, 50-day, or 200-day moving average on volume that is higher than the volume on any down day (the volume on up days is not a factor) over the prior 10 trading days. This concept is discussed in detail in our first book,* Trade Like an O'Neil Disciple: How We Made 18,000% in the Stock Market *(John Wiley & Sons, August 2010).*

Stops on short positions are still dependent on one's position size, personal psychology, and risk tolerance. When considering what type of stop-loss system to

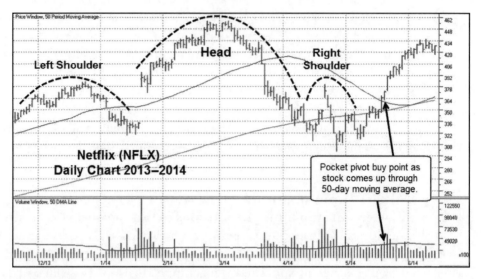

FIGURE 2.19 Netflix (NFLX) daily chart, 2014. A pocket pivot buy point shows up as the stock appears to be building a second right shoulder in an overall H&S topping pattern. Short-sellers that did not cover on the basis of this new buy point were painfully squeezed as the stock moved substantially higher.

Source: Chart courtesy of HGSI Investment Software, LLC (www.highgrowthstock.com), ©2014.

implement on the short side, it is important to remember one overriding reality of stops: there is no "magic" stop-loss point that guarantees you won't be whipsawed out of a position, only to see the stock roll over and head lower again. When it comes right down to it, where one sets their stop is primarily a function of how much money they are willing to lose if the trade does not work out and they are stopped out. It is this consideration that should rule your thinking in where and how to place to your stops on short positions. My general rule is that I never want to let a short position become more than a 1 percent loss to my total account equity, or value. Therefore, if one's account equity is $100,000, then the maximum loss you would be willing to take is $1,000. This means that a 10 percent short position could be allowed as much as a 10 percent stop, since 10 percent of $100,000 is $10,000, the dollar size of the position, and $1,000 out of $10,000 is $1,000/$10,000, or 1/10, which is equal to 10 percent. A position that is 25 percent of your total account equity or value is 25 percent of $100,000, or $25,000. A $1,000 loss is equal to $1,000/$25,000 which is equal to 1/25, or 4 percent.

As you gain experience short-selling, you might find a particular permutation of stop-loss policies that works best for you, but whatever the case, it is extremely important to always have a clear exit plan and point for any short position that is taken. Standing in the way of a sharp rally through indecision or hesitation, or what we refer to as *freezing up*, can be very dangerous.

One way to handle stops is to use a reverse-layering technique by peeling off portions of the position as a short position rallies against you, say one-third of the position when it is 3 percent above your short-sale price, another third when it is 5 percent above, and the last third once the stock has rallied 7 percent past your short-sale price point. Other permutations of this strategy might be half the position at 3 percent and the other half at 5 percent, or half at 5 percent and half at 7 percent.

Another technique that I favor is to simply pick a point at which to take a full short position in a short-sale target stock, using a short 2–3 percent upside stop, with the idea of covering if you get stopped out with the idea of re-shorting the stock if it fails higher up in the pattern. In some cases, one might be forced out rather quickly, only to see the stock roll over again on heavy volume. At this point it is possible to re-enter a short position, even if at a lower price than that which you covered the first time around. This is what I call "bobbing and weaving" with the stock as it rallies up into a logical area of resistance. Short-selling is a little trickier in this regard, and one must be persistent when pursuing short-sale target stocks as they rally. This is why you may sometimes need to take a number of small losses before hitting a stock just right and then watching it plummet. This will be covered in more detail in Chapter 4, where we discuss the mechanics of short-selling.

To summarize, Rule #5 can be revised to setting stops that are consistent with the maximum loss to your overall account equity/value that you are willing to take. There are no "magic" stops. Once you've figure out how much you are willing to lose if the trade goes bad, then your upside stop-loss level can be set within the context of the stock's price/volume action within its chart pattern and its associated upside resistance level.

Rule #6: Once a short position is showing a profit, set a downside profit target objective of 20–30 percent or use a "layering" technique, covering half the position once a 15–20 percent profit is showing and the other half at a 20–30 percent profit. Alternatively, once a short position is showing a good profit, one can use the 20-day moving average as a guide for a trailing stop. If the nearest moving average above the stock's current price is the 50-day or 200-day moving average, then that can be used in place of the 20-day moving average line. Watch also for undercuts of prior lows as potential rally points at which all or part of the position can be covered.

Because stocks will often have sharp upside rallies within their macro-downtrends, it is wise to set reasonable profit objectives for any downside move you expect a stock to make once you have taken a short position in the stock. In most environments, profit targets should be 20–30 percent. If you find that short positions are breaking closer to 15–20 percent before rallying and wiping out your profits, then you can adjust this, or again use a "layering" technique where you cover 1/2 the position when it is showing a 15- to 20-percent profit and the remainder when it is showing a 20- to 30-percent profit.

Alternatively, the 20-day moving average can sometimes be used as a guide for a trailing upside stop on any short position that is showing a decent profit. Once a stock has broken down from a proper short-sale set-up and topping formation and has been in a downtrend for at least a few days to a few weeks, the 20-day is often a useful reference point for a legitimate upside turn and rally in a stock, and hence offers what can be a nearby trailing stop.

Another method that I favor is working a short position based on the *undercut and rally* phenomenon I have observed in stocks as they top and begin their longer-term price declines. As a stock comes down, it will start to undercut prior support levels in the chart, and often these undercuts of prior lows in a pattern set up reaction rallies back to the upside. The reason for this is somewhat intuitive. If a breakdown through a "support" level is seen as bearish, this is where natural sellers will be washed out of the stock and short-sellers will swarm the stock on the short side as they see the breach of support as indicative of further, impending downside. Thus as everyone leans over to one side of the boat at the same time, selling is washed out in the short-term and the stock then rallies back up through the previously breached support level.

Pandora Media (P), shown on a daily chart from 2014 in Figure 2.20, gives some idea of how this undercut and rally method of working a short position might play out. In early March 2014, as the general market began what turned out to be a

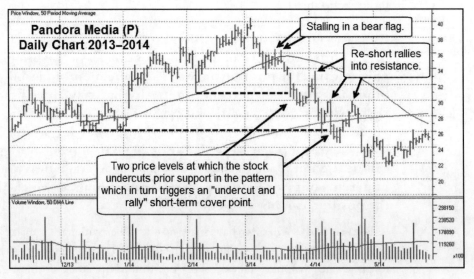

FIGURE 2.20   Pandora Media (P) daily chart, 2014. Two breaches of prior support in the pattern trigger *undercut and rally* moves back up through the broken support levels.

Source: Chart courtesy of HGSI Investment Software, LLC (www.highgrowthstock.com), ©2014

short-term correction, Pandora Media gapped down off of its peak price on heavy selling volume that was about three times average daily volume. The stock then found support along its 50-day moving average in the middle of March in a short *bear flag* formation. Within this short, six-day bear flag we can see two days where the stock tried to rally up and off of the 50-day moving but instead stalled out and closed back below the 50-day line. I actually shorted the stock right at this point and it immediately broke down and undercut the early February low delineated by the upper dotted line on the chart. That triggered an undercut and rally that carried up into resistance along the prior late February/early March lows in the 34 price level, more or less. The stock was shortable again on this rally, and it reversed very quickly and sharply, breaking to lower lows over the next two days. On the third day down, the stock undercut a more significant low that marked the bottom of a chart base that the stock had built in November and December of 2014, delineated by the lower dotted line. In this case there were two undercut and rally moves, with the first one moving below the late December 2013 low on an intra-day basis and then rallying back up to the 30 price level, where the stock was shortable again. This immediately broke down and again undercut the late December 2013 low, but this time the stock closed below the low. This triggered a second undercut and rally that carried right back up to the same 30 price level, where the stock was shortable yet a second time. This then led to a huge-volume gap-down that took the stock to new lows. In this manner, I will campaign a stock on the short side, hitting it heavily on the short side as it rallies into potential resistance and then covering on the downside breaks as the stock undercuts a key support level in the pattern. As a broken-down former leader trends lower over several weeks, this process can be repeated several times as the stocks breaks down, then undercuts a support level, rallies back to an overhead resistance level, and breaks down again to fresh lows.

In practice, this approach works best since flexibility is required at all times on the short side. While making a practice of taking 20–25 percent profits in short positions when you have them is sound, the practical problem with that is sometimes the downside move is more within the 10–20 percent range, and using the undercut and rally method is generally more accurate in determining when to take profits.

As we saw in our discussion of Rule #1, you never know exactly when and if you are in a short-term correction, an intermediate correction/bear market, or something much nastier and severe, such as the bear markets of 2000–2002 or 2007–2009. Therefore you never know when the market pullback and correction will end, sending stocks bouncing sharply back to the upside. And, as we saw with the example of Netflix (NFLX) in Figure 2.19, you also never know when what looks like a H&S topping formation will suddenly morph into the right side of a new, potential cup base. In this manner, I would say that playing the short side of the market requires more maneuvering and often more effort in terms of position monitoring and trading frequency. While it can be very rewarding when it works, short-selling can also be exhausting! If hard work and perseverance are concepts that don't frighten you, then you may have the potential to become an effective short-seller.

To summarize Rule #6, we can say that setting stops is primarily a matter of figuring out just how much you are willing to lose if the trade goes against you, and then mapping a logical stop-loss and profit-taking program around the technical aspects of the stock's chart pattern with respect to areas of prior support and current resistance. In general, the undercut and rally method is more accurate than just ascribing a rote rule of taking 20–25 percent profits when you have them. As we've illustrated in our discussion, there are a number of scripted techniques and methods you can use as part of your short-selling risk-management, but understanding some basic concepts can go a long way in helping you find out what works best for your style of trading.

Hopefully this chapter has given the reader a detailed working knowledge of the basics of OWL-style short-selling, as expressed through these six Golden Rules. In our first book, we touched upon these rules only briefly. In addition, you also understand that most of these rules have been revised over the past four years as our studies of short-selling in real-time help us too evolve and refine our methods. As we move through the rest of this book, you will gain a deeper understanding of how these basic rules are implemented as we repeat, review, and revert to these rules in the more detailed discussions presented in these pages.

CHAPTER 3

Short-Selling Set-Ups: Chart Patterns for the Dark Side

On the way up, leading stocks will form certain chart patterns that identify and confirm their technical health. These chart patterns result from the pattern of accumulation in the stock by institutional investors, including mutual funds, pension funds, hedge funds, and trusts as they build their positions over a period of time that may range from a few months to a few years. They are quite literally the "footprints" of institutional buyers as they conduct their intermediate- to longer-term operations in a particular big-stock leader. By the same token, institutional selling and distribution that occurs when these same institutions reduce their positions in a leading stock also has specific "footprints" in the various topping chart patterns that take shape as a big-stock leader ends its upside life-cycle and begins a period of decline characterized by a pattern of distribution. Short-selling is all about the techniques, as leading stocks generally top when the fundamental picture is quite rosy, so the price/volume action and the chart patterns it carves out are an important and primary driver in the analysis and decision process.

There are three primary short-selling set-ups that we use: the *head-and-shoulders (H&S) top*, the *late-stage failed-base (LSFB)*, and the *punchbowl of death (POD)*, which is essentially a massive double-top of sorts. Each has its own unique characteristics, but sometimes patterns can overlap and therefore can be interpreted as a hybrid between two or more of these formations, as we will see later in this chapter. Ultimately, the exact shape and label we assign to a particular topping formation is less important than the actual price/volume action within the pattern that indicates the stock is very likely under systematic and sustained distribution. It is important not to get overly "textbook" about these chart pattern labels. Markets are fluid and contextual, so the pattern labels only serve as a general guide.

As well, the patterns do not exist in a vacuum. The action of the general market figures heavily into how these patterns will ultimately play out in real-time. There is also the context of just where the stock is within its overall price run in terms of magnitude and duration. Tracking the flow of institutional sponsorship into and out of a big-stock leader can provide additional context for the formation of a topping pattern. Thus the context within which these chart patterns form requires some consideration and represents some of the broader analysis necessary when it comes to one's short-selling pattern recognition skills.

The basic, initial, and most immediately obvious feature of any topping pattern is generally a sharp downside price break right off the peak that occurs on massive downside volume after a steady upside price run of several months or more. Heavy volume selling off the top after a sustained uptrend is the first tip-off that an initial wave of distribution in a big-stock leader is at hand as institutions begin the distributive process. We should make it clear, however, that there can be some variation in the magnitude of these price breaks. Price breaks off the peak in some stocks can occur in as little as one quick week, while others can take several weeks. Regardless, this is the point at which a big-stock leader that was previously on your buy watch list should now be moved to your short-sale watch list. Screening for stocks with heavy-volume price breaks on a daily and weekly basis is the most effective way to catch potential short-sale targets once they start to come under distribution. Keep in mind that in not all cases will a price break down off the peak in a former leader result in the stock building an overall topping formation. Leading stocks can and often do simply correct and build new chart bases from which they begin new price advances, so such a breakdown can sometimes just be the start of a normal correction and base-building period in the stock. The price break, however, is the first technical signal that highlights the *possibility* that a leading stock may be topping for good. This is why, although it is possible to build elaborate screens that identify H&S formations, it is not necessary. Keeping a watch list of "broken" leaders that have had big-volume sell-offs off the peaks of big price runs in the immediately prior bull market phase is sufficient for compiling a short-selling "pool" of names from which to operate.

The Head-and-Shoulders Top

When it comes to something that could be considered a "template" for a classic H&S top, we would like to think that Crocs (CROX) in 2007–2008, shown on a weekly chart in Figure 3.1, is the poster child for such chart formations. The reality is that such a picture perfect example of a H&S topping pattern is more the exception than the rule. In practice, H&S formations come in a variety of imperfect forms. But the CROX example is still very useful for the purpose of understanding the basic components of a head-and-shoulders topping formation and aids in the pattern recognition process as one monitors big-stock leaders once they have begun to break down.

The essential prerequisite for any topping pattern is a strong prior upside price trend. The head-and-shoulders top is no different. As the stock continues higher, it suddenly breaks off the peak on huge volume. This massive-volume price break off the peak defines the right side of the head in the head-and-shoulders formation. Two left shoulders can now be seen in the pattern. Remember, prior to the big price break off the peak, the two left shoulders were just price consolidations within the prior uptrend. Not until that uptrend comes to an end with a high-volume price off

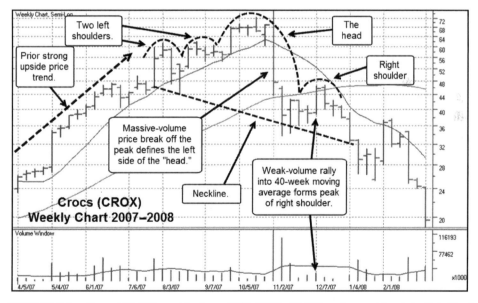

FIGURE 3.1 Crocs (CROX) weekly chart, 2007–2008. CROX can be considered the "ideal" of what a head-and-shoulders topping formation "should" look like. However, such a perfect short-sale set-up like this is more the exception than the rule.

Source: Chart courtesy of HGSI Investment Software, LLC (www.highgrowthstock.com), ©2014.

the peak are we able to determine that we are potentially dealing with the start of a head-and-shoulders top. Once the stock breaks off the peak, the initial context for a head-and-shoulders formation is put into place, and it is at that point a matter of watching to see whether and how any right shoulders form over the ensuing weeks and, in some cases, months.

The CROX example has only one right shoulder, giving it a very neat and orderly appearance as the stock rallies up to the 40-week moving average, corresponding to the 200-day moving average on a daily chart, on weak volume and then gives way as it rolls over to the complete the right shoulder in the pattern. By drawing a trend line along the lows of the right shoulder(s) and the terminus of the right side of the head, we can derive the neckline of the pattern. Generally, a descending neckline tends to be the weakest, although I've seen both ascending and flat necklines work as well. The pattern is also generally considered to be weaker when the right shoulder or shoulders in the pattern form below the peak of the left shoulder(s). Notice that in the CROX example the stock breaks out to the downside through the neckline, but then fakes short-sellers out by making one last rally back up through the neckline that eventually finds resistance at the 10-week (50-day on the daily chart) moving average. The last feature to note is that the general pattern of trading volume will appear to trend higher as you move your eye from left to right in the pattern. This can be "eyeballed" by observing a rising 10-week moving average of volume on the chart.

Whatever you do, however, don't get carried away with the idea that just because you can slap an H&S label on a stock's pattern it means instant short-selling profits are at hand. The example of Priceline.com (PCLN) in 2009–2010, which we show on a weekly chart from that period in Figure 3.2, looks almost too good to be true. Looking at this "textbook" H&S topping formation, one might marvel at how perfectly it matches the CROX example.

The pattern has all of the components we want to see in a head-and-shoulders short-selling set-up, from the high-volume break off the peak that defines the right side of the head in the head-and-shoulders formation to the descending neckline, theoretically the weakest such set-up. How could one go wrong shorting this? Easily, that's how. Figure 3.3 shows the ultimate resolution of this H&S formation as a rally to new highs, the "perfect" H&S set-up turned into a not-so-perfect cup-with-handle base breakout that catapulted the stock into all-time new high price ground. The market always does its best to fool the most people most of the time, so one should not get bogged down in searching for "perfect" H&S chart patterns. Sometimes, as we will see as we progress through this chapter, the least perfect head-and-shoulders formation can be the most rewarding for short-sellers.

Why did such a "perfect" head-and-shoulders formation fail to work? Well, mainly because such visual perfection is no guarantee that the stock will automatically go lower just because you can slap a neat label on the formation. In PCLN's case, the

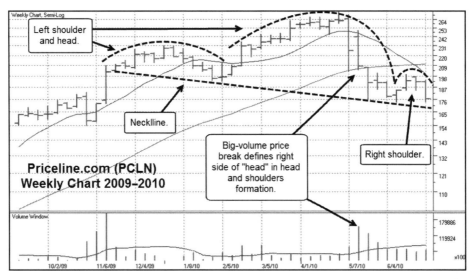

FIGURE 3.2 Priceline.com (PCLN) weekly chart, 2009–2010. A "perfect" H&S topping formation gets would-be short-sellers salivating.

Source: Chart courtesy of HGSI Investment Software, LLC (www.highgrowthstock.com), ©2014.

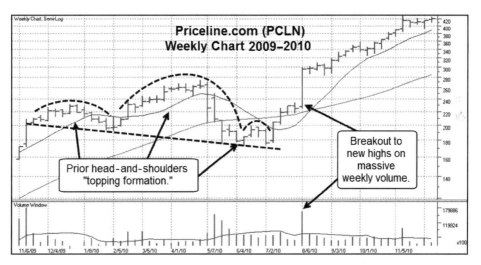

FIGURE 3.3 Priceline.com (PCLN) weekly chart, 2009–2010. What looked like a "perfect" head-and-shoulders topping formation on the verge of breaking down through its neckline fools short-sellers when it turns back to the upside, resulting in a breakout to fresh price highs.

Source: Chart courtesy of HGSI Investment Software, LLC (www.highgrowthstock.com), ©2014.

stock issued a pocket pivot buy point as it moved up through its 10-week (50-day) moving average in early July of 2010. As we discussed in Chapter 2, that is always a signal to cover any short position. Thus the only thing that tells you whether the pattern is going to work is, in fact, whether it works—if it stops you out instead, then at that point, and only at that point, can you know that the pattern isn't working on the downside. The general market is also a major factor in determining whether a given short-sale pattern will work or not, but PCLN actually bottomed before the market in the late summer of 2010 during the intermediate market correction that began with the Flash Crash of May 2010 and finally ended at the beginning of September 2010 as a new market rally phase took hold. In that particular case, the recovery of PCLN as it "shook off" its head-and-shoulders pattern and moved to new highs was one of the early clues that the market was about to bottom and move back into a new rally phase.

Mellanox Technologies (MLNX), shown on a weekly chart from 2012–2013 in Figure 3.4, is an example of a head-and-shoulders formation with an ascending neckline, which by default disproves the notion that only an H&S pattern with a descending neckline can work. Notice also the very large "dome-top" head and the relatively much smaller left and right shoulders, giving it a somewhat disproportionate look. This helps to illustrate the point that H&S formations can come in a variety of sizes and shapes which do not necessarily adhere to some ideal of a "perfect" and hence optimal pattern.

Nationstar Mortgage Holdings (NSM), shown on a weekly chart in Figure 3.5, below, shows a flat or horizontal neckline. If you study the chart carefully, you might

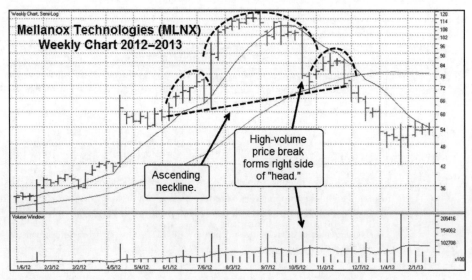

FIGURE 3.4 Mellanox Technologies (MLNX) weekly chart, 2012–2013.

Source: Chart courtesy of HGSI Investment Software, LLC (www.highgrowthstock.com), ©2014.

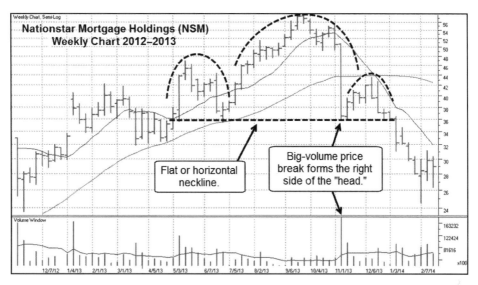

FIGURE 3.5 Nationstar Mortgage Holdings (NSM) weekly chart, 2013–2014.

Source: Chart courtesy of HGSI Investment Software, LLC (www.highgrowthstock.com), ©2014.

notice that the head is itself comprised of a smaller H&S formation with a rising neckline. In some formations, regardless of the slope of the neckline, you can have a situation where the head forms in this manner, and we will see more examples of this as we progress through the book and expand on the idea of "fractal" topping patterns.

NSM's massive breakdown along the right side of the head pushed below the 40-week (200-day) moving average in early November 2013 and then rallied up to the 40-week line over the next five weeks. The downside reversal in early December marked the peak of the right shoulder and offered a concrete short-sale entry point before the stock moved lower and eventually staged a downside breakout through the neckline.

While the right side of the head in a head-and-shoulders pattern will often be comprised of a sharp, high-volume price break off the peak, as the CROX, MLNX, and NSM examples show, sometimes it simply rolls over off the peak on above-average weekly volume in "slow-motion" fashion, as the example of Netflix (NFLX) in Figure 3.6 shows. In this case, the breakdown off the peak in July 2011 took four weeks to form the right side of the head. After the head finished forming, the stock then bounces once off of its 40-week (200-day) moving average to form the first right shoulder and then zig-zags below the 40-week line and then back above it to form a second right shoulder. Each shoulder is about two weeks in duration, which is pretty much the limit for how quickly any shoulder in the pattern can form. From there the stock blows apart and plummets about 50 percent in three weeks. Another interesting exception to the rule in this NFLX example is that the overall level of volume declined as you move from left to right in the pattern and did not increase

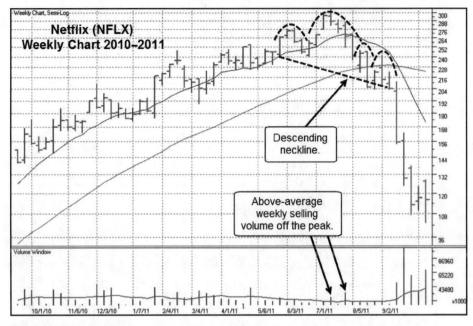

FIGURE 3.6 Netflix (NFLX) weekly chart, 2010–2011.

Source: Chart courtesy of HGSI Investment Software, LLC (www.highgrowthstock.com), ©2014.

until the stock began to plummet through the neckline. In many ways NFLX was not a "perfect" H&S formation, but its downside price move was very exciting for those playing it on the short side at the time. We will look at NFLX's 2011 top and breakdown in more detail when we review it as a Case Study in Chapter 7.

Driving home the point that not all head-and-shoulders patterns are created in the same image, we can find some humor in the example of LED-lighting manufacturer Cree (CREE), which we show on a weekly chart from 2013–2014 in Figure 3.7. During the period of July through September 2013, the stock started out building what looked like a classic head-and-shoulders topping formation. One left shoulder, a head with a massive volume and very steep price break off the peak, and one right shoulder all came together to form what looked like a textbook head-and-shoulders formation not too unlike the example of CROX in Figure 3.1.

But in October, as it appeared to be near the peak of the right shoulder, CREE took off and recovered right back up to its prior highs in just one week's time. The biggest part of that one-week move was a 15.9-percent one-day rocket ride up through the peak of what was looking like the right shoulder and the 10-week (50-day) moving average on the first day of October 2013. This attempt at new price highs failed within three weeks, as the stock gave up all of those early October gains with a −16.89-percent mid-air blow-up on October 23, following the company's third quarter earnings announcement. This breakdown formed the right side of a

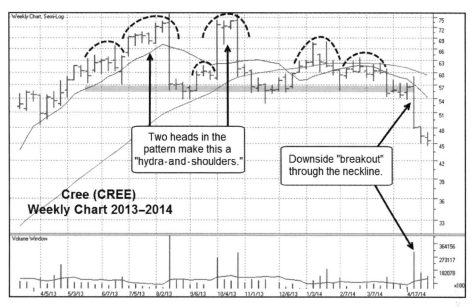

FIGURE 3.7 Cree (CREE) weekly chart, 2013–2014. A very unusual head-and-shoulders formation with two heads in the pattern, making it something of a "hydra" version of a normal H&S formation.

Source: Chart courtesy of HGSI Investment Software, LLC (www.highgrowthstock.com), ©2014.

second head in the pattern to create a multi-headed sort of "hydra and shoulders" formation.

This second head then led to the formation of two right shoulders that were of longer duration and during which the stock rallied further up in the pattern. This created a pattern with one left shoulder, a left head, a "middle" shoulder, a right head, and two right shoulders. The two right shoulders led to more significant reaction rallies in the stock, such that their peaks were above the peak of the middle shoulder, certainly not what you would call a "textbook" head-and-shoulders top. Notice how CREE formed a four-week bear flag in April 2014 before it broke out to the downside and plummeted through the long neckline of the 11-month "hydra and shoulders" formation.

Some readers might remember the old underground comic book character "Zippy the Pinhead." Adding to the humor of CREE's hydra-and-shoulders formation, we have Blackberry Ltd. (BBRY), formerly known as Research in Motion (RIMM) in 2008, and its "pinhead-and-shoulders" formation, shown on a weekly chart in Figure 3.8. I like to refer to these types of patterns as "Zippy" formations.

The head in this pattern took only two weeks to form, and was primarily a function of a brutal base breakout failure in mid-June 2008. But the big-volume price break off the peak, when taken in context with the ensuing rally that formed a right shoulder, means we can view this as an H&S variant.

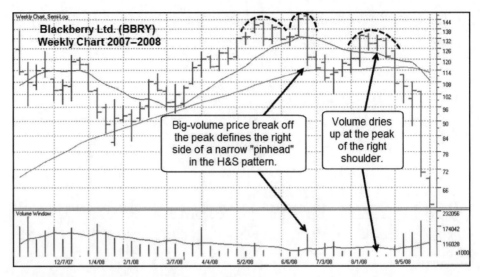

FIGURE 3.8   Blackberry Ltd. (BBRY), known in 2008 as Research in Motion (RIMM), weekly chart, 2007–2008. BBRY forms a "pinhead-and-shoulders" topping formation before blowing apart with the general market in the latter part of 2008.

Source: Chart courtesy of HGSI Investment Software, LLC (www.highgrowthstock.com), ©2014.

That right shoulder formed after BBRY broke down below its 40-week moving average in early July 2008 and then rallied back above both the 40-week and 10-week moving averages, corresponding to the 200-day and 50-day moving averages on the daily chart. The stock finally ran out of gas as buying volume dried up right at the peak of the right shoulder. Downside volume began to pick up as the stock sank through the 10-week and 40-week moving averages and broke to new lows. Looking at this pattern in Figure 3.8, the reader might notice that figuring out where to draw the neckline in this pinhead-and-shoulders type of formation is not necessarily all that easy to do. This is not uncommon for many head-and-shoulders formations, which is one reason why we generally look to short the stock somewhere in the upper part of the right shoulder rather than trying to discern where a downside neckline "breakout" might occur in a pattern where the neckline might be far too steep or too difficult to define with any meaningful precision to make it practical as a short-selling timing guide.

We can see that a great deal of variation occurs among head-and-shoulders patterns with respect to their shape, size, and duration. There are, however, clearly identifiable and essential features that can tip us off that a head-and-shoulders pattern is forming in a big-stock leader, particularly after a long upside price run, which of course provides the essential context for any topping formation. As well, sometimes head-and-shoulders patterns have "fractal" characteristics in that they can contain other short-selling patterns as subsets within them, or they themselves can be subsets of even larger short-selling formations, as we will see throughout this book.

The Late-Stage Failed-Base

When I first began studying head-and-shoulders formations back in the late 1990s, I began to notice that the huge-volume price break off the peak that defined the right side of the head in the pattern almost always resulted from a late-stage base breakout failure. These resulted in huge downside moves as the failed late-stage base breakout reverses hard to the downside, breaking through the lows of the prior late-stage base and, generally, the 50-day/10-week moving averages.

This was the genesis of the late-stage failed-base (LSFB) topping formation that provides us with our second, and more common, topping formation, which I wrote about in *How to Make Money Selling Stocks Short* (John Wiley & Sons, 2004), which I as a "co-author" essentially ghost wrote. As I studied more of these, I began to realize that an LSFB set-up can also just be a late-stage base from which the stock blows up and plummets, without first forming a left shoulder, as the example of Chipotle Mexican Grill (CMG) from 2012 shows us in Figure 3.9.

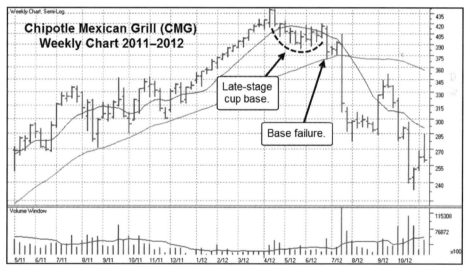

FIGURE 3.9 Chipotle Mexican Grill (CMG) weekly chart, 2011–2012. CMG closed up for 17 weeks in a row before forming a late-stage base from which it blows up to the downside, giving up most of those gains in one short week.

Source: Chart courtesy of HGSI Investment Software, LLC (www.highgrowthstock.com), ©2014.

Here we see that after closing up every week for 17 weeks in a row, CMG finally peaked out and began to correct, forming something of a "cup" base formation. As it rounded out the lows of the pattern and moved back above the 10-week (50-day) moving average, it suddenly broke to the downside as weekly selling volume picked up. This took the stock right down to the 40-week (200-day) moving average, where it then bounced back up to the 10-week line before rolling over and blowing to pieces. 17 weeks of consecutive gains were literally wiped out in one week.

In my experience, late-stage cup-with-handle formations seem to be particularly vulnerable, especially when they are very wide and loose. A cup-with-handle formation is often a very productive first-stage base to see when a stock is just starting a big upside price run, but when you start to see these sloppy late-stage cup-with-handle formations after a long upside price move, they can often mean that trouble is brewing, as was the case for Rovi Corp. (ROVI), shown on a weekly chart in Figure 3.10.

ROVI was engaged in a strong upside trend going into January of 2011, rising 14 out of 17 weeks in a row up to that point. It then built a short four-week flag formation from which it failed, breaking down through its 10-week (50-day) moving average in mid-February 2011. This was the first LSFB in the pattern, and it initiated a sharp break that bounced off the 40-week (200-day) before consolidating for about five weeks and then moving below the 40-week line. This downtrend off the peak that lasted from mid-January through March formed the left side of a big, ugly cup formation, with a one-week blast to the upside in early May 2011 that formed the right side of the cup. Right away, we can see just how sloppy this cup formation was,

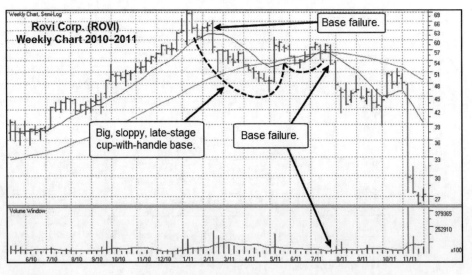

FIGURE 3.10 Rovi Corp. (ROVI) weekly chart, 2010–2011. ROVI's top in 2011 consisted of two LSFB short-sale set-ups, one right after the other.

Source: Chart courtesy of HGSI Investment Software, LLC (www.highgrowthstock.com), ©2014.

and things didn't necessarily improve as the stock built a handle from May through July. The handle itself also looked like a small cup-with-handle, but this eventually failed as the stock plummeted through the 10-week and 40-week moving averages on heavy weekly selling volume.

Note that as ROVI broke down in early August 2011, it found support along the lows of a base it built from July to September 2010 at the left side of the chart in Figure 3.10. It fully undercut the lows of that base in the first week of October, triggering an undercut-and-rally move back up to the 40-week moving average before the stock blew up in spectacular fashion in early November 2011, dropping 38.2 percent in one week.

In Figure 3.11, the weekly chart of Sunpower Corp. (SPWR) reveals another late-stage cup-with-handle formation that ultimately resolved as an LSFB. The pattern has several noticeable clues and flaws that aid in the interpretation of this as a potential LSFB. The first was the climactic sort of price run the stock had in the last three weeks of the upside price run leading up to the peak in early November 2007. The second clue was the extremely high-volume reversal off the peak, where the stock pushed up as high as 164.49 before reversing to close in the lower portion of the weekly price range.

The final clue was the narrow, v-shaped cup-with-handle formation that formed in November and December of 2007. After attempting to break out from the handle of the formation in late December, SPWR reversed to close at the intra-week lows

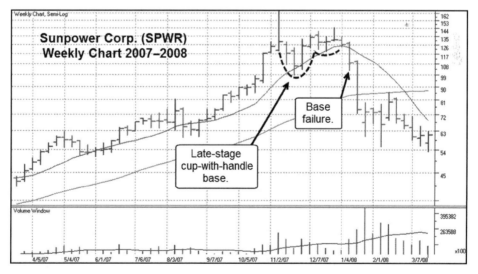

FIGURE 3.11 Sunpower Corp. (SPWR) weekly chart, 2007–2008. A big-volume reversal off the peak in early November followed by the formation of a narrow, v-shaped cup-with-handle set up a textbook LSFB.

Source: Chart courtesy of HGSI Investment Software, LLC (www.highgrowthstock.com), ©2014.

of the week during which it attempted to break out, not entirely unlike the first week of the pattern in early November. Once SPWR dropped below its 10-week (50-day) moving average, it blew up in spectacular fashion.

Video game retailer GameStop (GME) provides an example of an LSFB type of short-sale set-up that later morphs into an H&S formation which I've outlined on the weekly chart of the stock in Figure 3.12. GME formed a relatively flat base within an existing uptrend between the middle of August 2013 and the middle of October when it attempted to break out to new price highs. Some stalling on the breakout was evident, as the stock closed roughly mid-range at the beginning of November 2013 just as it was edging into new high price ground. This breakout attempt then failed in mid-November to complete the LSFB which later finished forming as a head-and-shoulders top (for which the LSFB formed the right side of the head) following the right shoulder rally in December that stalled out right at the 10-week (50-day) moving average.

LSFB set-ups are generally shortable as the stock drops back below the prior base breakout point and the 10-week (50-day) moving average. Usually this leads to a breakdown that will carry as far as the 40-week (200-day) moving average, after which the stock will try and rally off of the 40-week line, generally bouncing as high as the 10-week line where it becomes shortable again, as in the example of CMG in Figure 3.9. When the 10-week and 40-week lines are in confluence, as they were in the ROVI example in Figure 3.10 when its wide and loose cup-with-handle (the second LSFB that formed during its overall topping process) failed in July of

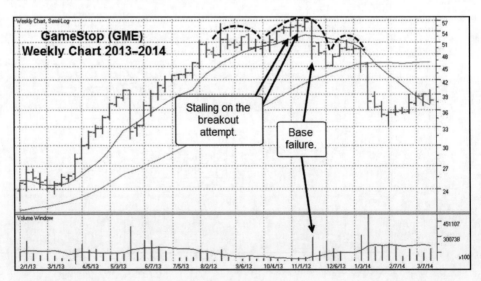

FIGURE 3.12 GameStop (GME) fails on a base breakout attempt to form an initial LSDB that eventually fills out and morphs into an H&S top.

Source: Chart courtesy of HGSI Investment Software, LLC (www.highgrowthstock.com), ©2014.

2011, then one should look for the breakdown to carry down to and undercut a prior area of support in the pattern.

The Punchbowl of Death

Arguably the most colorfully labeled short-sale set-up that we will discuss, the *punchbowl of death* (POD) short-sale set-up is simply a corollary to the LSFB concept. In my studies of topping formations, I found that one of the major clues that a leading stock is topping is when a previously coherent, well-defined uptrend starts to become wider, looser, and generally sloppier as the "character" of the stock's price trend begins to change. Like a smoothly flying jet airliner that suddenly encounters severe turbulence, a big-stock leader that has been trending in orderly fashion can often signal that a shift in trend may be at hand when it begins to pitch up and down, showing wide weekly price ranges and more erratic price swings that contrast sharply with the prior uptrend.

This type of action usually leads to big, wide, and loose cup or double-bottom types of formations that look somewhat exaggerated, even clown-like, in relation to the rest of the chart pattern. To get an idea of what I'm talking about, take the example of Cree (CREE) in 2010–2011, shown on a weekly chart from that period in Figure 3.13. CREE's uptrend from July 2010 into the middle of April 2011 was very orderly as it tracked above and along the 10-week (50-day) moving average

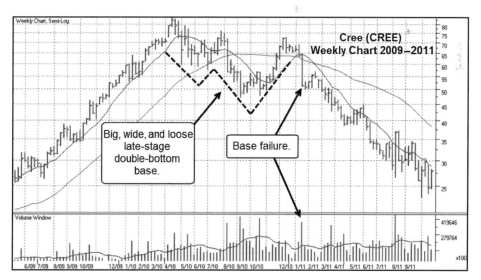

FIGURE 3.13 Cree (CREE) weekly chart 2009–2011. A big, wide, and loose double-bottom formation forms an LSFB that produces a downtrend that creates a mirror image of the prior uptrend leading into the top in April 2010.

Source: Chart courtesy of HGSI Investment Software, LLC (www.highgrowthstock.com), ©2014.

and was characterized by mostly tight weekly price ranges. A three-week downside break in mid-April 2011 marked the character shift in CREE's chart pattern that transformed it from a "Dr. Jekyll" uptrend into a "Mr. Hyde" top.

The peak in CREE occurred three weeks before the Flash Crash of early May 2010, and during the first three months of that ensuing market correction CREE built a 14-week late-stage cup formation that was wide and loose. That cup formation made up the right side of the "W" in the big double-bottom that lasted from April to December 2010. When CREE failed from that late-stage cup base in August 2010, it went crashing through the 10-week and 40-week moving averages and into new low price ground. The stock bottomed in early September and began coming up the right side of a new cup formation from September into December. This second cup formation made up the right side of the "W" in the pattern. In January 2011 CREE failed again, this time from a short five-week handle that it had been forming throughout most of December 2010, and from there the stock dropped all the way back below the June 2009 price levels.

The interesting point of the CREE example is that the second cup in the big double-bottom was a POD type of formation with a duration of 20 weeks from the left side in August 2010 to the right side in December. In this way we might consider that the left side of the double-bottom was an LSFB type of short-sale set-up, the right side of the double-bottom was a POD type of set-up, and the two sides together formed a big, ugly, "clown-like" double-bottom pattern that was wide, loose, and failure-prone.

Let's now take a look at JA Solar Holdings (JASO) in Figure 3.14. The solar energy group was a sizzling hot area of the market in 2007–2008 and a number of names within the group had huge price moves. When they topped, however, they fell faster than Icarus and his melting wings. JASO had a more-than-four-fold move before it finally topped in January 2008 as the general market began its second leg down in the bear market of 2007–2009. Right off the peak in January, the stock topped and broke very rapidly to the downside in a nine-week decline of −52.3 percent. At that point, the stock turned and rocketed back up to its old highs in about six weeks, forming a very deep cup formation of 15 weeks in duration. The stock built a short four-week handle and finally dropped back below its 10-week moving average, triggering its second and far more severe decline off the peak.

Besides fitting the definition of a POD, JASO's big 52.3-percent deep cup-with-handle can also be seen as a big, clown-like LSFB that looks quite out of place in relation to the strong, relatively far more coherent uptrend that preceded it. We will discuss JASO in greater detail in the next chapter. What distinguishes a POD is that it a) generally occurs in a "hot" stock that has a blistering upside run first, and b) it consists of a relatively sharp break followed by an equally sharp rally back up to the prior highs. The duration of the most effective POD formations is 15–28 weeks, although some can be longer, particularly among larger-cap leaders. In other words,

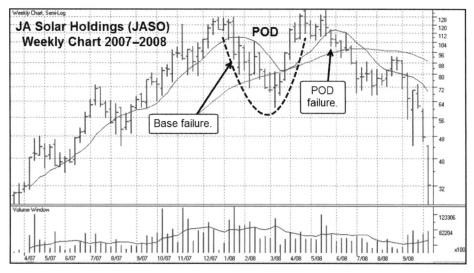

FIGURE 3.14 JA Solar Holdings (JASO) weekly chart, 2007–2008. JASO forms a 52.3 percent deep punchbowl before blowing apart in 2008.

Source: Chart courtesy of HGSI Investment Software, LLC (www.highgrowthstock.com), ©2014.

relative to the steep price run-up where a stock may have easily appreciated several hundred percent and on the way up had its share of normal corrections, which in turn spawn constructive basing patterns from which the stock emerges and continues its upward price run, the current base is too deep and too short, so it is highly failure prone when attempting to break out.

From a psychological point of view, the POD occurs when a hot-stock high-flyer breaks down severely, at which point it is able to bring in investors who missed the prior big price run and see the stock as "cheap." This sets off a very rapid price advance back up to the highs and the left side of the POD that is quite simply unsustainable. At that point, everyone who is going to buy the stock has, and the sellers who hit the stock at the left side peak of the POD can now finish distributing their stock. With fewer "suckers" left to buy it, the stock then breaks down in rapid fashion and in most cases to new lows.

Cepheid (CPHD), a hot biotech in 2007, had a huge price move throughout most of 2007 before breaking down from a flat base that formed at the peak in January and February of 2008, as shown in Figure 3.15. Notice that as CPHD breaks down through the 10-week (50-day) moving average in late February, it drops all the way down to the 40-week (200-day). This leads to a short bounce off the 40-week line that gives way in a couple of weeks and the stock breaks down below the 40-week line to fresh lows. This first breakdown is in fact an LSFB short-sale set-up that was very playable on the short side. We can see that this action is similar to the initial

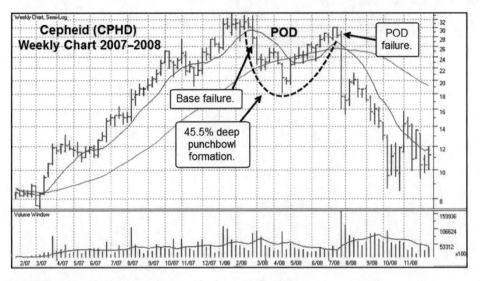

FIGURE 3.15   Cepheid (CPHD) weekly chart, 2007–2008.

Source: Chart courtesy of HGSI Investment Software, LLC (www.highgrowthstock.com), ©2014.

LSFB breakdowns in Chipotle Mexican Grill (CMG), shown in Figure 3.9, and Rovi Corp. (ROVI), shown in Figure 3.10.

That entire LSFB breakdown covered −45.5 percent on the downside in nine weeks and formed what would later evolve as the left side of a big POD formation. The right side of the POD was formed after the stock bottomed in April 2008 and began rallying back to the upside over the next eleven weeks, making the entire CPHD POD 20 weeks in duration. The huge weekly break in late July 2008 mostly consisted of a big one-day gap-down, so from a practical standpoint one would have had to short the stock a day or two before the gap-down. CPHD's initial base failure at the left peak of the POD was in fact much more playable given the mostly continuous price movement as the stock came down from the peak.

Another example that formed at around the same time is Diana Shipping (DSX), shown on a weekly chart from 2007–2008 in Figure 3.16. It is a much more irregular POD that looks like some sort of triple-bottomed "reverse H&S" beast. The breakdown off the peak took 11 weeks, while the ensuing rally, which had one higher high and one higher low, took 17 weeks for a total of 28 weeks.

Notice that DSX finished off its upside run in 2007 by having one massive shakeout to the 40-week (200-day) moving average before turning back to the upside and then closing on the upside every week over the final seven weeks leading right up into the top in early November 2007 as volume pulsated higher in a massive crescendo. There was no LSFB at the peak as the stock peaked into a wild climax top and then just blew up in mid-air.

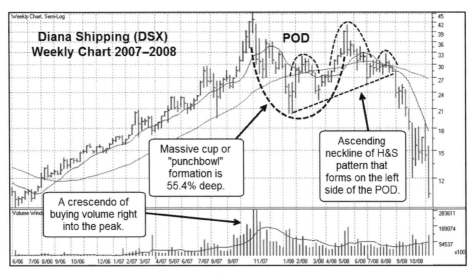

FIGURE 3.16   Diana Shipping (DSX) weekly chart, 2007–2008.

Source: Chart courtesy of HGSI Investment Software, LLC (www.highgrowthstock.com), ©2014.

The right side of DSX's POD eventually evolved into a head-and-shoulders formation with an ascending neckline. The head of the H&S has a massive-volume reversal right at the peak, which substitutes for a massive-volume price break off the peak that normally forms the right side of the head in a head-and-shoulders top. In this case, when DSX broke out to the downside and through the ascending neckline, it had so much downside velocity that the stock lost nearly two-thirds of its value in seven weeks from that point. In this manner we can see how a POD formation morphs and evolves into an H&S. In the prior examples we saw how an LSFB can sometimes be the precursor to a POD formation, and indeed sometimes we will see what starts out as an LSFB evolves into a POD which in turn evolves into an H&S.

Our final POD example might serve to illustrate this "LSFB into POD into H&S" phenomenon, but the reader will have to do a little work when studying the weekly chart of Exone Company (XONE) in 2013–2014, shown in Figure 3.17.

XONE was part of the 3-D printer mania that gripped the market in 2013, as it and other names in the group, such as 3D Systems (DDD) and Stratasys (SSYS), went on a tear to the upside. At that time, 3-D printing was hailed as a game-changing technology, which in many ways it was. But as is usually the case with hot stocks that possess an exceptionally compelling theme on the order of something like 3-D printing, they eventually become overdone.

This is why some of the most rapidly-rewarding POD formations to play can be those that occur in very hot IPOs such as the solar stocks in 2007–2008, of which JASO in Figure 3.14 is a prime example. Hot IPO merchandise starts "flying

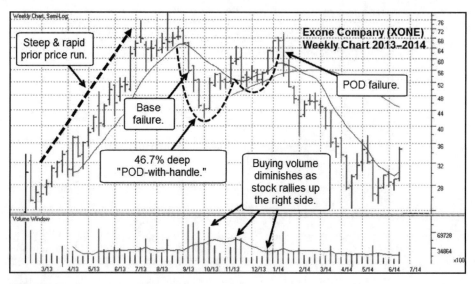

FIGURE 3.17 Exone Company (XONE) weekly chart, 2013–2014.

Source: Chart courtesy of HGSI Investment Software, LLC (www.highgrowthstock.com), ©2014.

off the shelves" when it comes with a compelling theme that catches the investing community's imagination, leading to blistering upside moves as the stocks go straight up in a speculative frenzy. But eventually the buying craze simply becomes saturated, and everybody who is going to buy the stock is already in it. At that point everyone piles out and the stock goes down as fast as it went up. XONE was one such situation.

XONE showed some heavy stalling action at the peak of the price run that lasted from the time the company went public in February 2013 to the peak in August of that year. Each time the stock tried to pierce the 70 price level while it was building a new base in July and August 2013, it turned tail, closing at the weekly low each time. That seven-week base failed in early September as the stock broke down through the lows of the base and the 10-week (50-day) moving average on big selling volume. XONE then dropped 46.7 percent from its highs in five weeks, forming the left side of the POD. The stock then spent the next 13 weeks working its way back up the right side of the pattern before once again running into resistance at the 70 price level. From there, XONE reversed in early January 2014 and began a 65.4% descent from the peak of the right side of the POD.

The alert reader might ask why one could not also look at this as a big, wide, loose, and very sloppy "late-stage" cup-with-handle formation. The fact is that it isn't really that different from an LSFB—except for the fact that it isn't a late-stage formation. At most, the POD would be a second-stage base, and as a short 18-week formation it has some of the features more typical of PODs as a "hot stock" topping formation. XONE came public in the midst of the 3-D printing mania, and as a fresh, exciting new IPO in the group, it immediately ignited as a hot new name in a hot group, despite the fact that it was and still is at the time of this writing a money-losing enterprise. We will discuss XONE in greater detail in the next chapter.

The POD short-sale set-up and topping formation can be a very rewarding one, particular if a short-seller is able to identify the "rush" up the right side of the POD and wait for the first high-volume reversal day to short the stock off the right peak. Some very quick, sharp profits can be gained thereby, as the examples we've discussed have demonstrated, but once the stock has broken down off the right side there are numerous points at which the stock can be shorted again as one "campaigns" it on the short side.

■ Using Livermore's "Century Mark" Rule Together With LSFB and POD Short-Sale Set-Ups

When it comes to short-selling, putting divergent pieces of a puzzle together is often part of the process. One "trick" that I have found is useful when dealing with LSFB and POD short-sale set-ups is based on the great trader Jesse Livermore's "Century Mark Rule," as I have dubbed it. The rule is derived from comments he made in what I consider to be something of a trader's and investor's bible, *Reminiscences of a Stock Operator*, regarding his play in Anaconda Copper back in 1907. As Livermore is quoted in the book, "it was an old trading theory of mine that when a stock crosses 100 or 200 or 300 for the first time, the price does not stop there but goes a good deal higher, so that if you buy it as soon as it crosses the line it is almost certain to show you a profit." When Anaconda Copper cleared the $300 price level for the first time in 1907, Livermore observed the action in the stock as follows: "I figured that when it crossed 300 it ought to keep on going and probably touch 340 in a jiffy." Anaconda, however did not act as it should, and Livermore noted that "Anaconda opened at 298 and went up to 302 3/4 but pretty soon it began to fade away. I made up my mind that if Anaconda went back to 301 it was a fake movement. On a legitimate advance the price should have gone to 310 without stopping. If instead it reacted, it meant that precedents had failed me and I was wrong; and the only thing to do when a man is wrong is to be right by ceasing to be wrong."

At that point Livermore went short with Anaconda Copper and made a killing on the trade. By going short a stock that should have moved straight through a century mark like 300 but which instead failed at that price level, Livermore was simply using his Century Mark Rule in reverse.

We can apply this same technique to getting a jump on LSFB and POD formations as they just start to break down. The weekly chart of Apple (AAPL) in 2007–2008, shown in Figure 3.18, illustrates how this works. Please note that the price scale on the chart is split-adjusted after AAPL split its stock 7-for-1 in June 2014. The 28

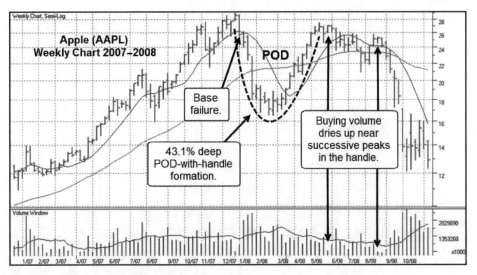

FIGURE 3.18 Apple (AAPL) weekly chart, 2007–2008.

Source: Chart courtesy of HGSI Investment Software, LLC (www.highgrowthstock.com), ©2014.

price level shown on the chart in Figure 3.18 roughly corresponds to the 200 price level for AAPL in 2007–2008.

We can see that as it was running to the upside in 2007, AAPL formed two v-shaped cup formations, one in August and one in November. The v-shaped cup in August worked as the stock broke out from that formation and moved higher to form the second v-shaped cup pattern. This time when the stock tried to break out and push through what was at that time the $200 price level, it failed. There was a lot of hype and hoopla surrounding this event, given that it was the first time that AAPL had printed 200 or better.

According to Livermore's Century Mark rule, since AAPL was going up through the 200 century mark for the first time, it should have a sustained price movement beyond that price point in much the same manner that Anaconda Copper in 1906 should have plowed right through the $300 price level and gone to $340, as Livermore surmised it should. Of course, when Anaconda Copper failed at the $300 level, Livermore turned around and shorted it. Savvy investors could have done the same thing with AAPL when it failed at the $200 price level in January 2008. One could have used Livermore's Century Mark Rule in reverse along with the v-shaped cup LSFB that formed at the time as a sound basis for shorting the stock at that point.

AAPL declined 43.1 percent from the January 2008 peak just above the $200 price level over the next eight weeks. From there it bottomed in late February 2008 and came rushing back to the upside over the next 12 weeks to complete a large cup or punchbowl formation that ended up failing in synchrony with the market as the indexes started their third leg down of the 2007–2009 bear market in September 2008.

In my view, whatever one can use in the way of additional techniques that might be additive or complementary to our basic short-sale method is likely to be helpful, particularly if it is rooted in the essence of the O'Neil–Wyckoff–Livermore (OWL) methods and philosophy. To the extent that using Livermore's rule in reverse helps you enter a possible LSFB pattern as early as possible on the short side of a broken-down big-stock leader, it is useful. On a practical level, shorting stocks in real time with real money, I have found this to be the case with respect to the Livermore Century Mark Rule.

■ Summary

In this chapter, you have become acquainted with the basic short-sale set-ups that we use to identify potential short-sale target stocks among former big-stock leaders that have begun to break down. You have also seen that these patterns are often *fractal*, in the sense that any one of these patterns can contain elements of the other patterns within them. The head of an H&S pattern can be composed of an LSFB or even another, smaller H&S, while a POD can start out as an LSFB and end up as an H&S later on in the pattern or even be composed of two PODs, side-by-side. Thus it becomes less a matter of trying to impose a label on a particular chart pattern, and more a matter of understanding when the elements of the pattern indicate that a big-stock leader has reached a point where it becomes failure-prone.

Being able to identify these patterns is the easy part of short-selling. The more difficult task lies in determining precise entry and exit points, including where and when to take profits. You have to know when to hold 'em and when to fold 'em, so stops are critical, but you also have to know when the stock deals you a new hand by giving you another actionable short-sale entry point even after you may have been stopped out trying to short the stock earlier. This is where the rubber meets the road, so to speak, in the short-selling game, and it is the topic of the next chapter.

CHAPTER 4

In and Out: The Mechanics of Short-Selling

A ny fool can go back with benefit of hindsight, pick out a pile of historical weekly charts of former big-stock leaders after they topped and broke down, and draw arrows with the caption "Short-Sale Point" at every spot on the weekly chart where the stock rolled over and went lower. Unfortunately, one's trading and investment operations, whether on the long side or the short side of the market, are conducted in real time, where one does not have the unrealistic advantage of being able to look backward and see exactly what happened and how a particular stock's trend unfolded. In my view, it is at best simplistic and at worst deceitful to pretend that one can master the art of short-selling without breaking it down to what is happening on the daily chart. This is the primary failing of the first book I wrote on short-selling as a "co-author" with William J. O'Neil, *How to Make Money Selling Stocks Short*, and it is something that I have sought to correct in subsequent books with which I have been involved that discuss the topic of short-selling. The truth is that if I lived in a world where I had the option of only looking at weekly charts or only looking at daily charts when implementing my short-sale methods, I would without hesitation choose daily charts. While understanding how the macro-patterns develop on the weekly charts is extremely useful to the short-selling process, determining exactly where and how I place my short-sale trades all occurs on the daily charts. Fortunately, there are no limitations on what types of charts we can look at, and we make use of both weekly and daily charts to derive a comprehensive analysis of a particular short-sale target stock.

■ Entry Points

Short-sale entry points can be broken down into two basic price/volume "signatures" that alert us to when we are at or at least approaching a potential short-sale point within a particular short-sale target stock's pattern. While it might seem odd, I rarely short a stock on a downside breakout where the stock drops to lower lows and through a prior support level such as the neckline of a head-and-shoulders top formation or the floor of a late-stage base from which the stock fails. Most of the time the short-sale points I choose occur from two basic set-ups on the daily chart where the stock is not in a downward trajectory, at least on a short-term basis. The first is a wedging rally, where the stock is bouncing on declining volume after a prior downside trend or price break. If you draw a trend line under the price as it rallies and a trend line over the corresponding volume bars on the chart, the price trend line is rising while the volume trend line is falling, such that the two trend lines together have the look of a wedge—hence the term *wedging*. As the stock moves higher, the volume moves lower, indicating that as the stock bounces in a natural *reaction rally*, buying demand is drying up. As the buying interest fades, the stock loses "airspeed," so to speak, begins to stall out, and then pitches back to the downside like a jet aircraft experiencing engine failure as it climbs.

This sort of action frequently can occur at the peak of a right shoulder in a head-and-shoulders (H&S) formation where it might also coincide with a move up into and around prior overhead resistance in the chart or a key moving average, such as the 50-day line. It can also occur as a reaction rally back up into the 50-day moving average and/or the prior breakout point in a late-stage failed-base (LSFB) short-sale set-up. Wedging rallies where the volume reaches extremely low levels, less than half to a quarter of average daily volume or more, after several days of upside movement can often signal when you are approaching a reversal point. This is what we refer to as a *volume dry-up*, or VDU for short. However, I have taken it a step further, giving it a much more mysterious flavor by referring to such days as "voodoo" days.

Because downside breakouts are less reliable as short-sale points, I prefer to short into rallies that occur within the overall bearish trend. Wedging rallies, in particular, have a higher probability of failure, so those are the types of rallies that I look to short into. Rallies that show heavy-volume stalling or big price reversals on heavy volume around a major point of potential resistance, such as the lows of a prior base or a key moving average like the 50-day line, are different than wedging rallies but also have a higher probability of working. While a wedging rally shows declining buying interest as a stock rallies within a weak overall pattern, stalling or reversing at resistance on heavy volume shows an increase in selling interest as the stock rallies. Frequently heavy-volume stalling or reversals can occur as a stock is trying to make higher highs.

The second set-up on the daily charts that I use is a common "Technical Analysis 101" pattern known as a *reverse* or *bear flag* that forms after a prior price break. I have also referred to it from time to time as "walking the plank." In the same way that a stock can move up sharply and then go tight sideways for a period of time in a so-called *high, tight flag* before it breaks out and moves higher again, what we might call a *bull flag*, a stock can do the same thing in reverse as it consolidates prior downside legs within an overall downtrend. While a bull flag looks like its name, with a long "flagpole" followed by the tight sideways movement that creates the "flag," a bear flag has the shape of a capital *L*. Generally, I will look to short into low-volume moves up to the top of the bear flag's price channel once I can determine a reliable high in the pattern. For example, sometimes the upper channel of a bear flag, as it moves sideways, will eventually meet up with a declining moving average like the 20-day or 50-day, for example. This then provides an additional reference point for upside resistance in the pattern.

If we think about a bear flag in reverse compared to a bull flag, we know that in a bullishly acting flag formation, a stock will pull back within the flag with volume declining as selling dries up. Flipping this around for a bear flag, we look for "pull ups" or movement to the upper end of the flag's price channel to occur on light volume as buying dries up. Just as selling volume drying up on downside moves within a bull flag can signal an impending upside breakout, buying volume drying up on upside moves within a bear flag can signal an impending downside breakout.

As well, if we continue to think about a bear flag in reverse compared to a bull flag, sometimes we will see upside shakeouts—what I like to refer to as *shake-ups*—where the stock breaks out of the flag to the upside but then quickly reverses and breaks back down through the lows of the flag. Thus the shakeout to the downside we might see in a bull flag has its mirror opposite in the upside shakeout that then results in a sort of downside breakout.

In both cases, the action of a wedging rally or a bear flag occurs after a prior price breakdown, and the two formations are really just different versions of the same phenomenon. The difference is that a wedging rally following a prior price break or downtrend occurs as a stock bounces while a bear flag occurs when there is not a significant bounce and the stock just moves sideways. In both cases, the stock is consolidating the prior downside move.

While you may need to wait two or three days for a stock to break down after taking a short position as the stock is engaged in the process of a wedging rally or a bear flag, these are generally more reliable entry points than buying downside breakouts. In fact, downside breakouts where a stock busts through a key support area such as the lows of a prior base in the pattern or the neckline of an H&S formation are often initially too obvious to the crowd to work. In our previous books, we have discussed the fact that in the modern age of investing, everyone has access to real-time charts and price data. Therefore, everyone sees the obvious "breach of support," and anyone and everyone who is going to sell at that price level does so, creating a temporary downside washout that leads to an undercut and rally situation. In this manner the crowd is fooled, and the stock heads back to the upside just as everyone either bails out of the stock or piles in on the short side.

There is a third type of entry point that can be described as a "shortable gap-down," although this is a rarer occurrence. The idea here is very simple. A massive-volume gap-down on the right side of any short-sale set-up can sometimes be treated as the opposite of a Buyable Gap-Up, or "BGU," an actionable type of buy point on the long side that is discussed in detail in our first two books. With a BGU we use the intra-day low of the gap-up day as our guide for a downside stop. In the case of a Shortable Gap-Down, or "SGU," we essentially reverse the rules for a BGU by using the intra-day high of the gap-down day as a guide for an upside stop. This type of short-selling entry point does not occur that often, but when it does it can be very profitable, as some of the examples we will discuss later on in the book demonstrate.

■ Exit Points

The most important aspect of any trade is not where and how you enter the trade, but rather how the trade is handled from that point on. While this basic axiom is often cited in reference to the process of buying and handling stocks on the long side, it applies just as much to the short side. This means knowing when and where to take profits by covering your short position and closing out the trade. One simple way to handle this is to set price objectives, and in the past we've recommended taking 20–25 percent profits in short-sale positions as a matter of policy. However, this too proves to be far too imprecise as a practical method, because in some environments the downside is not so pronounced and profits of 10–20 percent are more the norm. I find it far more accurate and profitable to use undercuts of prior support levels, downside moves to the tops of prior bases, and even moving averages as areas at which to cover my short position in a stock as it comes down.

In fact, this method of taking profits on various types of undercuts is based on the same truism that makes trying to short stocks on downside breakouts as they bust through areas of support or key moving averages less effective. As we discussed in the previous section of this chapter, we generally do not use downside breakouts as entry points because these are often far too obvious and only end up fooling the crowd as the stock shakes out and heads higher (the Shortable Gap-Down is one exception, however). This same concept, however, is why we use undercuts of support and key moving averages as points where we look to cover the stock, then let it rally from there and look at potentially re-entering the short trade if and as the rally fails. In practice, this method proves to be extremely effective.

■ Applying Entry and Exit Point Methods in Real Time

It is one thing to explain short-sale entries and exits in words alone, but nothing can replace the examination of the real-time application of my methods with real-world examples. As we progress through this chapter, I will examine the application of exit and entry points within the various macro-chart patterns we discussed in the previous chapter using real-world examples. But I want to throw the reader something of a curveball by starting out with an example from my own trading from March through April 2014 that doesn't quite fit what we've discussed so far with respect to short-selling set-ups on the weekly charts.

As a serious student of the short side of the market, my ongoing studies and practical, real-time experience have helped me to identify and develop what I might refer to as corollary techniques based on the fractal nature of short-selling chart set-ups. In this manner, I don't necessarily have to wait until an obvious short-sale chart set-up has developed on a weekly chart; I can begin to anticipate and act on concrete price/volume action that often leads up to a final top and trend reversal in a leading stock.

One of my most profitable short-sale plays in 2014 was Pandora Media (P), which emerged as a short-sale target in tandem with the early March 2014 market top illustrated in the daily chart of the NASDAQ Composite Index in Figure 4.1. While market tops are almost always spoken of in terms of what the major market indexes are doing, we should at all times understand that the action of the indexes is predicated on the action of the underlying stocks within those indexes. Some of the sharpest downside breaks in leading stocks can occur right around a peak in the indexes, so I am always alert to when something like this might be developing in the market.

As the market moved into the month of March 2014, some signs of distribution in the major market indexes, specifically the NASDAQ, around the peak began to show up. On February 28, the first high-volume churning and stalling day showed up, but this was immediately followed by a higher-volume gap-up two days later. Notice, however, that this big-volume gap-up move did not lead to further upside. Three days after that gap-up to new highs, volume picked up as the index stalled and reversed right off the peak. This was very subtle action right at the peak that was confirmed two days later when the second high-volume churning and stalling

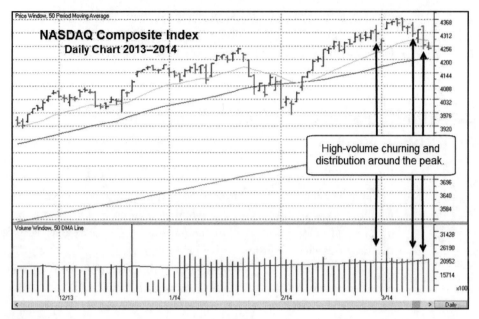

Price Window, 50 Period Moving Average

NASDAQ Composite Index
Daily Chart 2013–2014

High-volume churning and
distribution around the peak.

Volume Window, 50 DMA Line

FIGURE 4.1 NASDAQ Composite Index daily chart, 2013–2014. The index starts to show some signs of churning and distribution around the peak in late February to early March 2014.

Source: Chart courtesy of HGSI Investment Software, LLC (www.highgrowthstock.com), ©2014.

day hit the market. Notice that this was also an outside reversal day on increased volume from the prior day—a clear sign of distribution. After a "one-day wonder rally," as I like to refer to them, the market staged another outside reversal day on big volume. When I start to see this sort of action on one or more of the major market indexes, I begin to examine my buy watch list stocks very closely for signs of similar, potential topping action.

Pandora Media (P) was one stock that had been on my buy watch list for some time, and it was a favorite of short-sellers who stubbornly kept shorting the stock all the way up, as we can see on P's weekly chart, shown in Figure 4.2. The stock formed several bases on the way up, breaking out of each one and continuing higher. Pullbacks were relatively well contained to the 10-week (50-day) moving average and/or the top of the prior base, but by the time the stock was pushing above the $40 price level, it was now moving into possible late-stage territory. In early March 2014, I began to notice stalling action around the 40 price level that was occurring in tandem with the distribution around the peak in the NASDAQ Composite Index as can be referenced in Figure 4.1.

Observing the daily chart of P in Figure 4.3, we can see that the move up to the 40 price level in early March, which shows up as stalling action on the weekly chart in Figure 4.2, consisted of a very low volume move to the upside as the stock essentially drifted above the 40 price level. Right off the peak, the stock gapped

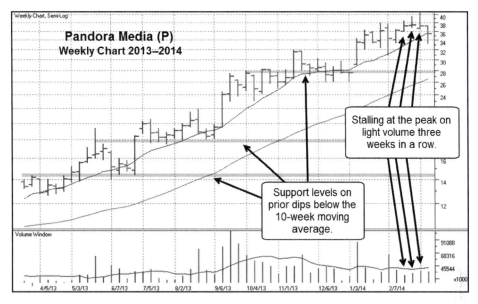

FIGURE 4.2 Pandora Media (P) weekly chart, 2013–2014. P was issuing subtle clues that it was ready to correct with the market in March 2014.

Source: Chart courtesy of HGSI Investment Software, LLC (www.highgrowthstock.com), ©2014.

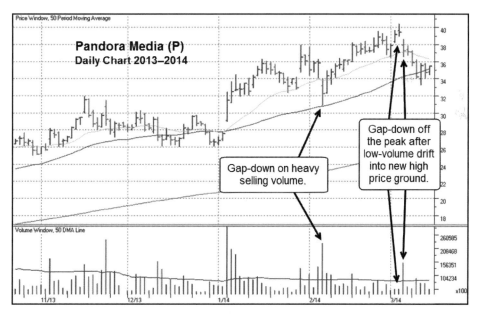

FIGURE 4.3 Pandora Media (P) daily chart, 2013–2014. P forms what is beginning to look like an H&S type of formation on the daily chart that is not so evident on the weekly chart shown in Figure 4.2.

Source: Chart courtesy of HGSI Investment Software, LLC (www.highgrowthstock.com), ©2014.

down on very heavy volume and then proceeded to move down to its 50-day moving average, where it found support for several days. Notice how the fractal nature of short-selling patterns makes itself evident here as we can start to see how the first heavy-volume gap-down in the pattern in early February now looks like the right side of a possible left shoulder while the gap-down off the peak around 40 is starting to look like a possible head in an H&S formation. Comparing the daily chart in Figure 4.3 to the weekly chart in Figure 4.2 illustrates how this action is not so evident on the weekly chart but becomes easier to detect on the daily chart.

As P continued to find support along its 50-day moving average it was basically building a short bear flag formation along the moving average, as we can see in Figure 4.4. This bear flag featured two days where the index tried to rebound back above the line but reversed to close down on higher selling volume, a sign of a potential and imminent breakdown through the 50-day moving average. It is here that a short-sale position could be initiated within the bear flag.

P then broke down in earnest, as we can see in Figure 4.5, and moved straight down to the top of a prior base in the pattern while also undercutting a key early February low in the pattern. As the stock dropped from roughly the 35–36 price level down to the 30 price level in about 6 days' time, the short position taken along the 50-day moving average showed a roughly 15 percent profit. Not bad for six days' work, and based on the stock undercutting the prior early February low and coming down on top of a prior base in the overall chart, the profit was banked

FIGURE 4.4 Pandora Media (P) daily chart, 2013–2014. P builds a short bear flag along the 50-day moving average following a breakdown from the peak around the $40 price level.

Source: Chart courtesy of HGSI Investment Software, LLC (www.highgrowthstock.com), ©2014.

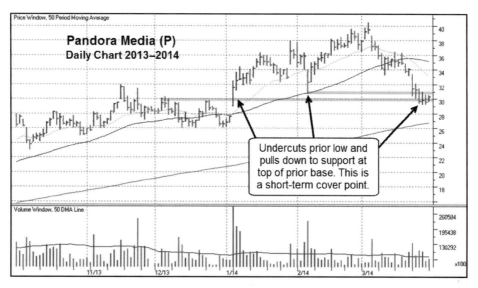

Price Window, 50 Period Moving Average

Pandora Media (P)
Daily Chart 2013–2014

Undercuts prior low and
pulls down to support at
top of prior base. This is
a short-term cover point.

Volume Window, 50 DMA Line

FIGURE 4.5 Pandora Media (P) daily chart, 2013–2014. P undercuts a key low where it finds temporary support.

Source: Chart courtesy of HGSI Investment Software, LLC (www.highgrowthstock.com), ©2014.

by covering the short position right here. In this case, we employed two reference points, the top of the prior base and the undercut of the early February low.

Notice that at the exact same time that P was breaking down through its 50-day moving average, the NASDAQ Composite, shown in Figure 4.6, also broke below its 50-day moving average before finding logical support around the 4131 price level. As the NASDAQ approached this support level, P was also approaching the top of the prior base and the early February low in its chart pattern. In this manner, you can easily see the relationship between what P was doing relative to the NASDAQ Composite Index, and that to some extent the price/volume action of each was intertwined. I always keep an eye on where my short positions are within their patterns relative to what is going on with the indexes, as this is a very important part of gauging where a stock might undercut and/or find support within its pattern as one or more of the major market indexes does the same.

As the NASDAQ bounced off of support along the 4131 on the chart in Figure 4.6, P did the same in a classic undercut and rally back up into the neckline of a small H&S formation that coincided with an area of overhead congestion and resistance along the 33–34 price area, as we can see in Figure 4.7. This provided a convenient short-sale re-entry point as the stock came up into resistance. At the same time, as we see in Figure 4.6, the NASDAQ was also rallying up through its 50-day moving average and into resistance at around the 4285 price area. At that point it reversed and broke back down through the 50-day line as selling volume balloons.

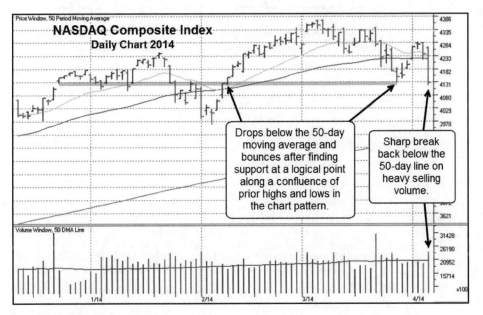

FIGURE 4.6 NASDAQ Composite Index daily chart, 2014.

Source: Chart courtesy of HGSI Investment Software, LLC (www.highgrowthstock.com), ©2014.

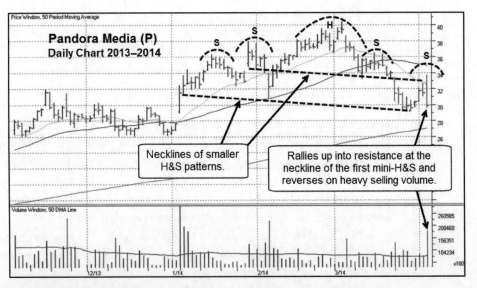

FIGURE 4.7 Pandora Media (P) daily chart, 2013–2014.

Source: Chart courtesy of HGSI Investment Software, LLC (www.highgrowthstock.com), ©2014.

As the NASDAQ reversed to the downside in the first few days of April, P followed right along, giving up its short rally up into resistance at around the 33–34 price area on a big outside reversal that took the stock all the way back down to the 30 price level, as we see in Figure 4.7. That reversal took place on a day where positive news regarding P's subscriber numbers was released, causing the stock to rally at the open before it gave way and reversed to the downside. Often, news-related rallies within weak overall chart formations provide opportunities to short into, and this is something for short-sellers to keep in mind. Notice also how the overall pattern was starting to look like a H&S complex with two discernible necklines (which is not evident on the weekly chart) that were effective in terms of timing short-sale entry points, but the downside movements were somewhat contained before the stock rallied again. The first downside breakout through the upper neckline did not yield much on the downside after the actual day of this breakout. If one had shorted the stock on that downside breakout, the stock would have simply rallied back up into one's face over the next eight trading days.

Looking at Figure 4.8, we can see that over the next two days after the big outside reversal in Figure 4.7, P continued lower down to its 200-day moving average, where it briefly broke through and undercut the 200-day line. The reader should make careful note of the fact that when P undercut its 200-day moving average, it was also finding support along the lows of the prior base in the pattern. Based on this, one could have taken profits on the short-sale position that was re-entered on the last rally up into resistance in the 33–34 price area, as we can see in Figure 4.8.

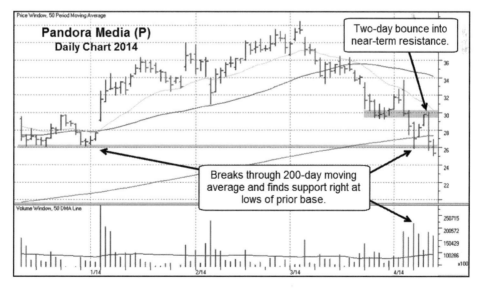

FIGURE 4.8 Pandora Media (P) daily chart, 2014. P undercuts the lows of a prior base in the pattern.

Source: Chart courtesy of HGSI Investment Software, LLC (www.highgrowthstock.com), ©2014.

P then engaged in a two-day wedging rally right up into near-term resistance at the 30 price level where the stock was once again shortable. It then broke back to the downside and this time pushed right through the 200-day moving average as it cleanly undercut the lows from the prior base and moved to lower lows in the pattern. If one had shorted the stock yet again on the quick bounce back up through the 200-day line and the 30 price level, this was a final cover point. The alert reader will also notice that after the gap-down off the absolute price peak in early March, P obediently followed below its 20-day moving average, which put a lid on any bounces that occurred on the way down.

With P moving below the 200-day moving average, the downtrend that started off the peak in early March was now getting somewhat long in the tooth. Confirmation of this was provided by the action of the NASDAQ Composite in Figure 4.9. Just two days after P violated its 200-day moving average and cleanly undercut the lows of its prior base formed in December of 2013, the NASDAQ undercut a key low of its own from early February 2014 at around the 3968 price level. This undercut of the prior 3968 low also coincided with the NASDAQ bouncing right off of its 200-day moving average, at which point the market correction reached its terminus and the market began to turn and work its way higher from there, eventually pushing to higher highs 10 weeks later in a new market rally phase.

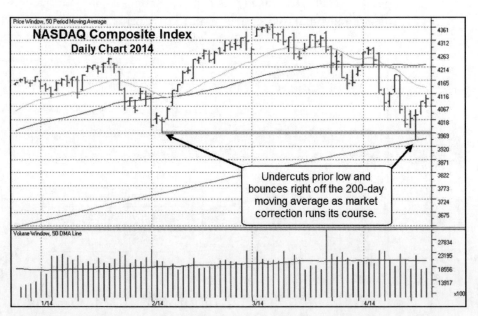

FIGURE 4.9 NASDAQ Composite Index daily chart, 2014. The NASDAQ undercut the 3968 early February low and simultaneously bounced off of its 200-day moving average, bringing its correction to an end.

Source: Chart courtesy of HGSI Investment Software, LLC (www.highgrowthstock.com), ©2014.

This Pandora Media (P) example in March and April 2014 illustrates how I seek to optimize the stock's downtrend, shorting into rallies that carry up into logical areas of resistance and covering as the stock breaks down and undercuts or finds support at prior lows in the pattern. Theoretically, one could have simply shorted P within the bear flag that formed in the 35–36 price area in the middle of March and held until the stock violated the 200-day moving average for a total gain of roughly 28 percent, but that assumes that one knows exactly how far the stock will go on the downside. The reality is that you never know exactly how far a stock will drop, and my method of working or, as I prefer to say, *campaigning* the stock on the short side as it zigs and zags its way lower achieves two objectives. First, it optimizes the exploitation of the downside move and, more importantly, it keeps you in a position where you are not susceptible to losing hard-won gains if a reaction rally and bounce in the stock carries much higher than you expect.

Let's look at another example from the same time period of March/April 2014 in big-stock 3-D name Stratasys (SSYS). To put this into proper context, we will first need to observe the daily chart of the NASDAQ Composite Index in Figure 4.10. Note that there were two general market corrections during the first half of 2014; the first was only 10 days in duration and extended from late January into early February, while the second lasted nearly 29 days. This is useful in understanding the entire top in SSYS at that time, as we progress through our discussion.

As we approached the end of February, SSYS was at the peak of what appeared to be an H&S formation where the head of a potential H&S topping formation during

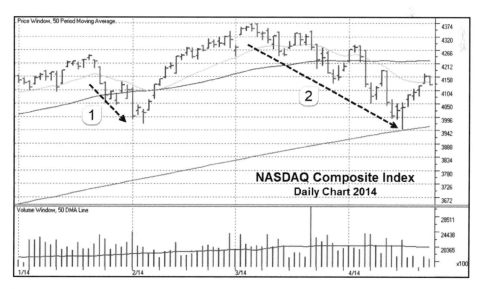

FIGURE 4.10 NASDAQ Composite Index daily chart, 2014. The general market had two short-term corrections in the first half of 2014.

Source: Chart courtesy of HGSI Investment Software, LLC (www.highgrowthstock.com), ©2014.

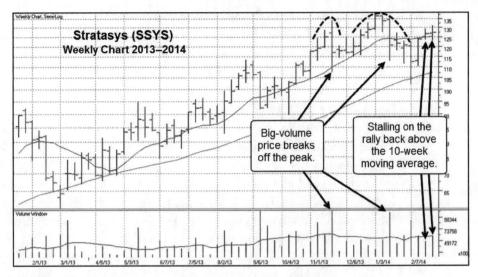

FIGURE 4.11 Stratasys (SSYS) weekly chart, 2013–2014. SSYS starts to form what looks like the peak of a possible right shoulder within a potential H&S topping formation.

Source: Chart courtesy of HGSI Investment Software, LLC (www.highgrowthstock.com), ©2014.

the general market correction of late January 2014. This was the second big-volume price break in the pattern, with the first one serving to create the left shoulder in the pattern. Notice that as the stock reached all-time highs in the first week of January 2014, at the very peak of the head buying volume was very light. In fact, the breakdown off the peak of the head was also a late-stage failed-base (LSFB), so we can consider this an example of an initial LSFB that evolved into an H&S formation.

The breakdown off the peak eventually took the stock all the way down to the 40-week (200-day) moving average and occurred during the late January correction that we observed in Figure 4.10. Once that short correction was over, SSYS rebounded with the market throughout February, clambering just above its 10-week (50-day) moving average, where it stalled out at what turned out to be the peak of the right shoulder.

In Figure 4.12 we get a more granular view of the same H&S formation on a daily chart. This illustrates why the daily chart can tune us into potential "tactical" short-selling opportunities that might not show up on the weekly chart. Notice that what we see as a head on the weekly chart in Figure 4.10 is actually a head with two small right shoulders in the daily chart. The first high-volume break off the peak formed the right side of the head, and then two more selling waves took the stock all the way down to the 200-day moving average.

Notice that the break on the right side of the head and the second selling wave that occurred in the latter third of February were each followed by short, wedging rallies back up towards the 50-day moving average. The first rally carried just above

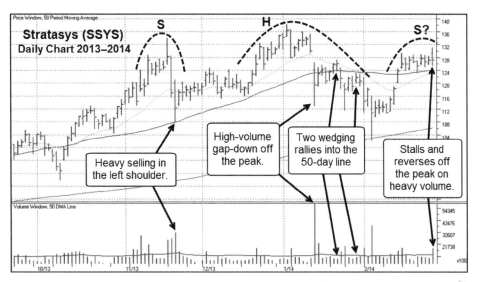

FIGURE 4.12 Stratasys (SSYS) daily chart, 2013–2014. The daily chart of SSYS's H&S top reveals many details that are not evident on the weekly chart.

Source: Chart courtesy of HGSI Investment Software, LLC (www.highgrowthstock.com), ©2014.

the 50-day line, while the second was weaker and carried right up to the 50-day line but no further. Note that each of these rallies could have been shorted into on the basis of the "voodoo" days that occurred at their respective peaks, after which they materialized into bona fide, failed right shoulder rallies. The observant reader will notice that the breakdown from the first wedging rally in the latter third of February undercut the lows of the high-volume price break off the peak that formed the right side of the head in the first third of February. The breakdown from the second wedging rally that took the stock down to the 200-day moving average also undercut the prior low in the latter half of January that also marked the bottom of the right side of the left shoulder. As with the example of P, we can see how wedging rallies are shorted into, and undercuts of prior price lows in the pattern are used in determining proper exit points.

By the time SSYS had fully "ripened" as a potential H&S formation, the market was in the throes of the longer correction that lasted from March to April as shown in Figure 4.10, the daily chart of the NASDAQ Composite Index. When SSYS stalled and reversed in a potential right shoulder as we moved through the third week of March the stock became shortable at that point. This led to a sharp price break that took the stock down to the neckline in a fully ripened H&S formation, as shown in Figure 4.13. Note some of the voodoo days around the peak of the right shoulder as the stock tried to push to higher highs. While the stock was trying to move up through the upper end of a short flag that made up the peak of the right shoulder and breakout through the 128 price level, upside volume was extremely

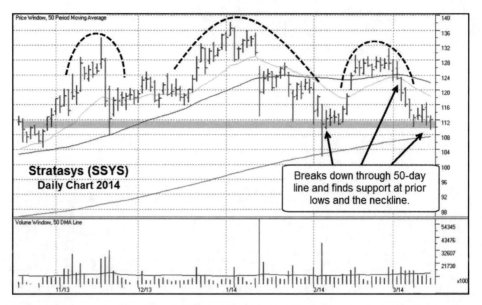

FIGURE 4.13 Stratasys (SSYS) daily chart, 2014. SSYS rolls over to complete the right shoulder in a fully ripened H&S formation and tests the neckline.

Source: Chart courtesy of HGSI Investment Software, LLC (www.highgrowthstock.com), ©2014.

low, indicating a lack of demand for the stock at that point. Once downside volume picked up sharply on the downside reversal after the stock "kissed" the 132 level on a breakout attempt right at the end of February 2014, the stock was done, and it broke down through the 50-day moving average on heavy volume.

Support at the neckline of the pattern was brief, however, as the stock rallied for two short days before reversing on the third day up. Figure 4.14 shows that the stock found resistance at the 20-day moving average, where it reversed on very little volume. Notice how the prior two-voodoo-day rally occurred on scant volume, the epitome of a wedging rally. SSYS then rolled over, piercing the neckline and continuing through the 200-day moving average on the third day down from the 20-day line. As it moved further below the 200-day moving average, it also undercut the early February low in the pattern, and this was a clear cover point for any short position in the stock.

The stock then rebounded off the $100 price level and back up through the 200-day moving average. This bounce and reaction rally took the stock up for six straight days, as we see in the daily chart in Figure 4.15. The reader will also notice the subtle churning on five out of six of those upside days before it finally reached the 50-day moving average and reversed on the seventh day, with selling volume picking up sharply. The 50-day moving average also coincided with the neckline of the prior H&S formation, providing two reference points for gauging where upside resistance might come into play.

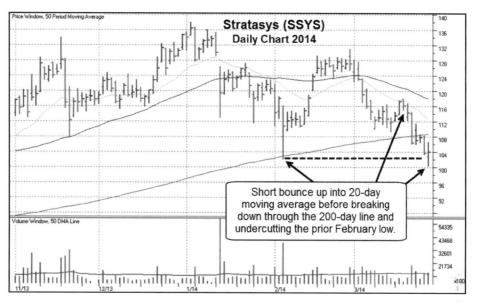

FIGURE 4.14 Stratasys (SSYS) daily chart, 2014. SSYS undercuts the early February low and the 200-day moving average.

Source: Chart courtesy of HGSI Investment Software, LLC (www.highgrowthstock.com), ©2014.

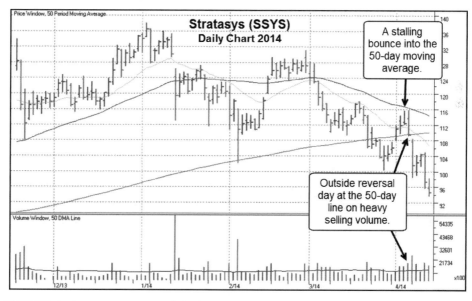

FIGURE 4.15 Stratasys (SSYS) daily chart, 2014.

Source: Chart courtesy of HGSI Investment Software, LLC (www.highgrowthstock.com), ©2014.

This rally right up into 50-day moving average was a clear short-sale point, and, assuming one had covered any short position on the prior undercut of the 200-day moving average and the early February low, would have served very well as a place to re-enter the previously covered short position in SSYS. Notice how the stock traded heavy upside volume as it moved up to the 50-day moving average, which would not qualify as "voodoo" type of action. However, the heavier volume was accompanied by noticeable stalling in the last two days' price ranges just before the stock reversed off of the 50-day line and back to the downside. The break from the 50-day moving average was very sharp, resulting in a greater than 20 percent short-sale profit in six days as the stock plummeted from the 116 price level down to a low of 93.70. With that kind of 20 percent–plus profit coming so quickly, it would be prudent to take some money off the table and cover at least part of the position.

As the need to sell SSYS became obvious, the stock rallied from the 93.70 low and again found resistance at the 20-day moving average, which it tested three times over the next three weeks, as Figure 4.16 shows. Eventually SSYS gapped down one last time after announcing earnings in early May, and because it came after a reasonably long prior downtrend, it was essentially a downside "exhaustion gap" that marked the end of SSYS's breakdown during the second general market correction in 2014. While the short rallies up into the 20-day moving average could have been shorted into for additional, smaller downside moves, at that point one could have felt that the selling in SSYS had run its course, at least for the time being. Indeed, from the

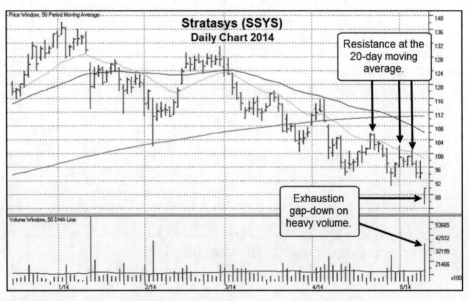

FIGURE 4.16 Stratasys (SSYS) daily chart, 2014.

Source: Chart courtesy of HGSI Investment Software, LLC (www.highgrowthstock.com), ©2014.

final exhaustion gap-down move to a low of 85.30, the stock turned tail and rallied all the way back up to a peak of 128.59.

SSYS is instructive in the way that it illustrates how topping patterns can begin their evolution over a series of two or more market corrections. In this example, we saw how SSYS's big-volume price break off the peak was formed during the brief market correction of late January 2014, and that the peak of the right shoulder formed and rolled over more or less in synchrony with the market's breakdown off of its own peak in early March, as the reader can check by referring back to the NASDAQ Composite Index daily chart shown in Figure 4.10.

The Pandora Media (P) and Stratasys (SSYS) examples give the reader a strong sense of how short-sale target stocks develop and evolve as they form their overall topping patterns in a synchronous "dance" with the general market. Sometimes a leading stock will top with the general market and closely mimic the action of the major market indexes, such as we saw with P and the NASDAQ Composite Index, during a correction or bear market. Sometimes a big-stock leader, such as we saw with SSYS, starts to show the first signs of weakness in its pattern during a minor short-term correction. By the time the next general market correction comes around, the pattern has evolved further into a more recognizable short-sale set-up, like an H&S top, at which point the stock is fully ripened and ready for a big fall.

Allow me now to shake things up by showing an example of a leading stock which topped and broke down while the general market remained in an overall uptrend. Trulia (TRLA) is an LSFB and H&S short-sale set-up that topped in early October 2013, as we can see in the daily chart shown in Figure 4.17. The breakdown in early October was in fact associated with a very short market correction of −5.26 percent that lasted six days. TRLA's September 2013 base breakout failed in synchrony with that brief market pullback, confirming an LSFB set-up. That breakdown on heavy volume also formed the head of an evolving H&S formation. On the sixth and final day of the short but sharp general market correction, TRLA bottomed at around the 41 price level. This short-term low occurred in synchrony with the market, but from there TRLA did not follow the market to higher highs, as it rallied weakly and just enough to form what was starting to look like the right shoulder of a still evolving H&S formation.

This rally carried up into and just beyond the 50-day moving average, and at the peak of the right shoulder the stock traded extremely light upside volume in "voodoo" fashion, indicating that demand for the stock was waning fast. At that point the stock began dropping back below the 50-day line. From the examples we've covered so far, the reader can see that wedging rallies up into the 50-day moving average, or any other moving average for the matter, rarely stop exactly at the moving average itself. It is very common for a stock to rally just past a key moving average, only encountering resistance once it has rallied 2–3 percent and sometimes as much as 5 percent or more beyond the moving average. The key is

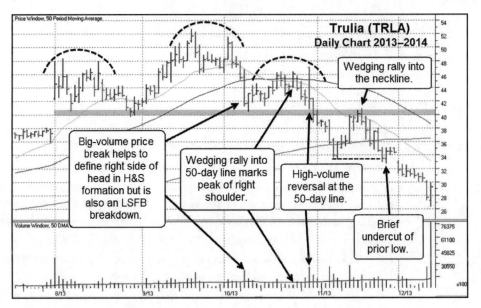

FIGURE 4.17 Trulia (TRLA) daily chart, 2013–2014.

Source: Chart courtesy of HGSI Investment Software, LLC (www.highgrowthstock.com), ©2014.

to watch how the stock acts as it moves above the moving average and be on the lookout for voodoo days or a high-volume outside reversals to the downside. We can see that at the peak of TRLA's right shoulder there is a clear voodoo day as volume dries up in the extreme.

I actually did not short the stock until I saw the huge-volume reversal day that occurred as the stock bounced off of the neckline of the H&S formation and back above the 50-day line at the end of October. TRLA had been placed on my short-sale watch list following the early October LSFB, and it is customary for me to scroll through charts of my watch lists in real-time during the trading day. The big-volume reversal indicated that the stock had become shortable at that time using the 50-day moving average as a reference for an upside stop. The next day the stock broke down through the neckline of the H&S formation, and over the next six days it made a beeline for its 200-day moving average, which it undercut on the final down day, signaling a cover point.

The stock hung around the 200-day line over the next three days, where one might have shorted the stock again, looking for it to break back down below the line. However, within the context of the prior downside break from an intra-day peak of 47.01 to an intra-day low of 33.43 in seven trading days, a move of −28.8 percent, the stock was likely "sold out" at the point. And indeed, the stock rallied from there right up into the neckline of the prior head and shoulders formation around the 41 price level, representing a reasonable short-sale re-entry point. Note the slight stalling action at the peak of that rally and right along the neckline followed by a downside reversal on the following day with volume picking up sharply.

From there, the stock broke back down to the 200-day moving average once again, bouncing there briefly for a day before reversing lower and breaking even further below the 200-day line. TRLA eventually bottomed in early December 2013 in synchrony with another general market correction that ended at the same time. That final low also coincided with an undercut of the lows of a prior base in the pattern, which we can see in the weekly chart of TRLA shown in Figure 4.18. If one had been short the stock from any point within the breakdown from the neckline down to the low of early November, this undercut of the lows of a big prior base in the pattern was a primary cover point. Once that undercut was completed, the stock remained in a big sideways price channel without moving lower for several months.

One of the richest examples of a massive, rolling top is Lululemon Athletica (LULU) during 2012–2014. The weekly chart of LULU from that period (Figure 4.19) has three big, ugly, wide, and loose late-stage base types of formations, all of which were shortable at their right side peaks. The first is a big cup-with-handle, where the handle forms near the left side peak of the cup, the second is a big double-bottom, and the third is a steeper and deeper cup-with-handle where the handle forms at roughly around the mid-point of the cup. If the reader studies this chart carefully, she will also be able to discern several smaller, "fractal" topping formations within the larger patterns. For example, the left side peak of the first big cup-with-handle is a late-stage failure from a short flag formation.

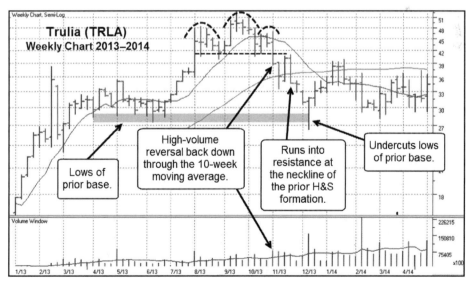

FIGURE 4.18   Trulia (TRLA) weekly chart 2013–2014.

Source: Chart courtesy of HGSI Investment Software, LLC (www.highgrowthstock.com), ©2014.

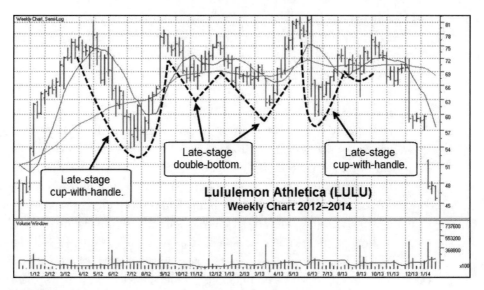

FIGURE 4.19 Lululemon Athletica (LULU) weekly chart, 2012–2014.

Source: Chart courtesy of HGSI Investment Software, LLC (www.highgrowthstock.com), ©2014.

The handle of this big cup-with-handle, which also forms the left side of the big double-bottom in the middle of the chart, is itself a smaller double-bottom that fails, and the right side of the big double bottom in the middle is another double-bottom. The breakout to new highs as the stock comes up and out of the big double-bottom in the middle of the chart is a late-stage failed flag formation from which the stock quickly plummets −27.8 percent off the peak in two weeks.

We can take this same chart and look at it in an entirely different way in Figure 4.20. Here I have outlined the same pattern in a manner that highlights two big left shoulders, a head, and three right shoulders in a big "rolling top" sort of H&S formation. Again illustrating the fractal nature of short-selling patterns, we can also see that the three right shoulders in the big head and shoulders formation form a smaller head and shoulders formation of their own. LULU's weekly chart can be investigated more closely on a daily chart in order to see all the short-sale and cover points in the overall topping pattern, and I invite the reader to do this on their own as an exercise. For our purposes we will focus on the right side of the pattern where the head and the three right shoulders form.

The first short-sale point actually occurred on the gap-down move coming off the peak of the head in early June 2013, as we can see in Figure 4.21, the daily chart of LULU from that period. This break was in fact an LSFB after a breakout attempt from a short flag formation that formed throughout most of May 2013. Trying to short a gap-down like this is normally very risky, but if the move clears a major moving average on the downside, and is trading near the moving average, it can provide a simple, nearby reference point for a quick upside stop. In this case LULU

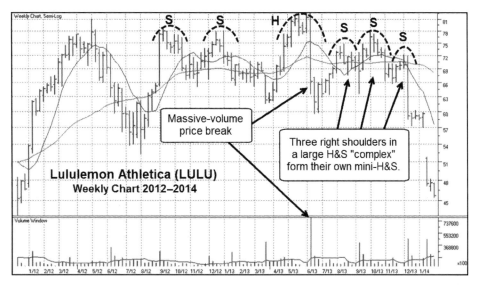

FIGURE 4.20 Lululemon Athletica (LULU) weekly chart, 2012–2014.

Source: Chart courtesy of HGSI Investment Software, LLC (www.highgrowthstock.com), ©2014.

gapped down and printed $70 a share right at the open, just under the 200-day moving average which was at the 71.46 price point at that time. One could have shorted the stock right there using the 71.46 price level as a hard stop or as a guide for a stop, adding 1–2 percent above the moving average to give the stock some leeway beyond the line. This keeps risk-control fairly tight while taking a shot at a short-sale target that might have some short-term downside velocity.

As we can see, LULU's downside velocity took it down to a short-term low of 59.60, where it undercut the late March low of 61.60. This would have been a cover point as the stock completed the formation of the head and then engaged in a textbook undercut and rally move that took the stock all the way back above the 200-day and 50-day moving averages where it formed the first right shoulder in the head and shoulders pattern.

Staying with Figure 4.21, we can see that the gap-down move as the stock rolled over to form the first right shoulder in the pattern did not work as a short-sale entry point. This gap-down opened up at 63.79, about 7 percent below the nearest moving average which was the 200-day line at 70.45. Remember that the gap-down off the peak of the head was shortable since the stock opened up within a couple of percent of the 200-day moving average. In this case, the 200-day moving average is too far away to provide a practical reference point for an upside stop.

The only practical way to try and short such a gap-down move would be to treat it as the inverse of a buyable gap-up. In a buyable gap-up, we use the intra-day low of the gap-up day as a downside selling guide. Conversely, if we want to short what looks like a breakaway gap to the downside, once we can establish an intra-day high

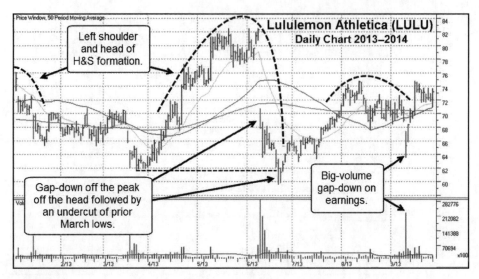

FIGURE 4.21 Lululemon Athletica (LULU) daily chart, 2013–2014. The initial break off of the peak of the head was also an LSFB short-sale set-up.

Source: Chart courtesy of HGSI Investment Software, LLC (www.highgrowthstock.com), ©2014.

we can put out a short position using that same intra-day high as our reference point for an upside stop. LULU opened up that day at 63.79, but on an intra-day basis it rallied all the way up to 67.38 before closing at 65.29. Therefore, one could short the position there using the 67.38 price level as an upside stop. In this case, however, LULU would have stopped one out on the very next day as it quickly rallied back up to its 50-day moving average and beyond. Notice that the rally back up to the 50-day and 200-day moving averages after the gap-down saw several above-average volume bars on the way up, so this was not a wedging rally that one would want to short into at the 50-day or 200-day moving averages. LULU pushed right through both as it moved to higher highs by early October.

That early October peak eventually became the second right shoulder in the larger head and shoulders formation we saw in Figure 4.20. Once that second right shoulder was completed, another rally formed the third right shoulder in the overall pattern. However, the three right shoulders also formed their own smaller head and shoulders formation, as I've outlined and labeled in Figure 4.22. Near the peak of the third shoulder, which was also the right shoulder of the smaller head and shoulders formation, the stock rallied up into the 50-day moving average and flashed an outside reversal day on big selling volume. That was a short-sale point, and two days later the stock blew apart on earnings, gapping to the downside.

It's instructive to break this down in greater detail, which is what I've done in Figure 4.23. Here we can see how the three right shoulders look like a bona fide head and shoulders all on their own. This is actually common in larger patterns

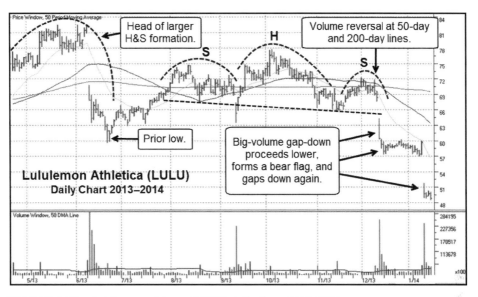

FIGURE 4.22   Lululemon Athletica (LULU) daily chart, 2013–2014.

Source: Chart courtesy of HGSI Investment Software, LLC (www.highgrowthstock.com), ©2014.

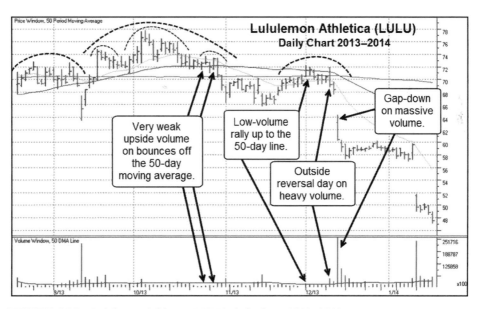

FIGURE 4.23   Lululemon Athletica (LULU) daily chart, 2013–2014.

Source: Chart courtesy of HGSI Investment Software, LLC (www.highgrowthstock.com), ©2014.

that approach or exceed 12 months in duration. The right sides of these patterns are generally of long enough duration to form their own fractal "sub-patterns." The final breakdown and collapse of LULU took about 15 months and was fairly symmetrical, as we saw in Figure 4.20, with the two left shoulders taking six months to form, the head taking three months, and the three right shoulders six months. Six months was plenty of time for the three right shoulders to form their own head and shoulders. I've also outlined on Figure 4.23 how the head of this short head and shoulders formation which was also the second right shoulder in the longer 15-month formation was itself a tiny six-week head and shoulders formation on the daily chart.

In the tiny right shoulder of that tiny H&S pattern, the stock began to dip below its 50-day moving average but bounced back up a couple of times on what were essentially voodoo days with only very slight buying volume. The next day volume selling then picked up at the end of October 2012, and the stock blew through its 50-day moving average. If one had shorted the stock at or just above the 50-day moving average, the following two days would have yielded a quick downside profit. Note, however, that this three-day drop below both the 50-day and 200-day moving averages also undercut the congestion area of lows in the left shoulder, leading to an undercut and rally move back up into the 200-day line. LULU zig-zagged between the 66 and 70 price levels for the rest of November and then finally bumped above its 200-day moving average and stalled right at the 50-day moving average at the beginning of December. Note that while volume is not very strong on the move to the 50-day line, it picked up as the stock stalled on that day, closing in the middle of its price-range. Adding weight to the 50-day moving average as a line of potential upside resistance was the fact that it coincided with the lows of late October, an area of overhead resistance. This all served to make the rally shortable around the 50-day line. That turned out to be the peak of the right shoulder in the six-month H&S formation and the peak of the third and final right shoulder in the 15-month formation. Two days later LULU gapped down and plummeted to the downside

That breakaway gap to the downside occurred after LULU issued a poor earnings report after hours on December 11, and the next day the stock gapped down and opened up at 63.15, briefly rallied up to an intra-day high of 64.38, and then continued lower to close at 60.39, eight cents above the absolute intra-day. In this case, if one was not short the stock prior to the earnings report and closer to the 50-day moving average, one could have taken a short position on the gap-down move once the intra-day high could be determined with a reasonable amount of certainty.

LULU also shows how a former big leading stock can stay on your short-sale watch list for a long time as you monitor it going through all of its breaks and rallies, breaks and rallies, and all the time metamorphosing into any number of topping formation fractals and permutations. LULU was a big retail leader that many felt was ridiculously overvalued all the way up. In the end, their thesis may have been right, but we can see that it was only when the technical action of the stock began to show the signs of forming a major top and after the stock had some time to ripen in the process that it finally blew apart. At the time of this writing in mid-2014, LULU is trading south of the 40 level, −52.6 percent below its all-time high of 82.50.

Flooring retailer Lumber Liquidators (LL) was a big, winning stock in 2013 that doubled as a favorite of obstinate short-sellers who insisted the company was something of a fraud. This did not keep the company from having a big upside price move before it finally began to build a big topping formation that was both an LSFB (in fact, two of them!) and an H&S short-sale set-up. This is a common theme on the short side, as big-stock leaders can go through several permutations of short-sale set-ups as they top, changing form and taking on new shapes as they evolve. Using each of these together to determine where the stock is in its overall topping formation provides a "macro-context" for the price action at any given point in the pattern and is helpful when timing short-sale entry points.

Figure 4.24 is a weekly chart of LL from that period that shows the initial breakdown in the stock occurring on a late-stage base breakout failure in the latter part of November 2013. This break also defined the right side of a head in what would evolve as an H&S top as well. The stock than rolled along the 40-week moving average, corresponding to the 200-day moving average on a daily chart. The stock bounced off of the 40-week line for one week and then rolled right back

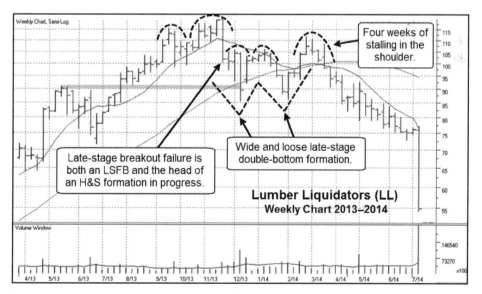

FIGURE 4.24   Lumber Liquidators (LL) weekly chart, 2013–2014. LL's overall top consisted of two late-stage failed-bases that also made up one larger head and shoulders topping formation.

Source: Chart courtesy of HGSI Investment Software, LLC (www.highgrowthstock.com), ©2014.

down through the line, undercutting some lows from early August 2013 and sliding into the upper end of a nine-week double-bottom base it formed in May through July 2013. From there, the stock found logical support and rallied back up into the 10-week moving average, corresponding to the 50-day on a daily chart, where it stalled and rolled over again. This move carried below the 40-week moving average for a second time, and ended up marking the second low in what then became a big, wide, and loose late-stage double-bottom formation. When LL moved to a higher high in late February 2014, it was in fact breaking out through the mid-point of the *W* in the double-bottom, and this breakout also served to form the third right shoulder in the larger H&S formation. It is at this point that the alert short-seller could put together both the second LSFB from this large but flawed double-bottom with what is also a third right shoulder in the larger H&S to determine an optimal short-sale entry point.

Let's break this entire LSFB/H&S/LSFB set-up into two daily charts in order to obtain a more granular view of the precise price/volume action. Starting with Figure 4.25, we can see that the initial base failure in mid-January 2014, which sees the stock streak to the downside following the publication of an article by a prominent hedge fund short-seller who panned the stock, occurred from what looks like a short cup-with-high-handle formation extending from mid-September to mid-November 2013. This break took the stock down to a point where it undercut a pair of lows that occurred near the end of September and the beginning

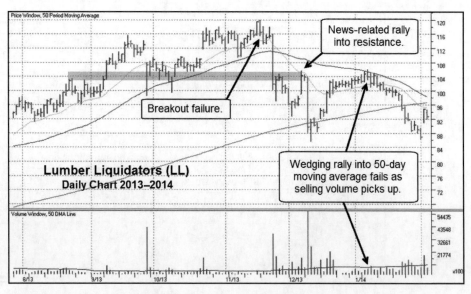

FIGURE 4.25 Lumber Liquidators (LL) daily chart, 2013–2014. A negative article triggers a sharp price break off the peak, leading to the formation of an H&S topping formation.

Source: Chart courtesy of HGSI Investment Software, LLC (www.highgrowthstock.com), ©2014.

of October 2013, and was not associated with any similar action in the major market indexes, which were all moving to higher-highs at the time. This undercut of the September/October lows led to a brief two-day rally right up into overhead resistance at the lows of the prior cup where it could have been shorted for a quick 10 percent–plus downside break from just above the 104 price level down to just below 93. This quick break undercut a prior low from late August 2013 at around the 96 price level, leading to another sharp rally back up into resistance at the lows of the prior cup, but this time it also met up with the 20-day moving average. Combining these two potential areas of resistance, we can then conclude that this is a short-sale entry point.

This short-sale point right around the 104 price area in early December 2013 led to a very sharp downside break two days later that took the stock down below the 200-day moving average. Referencing the weekly chart in Figure 4.24, we can see that this breakdown through the 200-day line also coincided with an undercut of the early August lows and the top of the prior double-bottom base the stock formed in May through July of 2013. That made it a major covering point for any existing short-sale position at that time.

From there, the stock engaged in a steady rally back to the upside, first sliding above the 200-day moving average before finally making it all the way back up to the 50-day moving average and that same 104 overhead resistance level that coincided with the lows of the prior cup formed in late 2013. Note that the peak of that rally formed a second right shoulder in the larger H&S formation outlined in Figure 4.24, and as the stock edged up into the 50-day line upside volume was drying up in near-voodoo fashion. Given that we have confirmed resistance at the 104 price level and likely resistance at the descending 50-day moving average, which has itself now reached the 104 price level, we could test a short position right there, using the 50-day line plus another 3–5 percent on the upside depending on one's risk-preference and risk-tolerance as a stop.

The short-sale at the 50-day moving average began to wobble in promising fashion as it began an accelerating, cascading descent back down to and below the 200-day moving average and all the way down to the early December 2013 lows. While the stock does not necessarily undercut those lows on an intra-day basis, it does undercut those lows on a closing basis. This also has to be looked at within the context of the prior breakdown from the 50-day moving average where the initial short-sale point was down to the lows of early December. That move lasted four weeks and took the stock from roughly the 104 price level all the way down to 89, a drop of at least −14.42 percent. Taking all that into account, taking profits underneath the 90 price level would have been prudent.

Recall that LL's initial price break off the peak when the stock was hitting all-time highs in late November 2013 did not occur in synchrony with a peak and correction in the general market indexes; it occurred when a negative article questioning the company's credibility was published. Generally such articles will have a short-term effect on a stock, but the fact that the stock never recovered up through 104 resistance and its 50-day moving average by early January 2014 was a clue that perhaps the article's negative claims about LL had a fair bit of substance behind them. Conversely, the breakdown from the 50-day moving average in the early part of January 2014 presaged by a few days a quick, sharp correction in the major market indexes. As the general market correction gathered momentum in the last few days of January, Lumber Liquidators cascaded through its 200-day moving average to complete a second, more fully-formed right shoulder in the larger H&S formation. The right side of this second right shoulder also formed what later became the second low in a wide, loose, double-bottom base that failed on the breakout attempt.

We get a much better view of this ensuing wide, loose, late-stage double-bottom base and its role in forming the larger third right shoulder in the overall H&S formation in Figure 4.26. Notice how LL gapped up off the second bottom and rallied up into the 200-day moving average. Volume was light as it spent several days bumping into the line, with some voodoo volume signatures present. One would be justified in taking a short position here, but given how much time the stock had already spent getting kicked around within the context of the overall top extending back to late November 2012, the need to sell LL was somewhat obvious at this point. However, there was a rationale for taking a short position here, however late

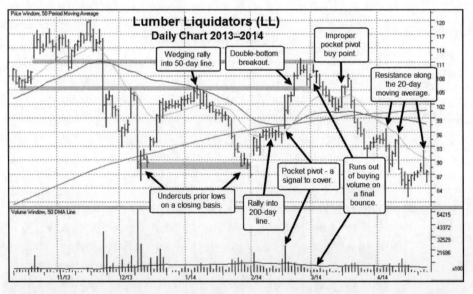

FIGURE 4.26 Lumber Liquidators (LL) daily chart, 2013–2014. The double-bottom breakout failure in mid-March 2014 also formed the third right shoulder in a larger H&S formation.

Source: Chart courtesy of HGSI Investment Software, LLC (www.highgrowthstock.com), ©2014.

in the pattern it might seem, with the idea of using the 200-day moving average as a quick upside stop. In this case. one would have been stopped out rather quickly when the stock gapped up and moved back above its 200-day and 50-day moving averages in the middle of February 2014 on a pocket pivot buy point, a move upon which any short position taken along the 200-day line should be covered.

LL's low at the end of January 2014 also marked the end of the general market's correction at that time, and as the general market rallied to higher-highs, including all-time highs in the S&P 500 and Dow Jones Industrials Indexes, the stock merrily rallied right along with the market. It eventually cleared resistance at the 104 level and broke out through the midpoint of the *W* it formed between late November 2013 and late February 2014. This double-bottom breakout pulled back to the top of the base and bounced in very early March, but buying volume was scarce as the stock logged a couple of voodoo days and bumped up against resistance along the lows in the 111 price area of the short handle/flag LL formed in late October and most of November 2013.

Recall from Figure 4.1, the daily NASDAQ Composite Index chart from March of 2014 shown at the outset of this chapter, that in early March the general market was just starting what turned out to be a 10-week short-term correction. Putting the action on the daily chart together with the general market action and the macro-context of a double-bottom LSFB that also forms the third right shoulder within an overall H&S formation, one had all the necessary conditions to initiate a short in the stock, using the 111 area as an upside guide for a stop.

From there LL immediately slid down to the 50-day moving average, whereupon it issued a pocket pivot buy point. However, this buy point was improper, as it came from a V-shaped position following a steady downtrend of several days' duration. That led to a short bounce that quickly failed, sending the stock back into the double-bottom base as the breakout failed once and for all. At this point it was possible to short LL just as it was dropping through the 106.03 mid-point peak of the *W* in the double-bottom, using the high of the post-pocket pivot bounce just above the 108 price level as a quick stop. As the March–April 2014 short-term market correction gathered some downside momentum, LL collapsed with the market. As it came down through the 50-day and 200-day moving averages, we can see how it finds resistance along the 20-day moving average as it bounced on the way down.

Lumber Liquidators (LL) is a great example of a stock that, like most topping leaders, has a large number of entry and exit points within a constantly shifting and evolving overall topping formation. This essentially allows one to "campaign" a short-sale target stock in question over many weeks and months, monitoring rallies for potential short-sale entry points and then covering at logical undercut and rally/support levels, ready to hit the stock again on the next feeble rally attempt.

■ Determining Entry Points for POD Short-Sale Set-ups

The punchbowl of death (POD) short-sale set-up can be thought of as being similar to an LSFB set-up in terms of short-sale entry points. The critical entry point generally occurs right at or near to the peak on the right side of the pattern as the steep rally off of the lows of the punchbowl quickly fails and reverses to the downside. The essence of a POD formation is that it also occurs in a very "hot" stock that has a sharp move to the upside, and the short-seller in such cases is looking for an equally sharp collapse to the downside once the pattern fails. Sometimes the failure and collapse off the peak of the right side of the pattern comes after the stock has built a flag or "handle" to the punchbowl formation. Sometimes the stock simply does an "about-face" right at the peak and then plunges to the downside.

There have been very, very few POD formations since the 2009 market bottom, primarily because we have not had a major bear market since then, at least at the time of this writing. There, were, however a number of PODs that occurred during the 2008 market period, which are discussed in Chapter 6 of our first book, *Trade Like an O'Neil Disciple: How We Made 18,000 in the Stock Market*. For our purposes, we can start with one of the few examples of a POD since 2009, Exone Company (XONE) during 2013–2014. During this period, XONE traded up to and around 1,000,000 shares a day, so it was on the cusp of what we might consider acceptable in terms of minimum daily trading volume and liquidity for a short-sale target.

XONE is an unusual type of POD, because its overall shape was not as symmetrical as most PODs tend to be. In fact, if we look at the weekly chart of XONE in 2013–2014 shown in Figure 4.27, we might also conclude that the overall POD is really just a big, ugly, improper cup-with-handle formation. At first it starts out looking quite symmetrical, as the five-week break off the peak on the left side of the pattern is immediately matched by a six-week rally back up towards the prior highs. That 11-week movement down and then straight back up could have been interpreted as a POD type of formation by the time it peaked out in mid-November 2013, as the stock broke down about 20 percent from there before finding support along its 10-week moving average and then rallying back up to new highs on a breakout from this POD-like cup-with-handle formation. That breakout in mid-January 2014 formed the right-side peak of the POD, and it immediately broke down at the same time that the general market started a short-term correction in the latter part of January 2014, as the daily chart of the NASDAQ Composite Index in Figure 4.1 shows. The breakdown from there was steeper than the prior run-up from February to September 2013, and took the stock all the way back down to the February price level. This sort of breakdown is what you are playing for when you enter a short-sale trade at or around where you believe the right-side peak of the POD is forming. In this sense, XONE's topping formation between September

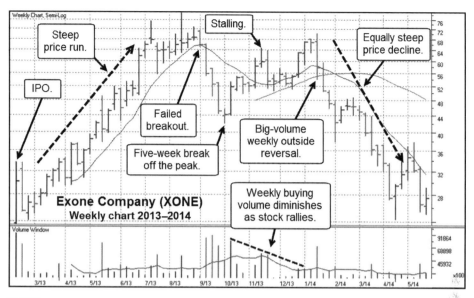

FIGURE 4.27 Exone Company (XONE) weekly chart, 2013–2014. XONE forms a POD that is also a wide, loose, and sloppy late-stage failed cup-with-handle base.

Source: Chart courtesy of HGSI Investment Software, LLC (www.highgrowthstock.com), ©2014.

2013 and January 2014 acted like a true POD. The formation itself was 20 weeks in duration, with five weeks making up the left side and the remaining 15 weeks making up the right side.

Figure 4.28 shows how the entire POD unfolded in detail, and one might surmise that there are three possible short-sale points in this overall formation. We have to remember that every POD pretty much begins its life as an LSFB, and XONE is no different in this regard. The stock attempted to break out in the first half of September 2013, but it immediately gapped down and failed. At this point, one could have looked at this as an LSFB short-sale set-up and attacked the stock on the short side on this basis. In this case, one could have used the rally back up to the breakout point at the end of September 2013 as a short-sale point, using the multiple stalling days up around the 72 price level as an indication of weakness in the stock at that point. Once two or three of these stalling days are seen in a row, one can then use the intra-day high of one of these days as a guide for an upside stop. From there, the stock broke down very quickly.

The midpoint of the XONE's POD formed in November 2013, and at that point one would have been justified in viewing that as the potential right side of a short 11-week POD. As the stock rallied up to the 64 price level, it began to run into congestion along the lows of the prior base it formed between July and August of 2013. My own view is that one would have had to be very shrewd and maybe a little lucky to pick this off as a short-sale point. There was one reversal day off the peak

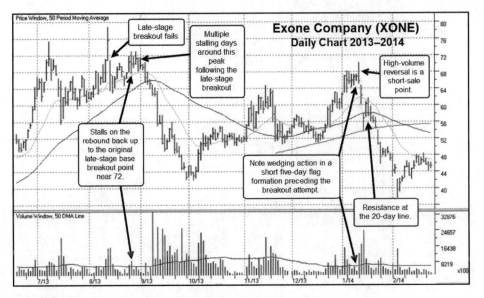

FIGURE 4.28   Exone Company (XONE) daily chart, 2013–2014.

Source: Chart courtesy of HGSI Investment Software, LLC (www.highgrowthstock.com), ©2014.

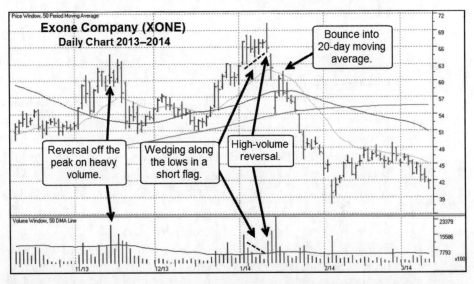

FIGURE 4.29   Exone Company (XONE) daily chart, 2013–2014. The right side of the POD is also a late-stage failed-breakout from a very wide, loose, and sloppy cup-with-handle formation.

Source: Chart courtesy of HGSI Investment Software, LLC (www.highgrowthstock.com), ©2014.

where the stock tried to push above the 64 level but reversed to close near the lows of the daily price range.

Figure 4.29 provides a close-up of the right side of the POD, where we can get a better view of this mid-November 2013 peak and reversal. You can see that the stock sprang back two days after the reversal day and briefly tested the 64 level before rolling over again. This took the stock down to the 50-day moving average where it swung back and forth for about a month, found support at the 200-day moving average, and charged back up the right side of the POD to make higher highs. Now as the stock approached the left-side highs of the POD shown in Figure 4.28, it broke out of the handle area of the formation and into a position where a POD breakdown is much more easily determined on the basis of a potential failed breakout attempt.

Once XONE broke out through the 63–64 peak of the handle that formed between mid-November and all of December 2013, it tried to move higher, but stalled and formed a short flag formation in the beginning of January 2014 that was wedging along the lows in voodoo fashion. A breakout attempt to higher-highs from this short five-day flag ran into a nasty downside reversal on heavy selling volume. This was a short-sale point, and the stock immediately blew apart, gapping through the 50-day moving average before finding support at the 200-day moving average.

This support was short-lived, as the bounce carried back up through the 50-day moving average before finding resistance at the 20-day moving average. In most right-side POD failures, once the stock breaks down it will generally carry through the 20-day moving average and then find support at the 50-day or 200-day moving averages, depending on where they lie within the overall pattern, and then try to rally. In most cases this rally will carry back up into the 20-day moving average, which presents a secondary short-sale entry point. The breakdown from there is nothing short of exhilarating for any short-seller short the stock at that point!

XONE is a valid hot stock POD example, and one should look for these types of formations among stocks that have been very hot upside movers within an overall hot group that gets investors frothing at the mouth, such as the 3-D printing group was in 2013. XONE fit into this theme as a hot IPO that came public right smack in the middle of the 3-D printing stock mania in 2013. Investors, looking for another "fix" in the 3-D printing area, immediately grasped onto XONE, even though the company was losing money hand over fist. In a similar vein, JA Solar Holdings (JASO), shown on a weekly chart in Figure 4.30, was a hot IPO that came public right in the midst of the solar stock frenzy of 2007.

We have to be realistic when assessing the short-sale entry point in JASO and realize that when the stock came back up to the left-side peak of the POD, one could have easily interpreted the action in late April 2008 as a potential POD breakdown. However, the stock did not break down at this point and instead formed a high-handle that lasted for five weeks before the pattern finally failed for good a month later. When it did fail in mid-May, the deciding factors were the two high-volume reversals as the stock tried to break out of the late-stage POD-with-handle. The pullback in the latter part of April did not see any real volume selling, so as was the case with XONE in Figure 4.29, the proper timing of the short-sale was associated with a high-volume reversal that carried below the 20-day moving average, and this

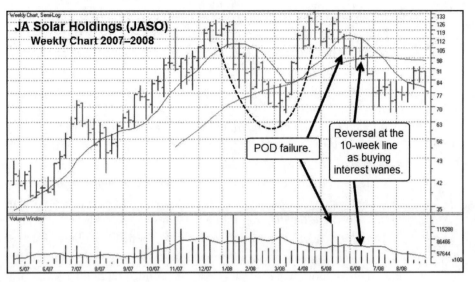

FIGURE 4.30   JA Solar Holdings (JASO), weekly chart 2007–2008.

Source: Chart courtesy of HGSI Investment Software, LLC (www.highgrowthstock.com), ©2014.

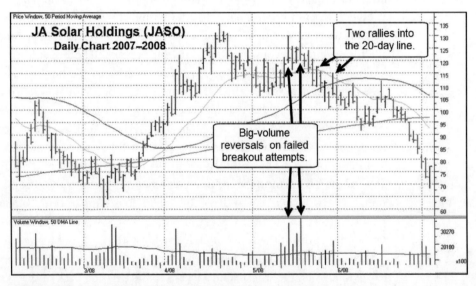

FIGURE 4.31   JA Solar Holdings (JASO), daily chart 2007–2008.

Source: Chart courtesy of HGSI Investment Software, LLC (www.highgrowthstock.com), ©2014.

did not occur until mid-May in JASO. Once the stock blew through the 20-day moving average, it had a couple of rallies back up into the line which presented additional short-sale entry points.

In most POD-type formations, you are looking for high-volume selling that comes in and hits the stock right along the right-side peak as a signal that the stock is now vulnerable to further downside and thus in a position to be shorted. My experience is that the 20-day moving average is usually the nearest moving average (I don't use the 10-day moving average) through which the stock must break down on heavy volume before I am comfortable coming after the stock on the short side.

XONE and JASO provide excellent examples of "hot stock" POD formations, but PODs can also be seen in larger-cap names that have had strong prior upside price runs and which also represented a very strong area of the market during the previous bull phase. These types of PODs tend to be longer in duration, and have less of a "straight-up-and-straight-down" look to them, although the final breakdown off of the right side peak can be very sharp. In fact, many of the elements essential to timing entry points in hot stock PODs are also seen in larger-cap PODs. Let's look at a couple of these.

Leading up to the market top in 2007, so-called *stuff stocks* (e.g., stocks that made "stuff" like coal, steel, copper, fertilizer, machinery, etc.) all had very strong group moves. Included in this category were related names, such as the stocks of companies that shipped all this stuff. Thus shipping stocks were a very hot area of the market leading up to the 2007 market top, and the big-stock leader among the shippers was Dryships (DRYS), shown on a weekly chart from that period in Figure 4.32.

DRYS' upside run in 2006–2007 was a very uniform, coherent, and, most importantly, extremely rapid price move that finally topped out in October of 2007 right in synchrony with the general market at that time. The stock then went on to

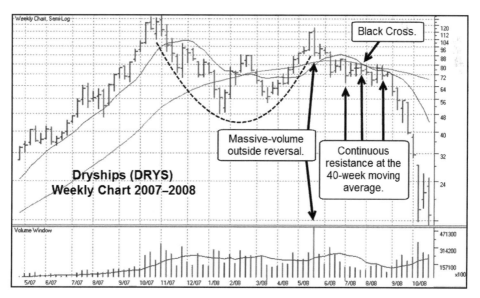

FIGURE 4.32 Dryships (DRYS) weekly chart, 2007–2008. Hot-stock shipper DRYS forms a 28-week POD topping formation that closely resembled that of Reading Railroad in 1906–1907.

Source: Chart courtesy of HGSI Investment Software, LLC (www.highgrowthstock.com), ©2014.

build what became a 29-week POD formation. We can again de-emphasize the need for a label and understand that the POD is really just an overly exaggerated LSFB formation. As I discussed in Chapter 3, stocks can often begin an overall topping phase with the formation of a big, ugly pattern whose dimensions are so exaggerated as to resemble something outlandish, which we might refer to as "Clown's Foot Syndrome." They're like the oversized shoes that clowns typically wear and which look woefully out-of-place within the context of the overall picture. The same is true for PODs and many other LSFB types of set-ups and is something to keep in mind when assessing these types of topping formations.

Here we can see the rapid eight-week run up the right side of the POD that culminates with a high-volume outside reversal week at the right-side peak. This starts the stock in motion to the downside. The initial break below the 10-week moving average carries below the 40-week moving average, and over the next 10 weeks the stock has what amount to three rallies back up into the 40-week moving average before the stock plummets to the downside in synchrony with the market break in September 2008.

Probably the most interesting thing about this particular POD in DRYS during 2008 is that it is a very close replica of a POD formed by Reading Railroad in 1906–1907, which Jesse Livermore discusses shorting in one of what we consider to be among the great trading "bibles," *Reminiscences of a Stock Operator*. Livermore had been playing the stock on the upside as it rallied during 1906, but it eventually topped and formed a big, ugly late-stage double-bottom that resembled a 38-week POD with the same general shape as DRYS's formation in 2007–2008. Like DRYS, Reading Railroad's pattern was a big double-bottom with the second low forming above the first low, something that is generally a failure-prone formation. As it broke down from the right side of the POD, Livermore eventually took advantage of the stock's long, steep downside break by going short the stock about midway down off the peak. As he puts it, "You ought to have seen that cornered stock that it was sure suicide to go short of, take a headlong dive when those competitive orders struck it. I let 'em have a few thousand more. The price was 111 when I started selling it. Within a few minutes I took in my entire short line at 92. I had a wonderful time after that, and in February of 1907 I cleaned up."

It is interesting to note that while Livermore began shorting the stock at 111, our knowledge of how POD formations play out would have indicated a short-sale entry point nearer to the right-side peak of the formation, at about 145. Had Livermore been more acquainted with these types of formations back then, he might have "cleaned up" quite a bit more. If we can imagine DRYS as Livermore's Reading Railroad of 2007–2008, we can understand how this would be so.

Figure 4.33 is a daily chart showing a close-up view of the right side of DRYS's POD in 2008. This chart illustrates quite effectively one method of determining when the right side peak of the POD is imminent. In this case, we can see that

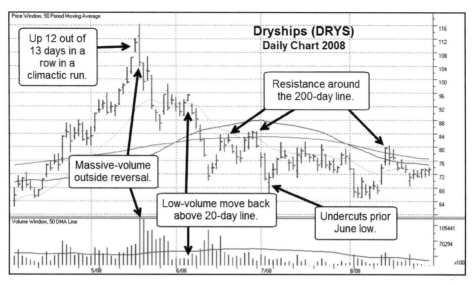

FIGURE 4.33 Dryships (DRYS) daily chart, 2008. A climactic run marks the peak of the right side of the stock's 2007–2008 POD formation.

Source: Chart courtesy of HGSI Investment Software, LLC (www.highgrowthstock.com), ©2014.

DRYS rushed up the final 25 percent or so of the right side of the POD in a move that saw the stock up 12 out of 13 days in a row. The 13th day of this climactic run was a gap-up move, and the next day the stock reversed on huge downside volume. Climactic types of moves as a stock blasts up the right side of a potential POD are something to watch for. If one was very alert to DRYS's set-up at the time, one could have simply shorted the stock as it was reversing in the middle of May 2008. From there the stock dropped below the 20-day moving average in a 6-day break off the peak and began bouncing up and around the 20-day line in late May. Note very carefully that as the stock was trying to rally back above the 20-day line, volume began to dry up significantly, and the final attempt to rally above the line occurred on a voodoo type of day. Volume immediately picked up as the stock gapped below the 20-day moving average, and the stock plummeted through the 200-day moving average over the next five days. At this point most of the downside "juice" was out of the stock, and it spent roughly the next three months bouncing up into its 200-day moving average. The reader will notice that the first couple of rallies into the 200-day line ended with voodoo days as upside volume dried up sharply. These are actually reasonable entry points for a short-sale, and the stock drops once more in early July where it briefly undercuts the early June low and then begins to chop back and forth in a somewhat tighter range.

As DRYS chopped around through the summer of 2008, it mostly found resistance along the underside of its 200-day moving average until mid-August 2008, when it flashed a sort of "bottom-fishing" pocket pivot buy point, which I use as a signal

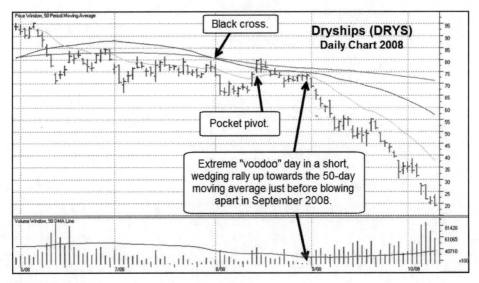

FIGURE 4.34 Dryships (DRYS) daily chart, 2008. A pocket pivot creates an upside "head fake" shortly before the stock sets up for a steady break to the downside.

Source: Chart courtesy of HGSI Investment Software, LLC (www.highgrowthstock.com), ©2014.

to cover in the event I'm short the stock at the time (see Figure 4.34). Generally, however, while these pocket pivots can serve as valid buy points when they occur in real-time, the subsequent failure of the pocket pivot puts the stock back in play as a short-sale target. Thus it is a matter of maintaining flexibility and allowing the market to function as a feedback mechanism. If the pocket pivot should fail, which in this case is confirmed by the quick violation of the 50-day moving average five days after the pocket pivot, the alert short-seller should then be vigilant for a new short-sale entry point.

This new short-sale entry point occurred at the end of August while the stock's 50-day moving average remained in a "black cross" and came in the form of a short wedging rally up towards the 50-day moving average that, to be more precise, actually halted at the 20-day moving average. The extreme volume dry-up was evident at that point as the stock drifted higher; this was a viable short-sale entry point. Once volume picked up on the downside, that was your final chance to enter the stock on the short side, and it quickly dropped away from the 50-day and 20-day lines. This breakdown occurred in synchrony with the start of third and final down leg or selling wave of the 2007–2009 bear market, which was discussed in Chapter 3.

Another big-cap POD is Charles Schwab Corp. (SCHW) during the period of 1999–2000, shown on a weekly chart in Figure 4.35. SCHW actually had a huge upside move from October 1998 to April 1999, before the mad rush to the peak that occurred at the height of the dot.com market bubble from late 1999 into

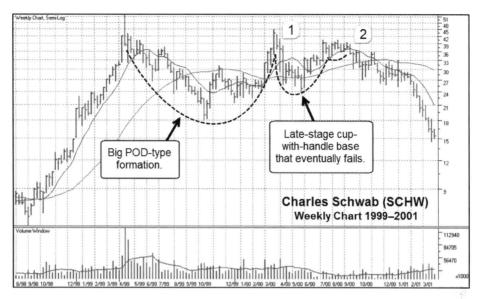

Late-stage cup-
with-handle base
that eventually fails.

Big POD-type
formation.

Charles Schwab (SCHW)
Weekly Chart 1999–2001

FIGURE 4.35 Charles Schwab (SCHW) weekly chart, 1999–2001.

Source: Chart courtesy of HGSI Investment Software, LLC (www.highgrowthstock.com), ©2014.

early 2000. It shows how a POD forms within a particular market context. SCHW topped in April 1999 in what was a classic climax top. This led to a 27-week trudge to the downside that didn't stop until the stock was −58.7 percent from its April peak. When the general market began its run from late October 1999 into March 2000, SCHW turned with the market in October 1999, but lagged the otherwise parabolic, ascending market trend during that time period, instead moving roughly sideways between late October 1999 and late February 2000. The mania of that general market period eventually got to the laggard stocks so that even the turkeys started flying, and SCHW joined the dot.com party in late February 2000. At that point the stock flared back to life with a rapid four-week run-up the right side of what became a 50-week POD formation.

The right-side peak of SCHW's POD formation occurred in synchrony with the general market top at point #1 on the chart in Figure 4.34. This shortable break in the stock later led to the formation of a second POD-like formation that was much smaller and which resembled a big, ugly, late-stage cup-with-handle formation. This second formation failed at point #2 on the chart. These are two distinctly different types of right-side POD breakdowns, the first being extremely sharp and quick to the downside, while the second break led to a slow roll down the 10-week (50-day on the daily chart) moving average that culminated with a deep, steady breakdown to new lows in January of 2001.

The short-sale point at #1 in Figure 4.35 can be viewed in greater detail on the daily chart shown in Figure 4.36. Here we see the climactic run up the right peak

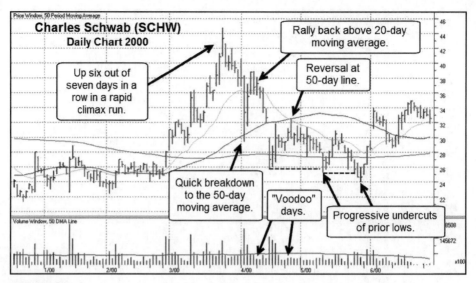

FIGURE 4.36 Charles Schwab (SCHW) daily chart, 2000. The sharp breakdown off the right-side peak of the POD formation is characterized by some extreme, but shortable, volatility.

Source: Chart courtesy of HGSI Investment Software, LLC (www.highgrowthstock.com), ©2014.

as the dot.com bubble market mania reached a crescendo in late March 2000. The stock ran up six out of seven days in a row and then finally pulled an "Icarus-like" move by simply falling out of the sky and plunging to its 50-day moving average. It bounced very sharply off of the 50-day line and retraced a good portion of the prior downside break. This extremely volatile, ultra-V-shaped bounce lost momentum as it glided back over the 20-day moving average, and the final up day that closed above the 20-day line occurred on a voodoo volume signature, indicating that buying demand is waning rapidly. This is a short-sale entry point. The stock holds along the 20-day line for one more day before plunging through the 50-day and 200-day moving averages over the next three days.

Notice that as SCHW blew through the 200-day moving average in mid-April, it was coming down on top of a prior base that it formed between late December 1999 and late February 2000. This is a logical cover point, and the stock then bounced up to its 50-day moving average, where it could have been shorted on the voodoo bounce up into the 50-day line. The stock then moved back down and undercut the mid-April low, rallied up to a point just above the 20-day moving average, lost upside momentum, and broke to new lows where it undercut the early May 2000 low. At this point, after a couple of successive undercut and rally moves around prior lows, things are a bit played out on the short side for the time being.

The reader should make note of the fact that the most concrete short-sale entry point occurred on the sharp V-shaped bounce off the 50-day line and back above the 20-day moving average, something that is actually quite common in POD breakdowns. However, as we have seen with the DRYS example as well, if one is highly attuned to and aware of the position of the stock within the overall POD formation as it comes up the right side and is then able to correlate this to simultaneous climax run type action as the stock approaches the right side peak, one can anticipate and short into the climax top once it shows signs of reversing. In Figure 4.36, we can see how SCHW ran up 6 out of 7 days in a row, and then on the eighth day gapped down and reversed on heavy volume, and this can also serve as a potential short-sale entry point.

Now let's look at the breakdown at point #2 on Figure 4.35 that occurred from the handle of a big, wide, and loose cup-with-handle formation that was 23 weeks in length and −46.4 percent deep. This progressed in classic style, with the handle breakout failing in the earlier part of August 2000 and the stock moving down to the 50-day moving average. As we can see in Figure 4.37, that led to a bounce back up towards the original breakout point near the 40 price level. This gapped and stalled on above-average volume in early September 2000, and the stock dropped through the 50-day moving average six days later. On the seventh day, the stock briefly tried to rally back up into the 50-day line, presenting short-sellers with a perfect entry point on the handle breakout failure. The stock dropped right down to and then through the 200-day moving average, where it became coverable. From there it rallied back up into overhead resistance at the underside of the prior handle and the 36 price area. Volume dried up on that move right at the peak in late September, and the stock again gave way to the downside, bouncing off the 200-day moving average

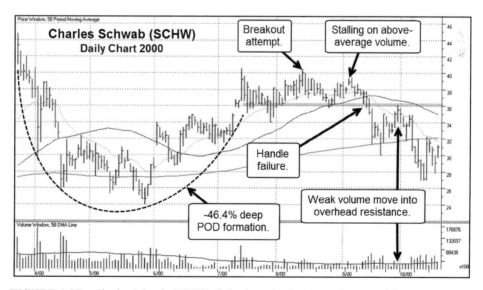

FIGURE 4.37 Charles Schwab (SCHW) daily chart, 2000. A second, 23-week long POD forms as a late-stage cup-with-handle base.

Source: Chart courtesy of HGSI Investment Software, LLC (www.highgrowthstock.com), ©2014.

for two days before rolling over and busting even further through the 200-day line as its moved into mid-October.

The practical aspects of short-selling require more thought than just looking for "entry points" on a weekly chart. This is because the uncertainty of what is going on with respect to the action of the individual short-sale target stock as well as that of the general market at large must be managed in real-time. That can only be done at the granular level on a daily chart. As well, short-selling is very much about searching for clues at the scene of a crime. Once a big, leading stock begins to break down and starts to produce the initial rumblings of a potential overall topping formation, the crime scene is set, and now one must search for those minute clues that tell you when and where the precise short-sale entry and cover points are. This requires some creativity and the development of a good "chart eye" on the short side, which can only be developed through experience.

Exercising some creativity and resourcefulness in the short-selling process is illustrated quite well by my experience with four of the biggest leading stocks in the early part of 2014: Yelp (YELP), Workday (WDAY), Tableau Software (DATA), and Splunk (SPLK). Each of these stocks had strong upside price moves in the early months of 2014, and each one managed to clear the $100 "century mark" level as we moved towards the early March short-term market top, which I discussed at the outset of this chapter with Figure 4.1, the daily chart of the NASDAQ in the early part of 2014.

Recall in Chapter 3, we discussed using Jesse Livermore's Century Mark rule in conjunction with LSFB and POD short-sale set-ups. Livermore used this rule of his on the long side, but would also use it in reverse as a rationale and method of shorting big, leading stocks that were on the verge of topping. As we quoted in Chapter 3, Livermore described this rule in *Reminiscences of a Stock Operator*, where he said, "it was an old trading theory of mine that when a stock crosses 100 or 200 or 300 for the first time the price does not stop there but goes a good deal higher, so that if you buy it as soon as it crosses the line it is almost certain to show you a profit." When Anaconda Copper cleared the $300 price level for the first time in 1907, Livermore observed the action in the stock, "I figured that when it crossed 300 it ought to keep on going and probably touch 340 in a jiffy." Anaconda, however, did not act as it should, and Livermore noted that "Anaconda opened at 298 and went up to 302 3/4 but pretty soon it began to fade away. I made up my mind that if Anaconda went back to 301 it was a fake movement. On a legitimate advance the price should have gone to 310 without stopping. If instead it reacted it meant that precedents had failed me and I was wrong; and the only thing to do when a man is wrong is to be right by ceasing to be wrong." At that point, Livermore shorted Anaconda Copper and made a killing in the process.

In March of 2014, however, as I was flipping through daily charts of the stocks on my watch lists I noticed that four strong leaders, YELP, WDAY, DATA, and

SPLK, had all pushed above their first century mark at the $100 price level but were suddenly breaking back down through that same century mark as the general market was starting to roll over, as shown in the daily charts of all four in Figures 4.38 through 4.41. In each case, the stock could have been shorted right as it failed at the $100 price level, and doing so would have resulted in huge short-sale profits over the course of the general market correction that lasted from early March to

FIGURE 4.38 Yelp (YELP) daily chart, 2014.

Source: Chart courtesy of HGSI Investment Software, LLC (www.highgrowthstock.com), ©2014.

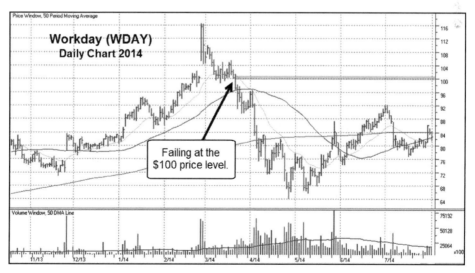

FIGURE 4.39 Workday (WDAY) daily chart, 2014.

Source: Chart courtesy of HGSI Investment Software, LLC (www.highgrowthstock.com), ©2014.

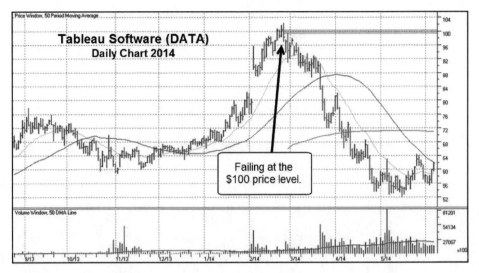

FIGURE 4.40   Tableau Software (DATA) daily chart, 2014.

Source: Chart courtesy of HGSI Investment Software, LLC (www.highgrowthstock.com), ©2014.

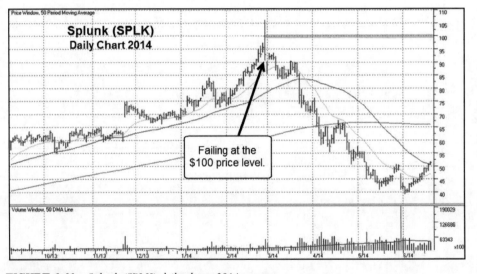

FIGURE 4.41   Splunk (SPLK) daily chart, 2014.

Source: Chart courtesy of HGSI Investment Software, LLC (www.highgrowthstock.com), ©2014.

roughly mid-April 2014. Each of these stocks was also a hot, high-flying tech name that was also a recent IPO within the past couple of years, with YELP having come public in March 2012, WDAY in October 2012, DATA in May 2013, and SPLK in April 2012. I did not short all four, but focused instead on YELP. While my premise was quite correct, I did not fully understand what I had stumbled onto, and I covered my YELP short far too soon. All of these stocks eventually cratered 40–50 percent or more.

The main point I am trying to make here is that the short-selling game is constantly evolving, and one must make the most of cumulated knowledge in a highly resourceful way. This includes employing a little creativity and thinking outside the box. In my view this is what make short-selling so rewarding and, more importantly, so much fun. I find that so many traders and investors desire the crutch of mechanical "rules" that they can follow by rote without engaging their brain. But successful investing is not about being a robot—it is about being a human being. And as human beings we have the ability to exercise all of our intellectual, creative, and psychological faculties in the process of solving the real-time puzzle that short-selling is.

■ Summary

I cannot possibly cover all the various permutations of short-sale entry points in one book, but as this chapter shows they do have certain common elements that one can look for in real-time. This generally requires monitoring a previously created short-sale watch list very closely, often over a period of several weeks and/or months as the overall topping pattern develops. We have seen how a single broken former leader can offer a multitude of short-selling entry points and opportunities while it remains in the process of breaking down, rallying, breaking down again, and rallying again as it continues to build an overall, larger topping formation. The fractal nature of the patterns and subpatterns in the overall topping formation is what makes this possible. In addition, we have also established a concrete method for taking profits and gauging when a downside "leg" in an overall topping formation has run its course, at least in the short-term.

Understanding short-selling is also a lot like listening to and understanding a musical symphony—you know that it has general movements and can label and understand those movements and the role they play within the overall structure of the symphony, but you do not know what the precise notes written down by the composer will be or how the various melodies, both melodic and percussive, will sound. In this manner, the weekly charts help you figure out where you are with respect to the overall "movements" of a major topping formation, but it is the daily charts where the actual "notes" are written. Short-selling requires a fluid, contextual, and inductive use of both.

In essence, I have provided you with the tools, but how you use these tools, either alone or in combination, or perhaps even in entirely new ways, and what you build with those tools is all subject to your own creativity and resourcefulness.

If some of this makes your head spin, do not fret. These concepts will be reinforced as we move through the rest of this book, and indeed there is much more to come. Now let's move on to the next chapters, where we look at some detailed case studies of short-sale "model stocks."

CHAPTER 5

Case Study #1: Apple (AAPL) in 2012–2013

Probably no other stock in the post-dot.com era of the New Millennium epitomizes the concept of a "big stock" more than Apple (AAPL) from 2004 to the time of this writing. The company's success at reinventing itself began with an entirely new product that bore no resemblance to the personal computers upon which it had previously built its name. This new product was nothing more than an MP3 music file player known as the iPod. It is useful to understand that Apple's business model after the dot.com era, the so-called "Internet bubble" of the late 1990s, was in fact enabled by the Internet itself. The idea of providing consumers with the ability to download music from the Internet through Apple's iTunes online music store rather than having to go into brick and mortar music stores illustrates how one wave of innovation can drive a second wave of innovation. Clearly, there is no shortage of evidence that the Internet has since spawned what is truly an entirely new universe of products and services, including "Internet appliances," that add significant value and productivity to consumers' day-to-day lives. The rebirth of Apple is a big piece of that evidence.

The iPod helped to fuel new growth for Apple, and the stock began to ride this wave in 2004 as it began a massive price run. In 2007 the concept of the iPod was married to that of the cell phone, and the iPhone was born. The iPhone essentially turned a cell phone into a miniature PC, and the concept of *apps*, or small, easily installable software applications, helped to drive its popularity and the popularity of rival products like Samsung's Galaxy phones. The utility of the iPhone as a sort of miniaturized PC then led to the idea of a slightly bigger version in the iPad. At the time of this writing in 2014, Apple is pushing the envelope even further by miniaturizing the iPhone with the iWatch, amidst the new concept of "wearable" Internet appliances. And so the beat goes on.

Apple's immense price run from 2004 through 2012 can be divided into two major phases: one phase from 2004–2008, after which the stock topped with the market during the financial crisis of late 2008, and one phase from 2009–2012 that saw the top form in late 2012. For our purposes, we will focus on the 2009–2012 phase. Figure 5.1 shows most of that move from early 2010 to the peak in late 2012. If we were going to take a simplistic view of shorting Apple following this top, we would simply draw an arrow at the downside "breakout" through the neckline of a large, roughly nine-month head-and-shoulders (H&S) top that formed from March 2012 to November 2012, and write "Short-Sale Point" in the text callout box. As we shall soon see, however, the situation was far more complex than that, and there are far more details to the story of how this top played out than might initially meet the eye.

Let's start by examining the weekly chart of Apple right around the top in the close-up view provided by Figure 5.2. We can see that the overall formation topped out at the peak of the head in mid-September 2012. At that point, the stock stalled and churned on average weekly volume before selling volume picked up sharply

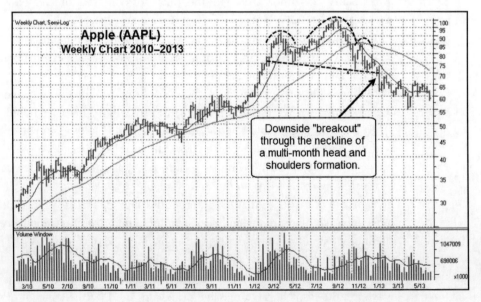

FIGURE 5.1 Apple (AAPL) weekly chart 2010–2013. A head and shoulders top marked a major top in AAPL shares following a strong upside price run from early 2009 into late 2012.

Source: Chart courtesy of HGSI Investment Software, LLC (www.highgrowthstock.com), ©2014.

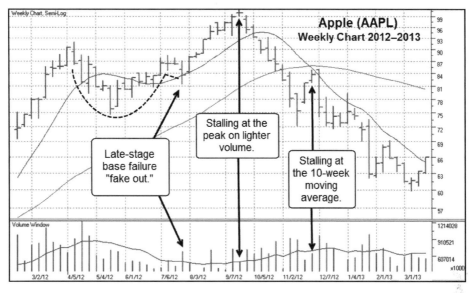

Weekly Chart, Semi-Log

Apple (AAPL)
Weekly Chart 2012–2013

Stalling at the peak on lighter volume.

Late-stage base failure "fake out."

Stalling at the 10-week moving average.

Volume Window

FIGURE 5.2 Apple (AAPL) weekly chart 2012–2013. The head and shoulders formation AAPL formed around the late 2012 peak.

Source: Chart courtesy of HGSI Investment Software, LLC (www.highgrowthstock.com), ©2014.

and the stock plummeted well below its 40-week moving average (200-day on the daily chart) over eight straight weeks of lower weekly closes. At the terminus of this price break, the stock undercut the lows of the late-stage cup-with-handle base, the left side of which formed the left shoulder in the overall H&S pattern. That undercut of a major low led to a sharp rally back up to the 10-week moving average, where the stock stalled as it ran into resistance right at a "black cross" where the 10-week line had crossed below the 40-week line, as Figure 5.2 shows. That was a short-sale entry point, and more in line with the types of short-sale entry points that I look for. From there the stock broke down and just barely undercut the lows of mid-November 2012, bounced back up into the 10-week line, and then broke out to the downside and through the neckline in late January 2013. This breakout through the neckline is labeled as such in Figure 5.1.

Notice that in early August 2012, the stock was in fact breaking out of a late-stage cup-with-handle that it had started to build in April 2012. The handle was moving straight sideways for two weeks before it "cracked" to the downside as it appeared to be moving into a late-stage base-failure. In Figure 5.3, we break Figure 5.2 down further and take a closer look at the left side of the formation that includes this late-stage cup-with-handle on the far more granular view that a daily chart provides. Here we see the cup-with-handle formation that took shape between early April and early August 2012. Seventeen trading days into August, the stock gapped down below its 50-day moving average on huge trading volume. This immediately looked

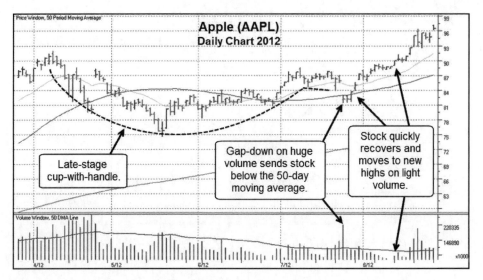

FIGURE 5.3 Apple (AAPL) daily chart 2012.

Source: Chart courtesy of HGSI Investment Software, LLC (www.highgrowthstock.com), ©2014.

like an LSFB short-sale entry point where one might play for a quick move to lower lows, perhaps undercutting the mid-May 2012 low of the cup down around 75. Had one shorted this gap-down with the idea of using the 50-day moving average as a reference point for an upside stop on the trade, one would have quickly been stopped out, as the stock turned and eventually moved to all-time highs in the latter part of August. So in this manner what initially looked like an LSFB simply ended up as a "shakeout and breakout" to new highs, illustrating the reality that short-selling is not always a profitable venture.

The breakout from this late-stage cup-with-handle in late August led to a move to all-time highs that carried another 15 percent or so before it finally topped in mid-September 2012. This top is shown on a daily chart in Figure 5.4, and the reader should make careful note of the fact that these charts are showing split-adjusted prices, so the $100 level on the chart is equivalent to the $700 level prior to Apple's 7-for-1 stock split in June 2014. The peak is marked by two days where Apple tried to move to new highs but stalled, the first day on light volume and the second day on heavier volume, indicating that sellers were coming in more aggressively. The stock came down from there, retesting the prior September lows around the 94 price level and building a couple of small right shoulders in a tiny fractal H&S formation. This small H&S in fact made up the upper part of the head in the larger H&S formation we see on the weekly charts in Figures 5.1 and 5.2.

The neckline of this fractal H&S formed along the 94 price area, as is highlighted in gray in Figure 5.4, and coincided with the 50-day moving average in early October. When Apple bounced off the 50-day moving average and ran into the 20-day

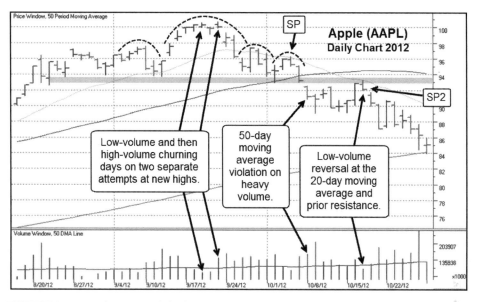

FIGURE 5.4 Apple (AAPL) daily chart 2012.

Source: Chart courtesy of HGSI Investment Software, LLC (www.highgrowthstock.com), ©2014.

moving average on the fourth day of October, it became shortable, labeled SP on the chart.

The daily chart of the NASDAQ Composite Index in Figure 5.5 shows the simultaneous general market action, and we can see that the NASDAQ topped on the same day that Apple did in mid-September. Later on, at the point labeled SP in Figure 5.4, Apple's daily chart, the NASDAQ took one more day to roll over with an outside reversal to the downside on the fifth trading day of October. From there, Apple and the NASDAQ both broke down through their 50-day moving averages, and then both rallied back up to their 20-day moving averages right in the middle of October. Apple's rally up into the 20-day line, shown in Figure 5.4, reversed on low-volume and sent the stock down to lower lows. Notice that the rally into the 20-day line also ran into resistance at the neckline of the small head and shoulders the stock formed around its peak in September and very early October, around the 94 price area on the chart. This is a short-sale entry point, labeled SP2 on the chart. The three-day downside break from there turned into a very quick undercut and rally, as Apple flipped back to the upside and pushed just above the 90 price level for a single day before reversing the next day and then sliding all the way down to the 200-day moving average at the far right of the chart in Figure 5.4. Meanwhile, the NASDAQ's action in Figure 5.5 closely correlates with that of Apple.

As Apple reaches its 200-day moving average, it paused for one day in a vain attempt to bounce off the line and then broke below the line to lower lows, as can be seen in a wider view of the daily action shown in Figure 5.6. We can see how

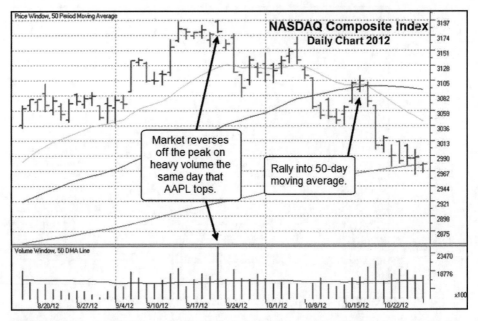

FIGURE 5.5 NASDAQ Composite Index daily chart, 2012. The NASDAQ's breakdown off the peak in September 2012 closely correlated with Apple's breakdown off of its own peak at that time.

Source: Chart courtesy of HGSI Investment Software, LLC (www.highgrowthstock.com), ©2014.

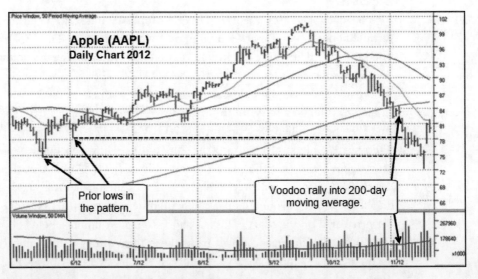

FIGURE 5.6 Apple (AAPL) daily chart 2012.

Source: Chart courtesy of HGSI Investment Software, LLC (www.highgrowthstock.com), ©2014.

Apple made one attempt to rally back up into the 200-day moving average on what is a very low-volume voodoo type of move, and then it gapped down to lower lows. At this point, the wider daily chart view comes in handy, because we can see that the stock was approaching a major low on the left side of the chart near the 75 price level. If one had been working the stock on the short side from the two prior short-sale entry points labeled SP and SP2 in Figure 5.4, it was then time to think about covering the position for good. The final undercut of the 75 low, actually the low of the cup-with-handle base shown in Figure 5.3, led to a sharp undercut and rally move that saw the stock gap-up into the 20-day moving average. At that point, the right side of the head in the overall H&S formation seen in Figure 5.1 was complete, and it remained to be seen whether Apple would go on to form any right shoulders as the H&S formation continued to evolve.

As Figure 5.7 shows, Apple's gap-up rally into the 20-day moving average showed a voodoo day at the peak, and one might have looked to initiate a short-sale re-entry at this point. However, the stock pushed right through the 20-day line and continued higher, leading to a quick stop-out. The rally continued a little further up towards the 200-day moving average, with a second voodoo day marking the peak of that rally.

At the same exact time, we can see that the NASDAQ Composite Index was running into resistance at its 50-day moving average, as its daily chart in Figure 5.8 shows. The alert reader will notice that for the most part, since the mid-September peak, the charts of Apple and the NASDAQ Composite correlate very closely. Apple peaked with the market in mid-September and bottomed with the market in

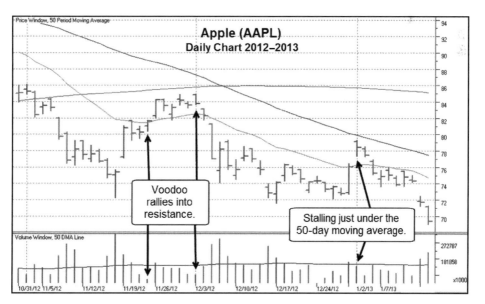

FIGURE 5.7 Apple (AAPL) daily chart, 2012–2013. Apple forms a large right shoulder.

Source: Chart courtesy of HGSI Investment Software, LLC (www.highgrowthstock.com), ©2014.

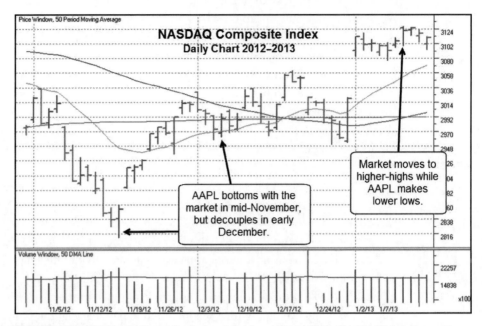

FIGURE 5.8 NASDAQ Composite Index daily chart, 2012–2013. The NASDAQ Composite Index chops around in a sideways movement during the month of December 2012.

Source: Chart courtesy of HGSI Investment Software, LLC (www.highgrowthstock.com), ©2014.

mid-November. This was actually not surprising at the time, since many considered Apple, as one of the biggest big-stock leaders and one of the largest components of the NASDAQ, to literally "be the market." But this phenomenon did not last forever. The ensuing rally off of the mid-November lows rally served to form the first and largest right shoulder in Apple's overall H&S formation. It was at the peak of this right shoulder that Apple decoupled from the NASDAQ and began to move in the opposite direction.

As the NASDAQ chopped around throughout the month of December, Apple completed a right-shoulder-rally, or RSR as I like to refer to it, and rolled over to retest the neckline in its H&S formation before eventually forming a second, much smaller right shoulder at the outset of December and heading to even lower lows as it gapped down through the neckline in January 2012, as Figure 5.7 shows. Meanwhile, the NASDAQ in Figure 5.8 gaps up to higher highs in January as the decoupling between the index and Apple is fully confirmed.

If we go back to a weekly chart of Apple in Figure 5.9, we can see how the peak of the right shoulder that formed in late November stalled right at the 10-week moving average, which in turn had moved below the 40-week moving average in a bearish black cross. This is a good illustration of how one needs to monitor the action on the daily chart closely and within the context of what is going on with the weekly chart. For example, in Figure 5.7, that first voodoo rally into the 20-day moving average

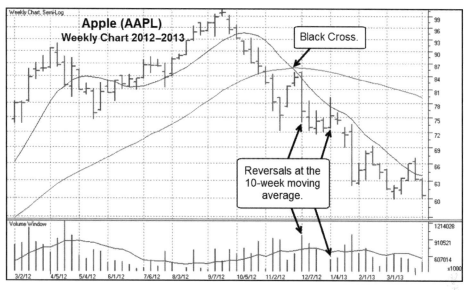

FIGURE 5.9 Apple (AAPL) weekly chart 2012–2013. Weak, stalling action is evident at the 10-week moving average and the peaks of the two right shoulders in the overall H&S formation.

Source: Chart courtesy of HGSI Investment Software, LLC (www.highgrowthstock.com), ©2014.

was not a successful short-sale entry point, and one clue that it might not work could have been found in the corresponding action on the weekly chart. Apple's weekly chart did not show any churning or stalling until it reached the 10-week line. At that point, the second upside bar in the bounce off of the mid-November lows, correlating to the move up towards the 200-day moving average, and the second voodoo day in Apple's daily chart in Figure 5.7 failed at the 10-week line and rolled over from there.

The second right shoulder in the pattern peaked right at the beginning of January 2013 and was a very short-lived affair. The daily chart in Figure 5.7 shows this as a stalling gap-up move into the 50-day moving average while the weekly chart in Figure 5.9 shows this as a big stalling week on light volume as the stock closed in the lower half of the weekly price range. From there Apple blows through the neckline in the pattern in a big downside "breakout" that lasts all of one week before the stock finds a low and begins chopping around in February and March of 2013.

The main point of our entire analysis so far in this particular case study is that short-sale points in Apple appeared in the upper part of the head, and would not have been evident to someone relying solely on the weekly chart and the completed formation of the H&S topping pattern. As Figure 5.4 showed, there were two clear short-sale entry points as the stock came down along what eventually became the right side of the head in the formation. By the time the stock broke out through the neckline of a fully-formed and completed H&S formation, a good chunk of the short-sale profit potential had already been wrung out of the pattern.

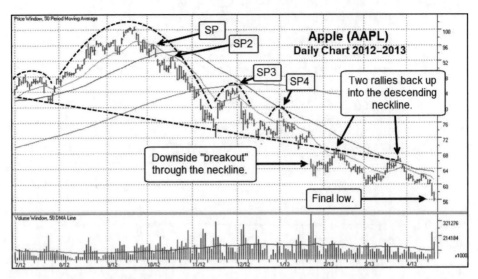

FIGURE 5.10 Apple (AAPL) daily chart, 2012–2013. The downtrend from peak to trough shows that the "fat" part of Apple's top and subsequent downtrend from a short-seller's perspective occurred before the neckline breakout.

Source: Chart courtesy of HGSI Investment Software, LLC (www.highgrowthstock.com), ©2014.

We can confirm this by observing Figure 5.10, a daily chart showing the entire peak-to-trough move in Apple from September 2012 to the final low in April 2013. The initial entry points at SP and SP2 occur quite early in the pattern at the peaks of two right shoulders within the "fractal" and smaller head and shoulders (see Figure 5.2) that formed in the upper half of the head of the larger H&S formation. The larger H&S formation is outlined in Figure 5.10. The entry point at the peak of the right shoulder, labeled SP3, was a viable entry point, particularly if one was using both the daily and weekly chart action to figure out exactly what was going on. The entry point at SP4 was a little less well-defined on the daily chart, but when taken into context with the weekly chart action, which showed a big stalling week with the stock closing in the lower half of the weekly range in Figure 5.9, could have been deciphered as a short-sale point.

Once Apple crashed through the neckline of the head and shoulders formation, the downward trend actually became somewhat shallower, something that is visually evident on the chart. Notice that even what looks like a brutal gap-down through the neckline on massive selling volume almost has more of an "exhaustion" feel to it as the stock rallied right back up to the 20-day moving average and the descending neckline. That rally would have offered another late short-sale point, and it would have worked when the stock moved to lower lows in early March. The second rally into the neckline in late March would also have offered a second such short-sale entry point. This also would have been successful as the ensuing downside move ended at the final low in Apple's 2012–2013 descent.

The reader should study this chart carefully and note all the little undercut and rally moves in the pattern all the way down that would have offered reference points for covering part or all of a concentrated position and then re-entering on the ensuing short bounces up into resistance. This is the way I tend to work and campaign stocks on the short side, but one can also take more of an intermediate-term view, giving the stock a little more room once a proper short-sale entry point has been determined and a position taken. If one recognizes such a short-sale point early in the pattern, as was possible with Apple near the peak as it formed a small, fractal H&S formation in the upper half of the larger head in Figure 5.2, and one had gotten short Apple at SP or SP2, then it would have been possible to hold the position all the way down to the 200-day line or further.

It is also instructive to compare the short-sale entry points in Apple's daily chart from July 2012 to April 2013, shown in Figure 5.10, to the daily chart of the NASDAQ Composite Index for the exact time period. Figure 5.11 shows Apple's short-sale points from the mid-September 2012 top to its final low in April 2013, as they would have occurred on a corresponding NASDAQ Composite Index daily chart. We can see how Apple, which had been considered to be "the market," fully decouples from the NASDAQ Composite Index in January of 2013 as it moves in the opposite direction from there over the next four months.

One of the most interesting characteristics of Apple stock right around the top was that as the stock initially sold down from what was then the absolute peak

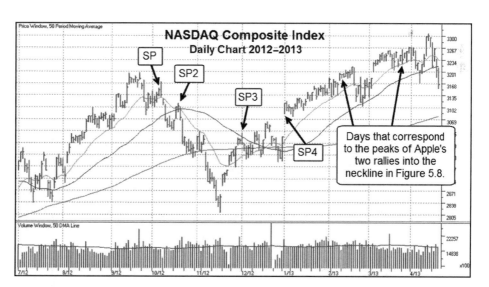

FIGURE 5.11 NASDAQ Composite Index daily chart, 2012–2013. An overview of the NASDAQ Composite Index's action as it corresponds to Apple's from July 2012 to April 2013 as shown in Figure 5.10.

Source: Chart courtesy of HGSI Investment Software, LLC (www.highgrowthstock.com), ©2014.

at $705.07, pre-split adjusted, Apple was valued at 13 times forward earnings estimates right around the price levels at SP2 in Figure 5.10. For many, especially those who missed the stock on the way up, this was an extremely compelling and "cheap" valuation for such a great company. The incredible "value" that Apple stock selling at 13 times forward earnings estimates allegedly presented did not prevent the stock from continuing much lower. At that time the stock was trading in the low 600s, and eventually went on to hit its nadir at 385.10.

The other interesting characteristic of Apple's stock during its topping process and the ensuing steady, seven-month downtrend from a high of 705.07 in September 2012 to a low of 385.10 in April of 2013, pre-split adjusted, is that it mostly countertrended the NASDAQ Composite Index. Figure 5.12 shows a comparison chart of Apple versus the NASDAQ Composite index at that time. We can see that the right side of the head in Apple's larger H&S formation all occurred in synchrony with the NASDAQ's top and downtrend into the November low. From there Apple rallied another couple of weeks with the NASDAQ, but over the next several months the stock and the NASDAQ went in opposite directions. This period where Apple underperformed the NASDAQ is shown within the smaller gray box that extended from November 2012 to July 2013. Thus, even the biggest of big-stock leaders continued to be shortable within a market uptrend, despite being considered a stock that could serve as a proxy for the market itself. In fact, Figure 5.12 proves that there were a number of periods during 2011–2014 where Apple both underperformed

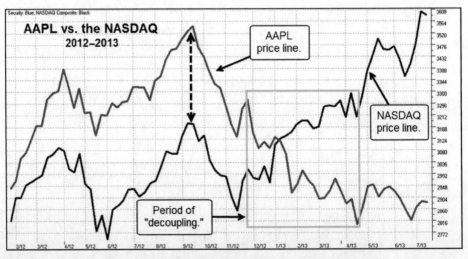

FIGURE 5.12 A comparison chart of Apple (AAPL) versus the NASDAQ Composite Index daily chart, 2012–2013. From early December 2012 into mid-April 2013, Apple and the NASDAQ went their separate ways.

Source: Chart courtesy of HGSI Investment Software, LLC (www.highgrowthstock.com), ©2014.

and outperformed the NASDAQ Composite. It also proves that big-stock former leaders can be shortable during market uptrends.

■ Summary

From the period 2004–2012, Apple was a massive consumer-tech juggernaut that truly set the gold standard for what a "big stock" is all about. However, we also know that Apple had two major corrections during that period (2007–2009 and 2012–2013) that offered some very substantial short-selling opportunities. Even the biggest of the big stocks are not immune to such sell-offs, and Apple certainly proved that point.

CHAPTER 6

Case Study #2: Netflix (NFLX) in 2011

There are few stocks in market history that have confounded short-sellers as much as Netflix (NFLX) did in the post-financial crisis bull market that developed off the lows of 2009. As we discussed in Chapter 1, NFLX was a frequent target of high-profile hedge fund short-sellers, several of whom found it necessary to pump their short position by appearing on financial cable TV and writing articles on financial websites detailing why NFLX was atrociously "overvalued." Such short-sellers were what we call *valuation short-sellers* who short a stock based on the idea that a) the stock is overvalued and b) the stock market doesn't know this, but they, in their preeminent prescience, do. In our view, arguing with the market, as much as on the long side as the short side, can have disastrous results, and the steady, albeit choppy, upside trend of NFLX shown in Figure 6.1 attests to this.

Had these persistent shorts been more attuned to listening to the market instead of telling it what to do, they could have just waited until NFLX finally showed signs of topping in mid-2011. After a strong surge to the upside that slowed down in April 2010, NFLX continued to chop its way higher. Each time it broke out of a short base it ran up a short way and then pulled right back to the top of the prior base. This was a fairly consistent pattern for NFLX all the way up until the stock finally began to show a change of character in mid-2011. The primary indication of this change of character was the breakdown below the 50-day/10-week moving

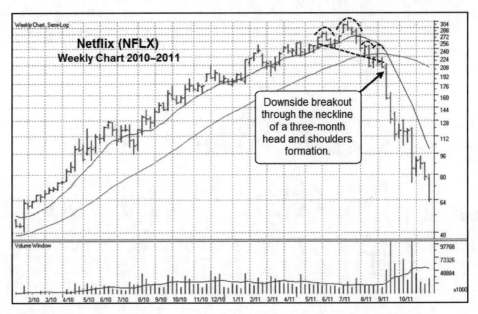

FIGURE 6.1 Netflix (NFLX) weekly chart (2010–2011). NFLX's steady upside trend off the lows of early 2009 chopped up short-sellers who fervently believed that they were smarter than the market.

Source: Chart courtesy of HGSI Investment Software, LLC (www.highgrowthstock.com), ©2014.

averages on the daily and weekly charts, respectively, and the subsequent formation of a clear head and shoulders (H&S) pattern.

What sets NFLX apart as a case study is the fact that it was immediately and immensely profitable right at the downside breakout, as the stock gapped through the neckline of its H&S formation and collapsed with furious velocity. This is plain to see in Figure 6.1. There were other short points earlier in the pattern, but the time to be short NFLX was right at the neckline breakdown. This, however, took some time to develop.

On the daily chart of NFLX during the time period surrounding its mid-July 2011 peak (Figure 6.2), we can see that its uptrend ended with a late-stage breakout failure in early July 2011. This breakout failure started with a buyable gap-up move that then drifted to a marginal new high (Point 1) over the next six trading days. On that peak day, the stock stalled on heavy volume and then began to come in to retest the intra-day low of the buyable gap-up day. As things progressed into the second half of July, NFLX dropped below the buyable gap-up's intra-day low just under the 276 price level and then bounced above its 20-day moving average, where it stalled on heavy volume (Point 2). The very next day it gapped below its 50-day moving average on very heavy volume, but managed to close just above the line. The next day, the stock stalled a bit just above the 50-day line. This is an initial short-sale

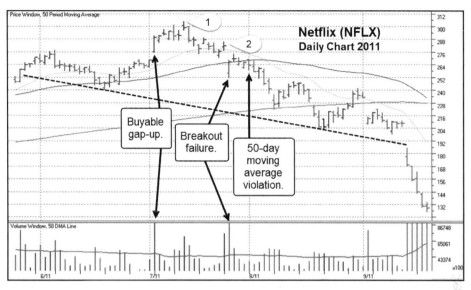

FIGURE 6.2   Netflix (NFLX) daily chart 2011.

Source: Chart courtesy of HGSI Investment Software, LLC (www.highgrowthstock.com), ©2014.

point on the basis of a late-stage failed-base (LSFB) set-up. When entering at this point, the top of the gap-down day at around 276 serves as a reasonable upside stop.

From there NFLX drifted lower and technically violated its 50-day moving average. Readers of our prior books will remember that a moving average violation occurs when a stock first closes below the moving average and then later moves below the intra-day low of that first day that the stock closed below the moving average. Once NFLX violated the 50-day line, it slid right down to the 200-day moving average, which could have been considered a short-term cover point given that the stock also gapped down and collapsed well below the prior 240 low in the pattern from mid-June.

At the same time, the NASDAQ Composite Index, shown in Figure 6.3, had already topped four days before NFLX's peak at Point 1 in Figure 6.2. The NASDAQ formed a little double-top type of formation and broke to the downside on a gap-down move. This coincided with NFLX's violation of its 50-day moving average, and as NFLX broke down away from its 50-day moving average and proceeded to meet up with the 200-day moving average, the NASDAQ was blowing right through its own 200-day moving average. As NFLX found support at its 200-day moving average, the NASDAQ also found support, and both bounced in synchrony over the next several days before peaking at the point labeled SP2 in Figure 6.3. Comparing the two charts in Figure 6.2 and 6.3, it is interesting to note that the NASDAQ appears to bottom right in mid-air, while NFLX bottoms right at a "logical" point, the 200-day moving average. Thus the NASDAQ low coincides with NFLX's low

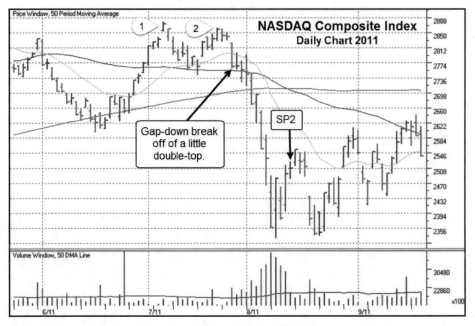

FIGURE 6.3 NASDAQ Composite Index daily chart, 2011. The NASDAQ topped just four days before NFLX in July 2011.

Source: Chart courtesy of HGSI Investment Software, LLC (www.highgrowthstock.com), ©2014.

at its own 200-day moving average. In a sense, the tail was wagging the dog, since we would normally expect to see the index providing support to individual stocks as the index pulls down into a key moving average like the 50-day or 200-day.

The move to the 200-day moving average combined with the undercut of the low in the prior base from mid-June, as the dotted line in Figure 6.4 indicates, represented a short-term cover point. There followed a rally up into a zone of resistance along a confluence of lows in the 252 price area, as highlighted in gray on the chart. The peak of this short rally occurred on a voodoo day, where volume was extremely light. This is a second short-sale entry point, labeled SP2 on the chart, and that corresponds to where I placed the SP2 label on the NASDAQ chart in Figure 6.3. From there, both NFLX and the NASDAQ rolled over, but NFLX broke below its 200-day moving average and made lower lows, while the NASDAQ merely retested and held at its early August low. The NASDAQ bounced off of that retest, and NFLX rallied with the index and back above its own 200-day moving average.

Another divergence occurs as the NASDAQ made a pair of higher highs, which we can see in Figure 6.5, but NFLX, shown in Figure 6.4, made a lower high and then gapped down to test the lows around the 210 area. Notice that the gap-down moves in NFLX correspond to similar gap-down moves in the NASDAQ Composite Index, but NFLX was in a downtrend while the NASDAQ was in an uptrend. NFLX

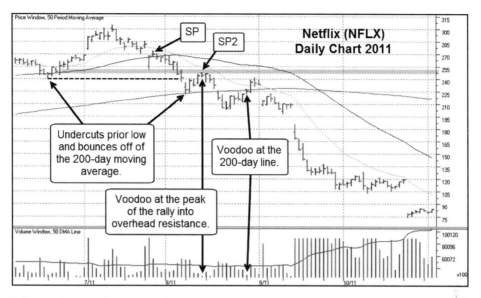

FIGURE 6.4   Netflix (NFLX) daily chart, 2011. Two short-sale points, one following a late-stage breakout failure in July 2011.

Source: Chart courtesy of HGSI Investment Software, LLC (www.highgrowthstock.com), ©2014.

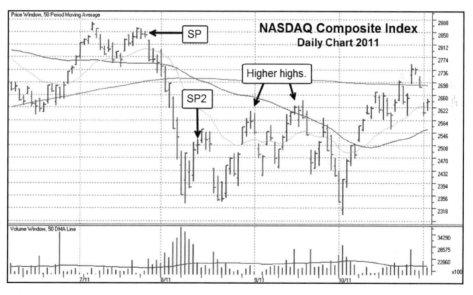

FIGURE 6.5   NASDAQ Composite Index daily chart, 2011. After bottoming in early August, the NASDAQ went on to make two higher-highs before breaking to new lows again.

Source: Chart courtesy of HGSI Investment Software, LLC (www.highgrowthstock.com), ©2014.

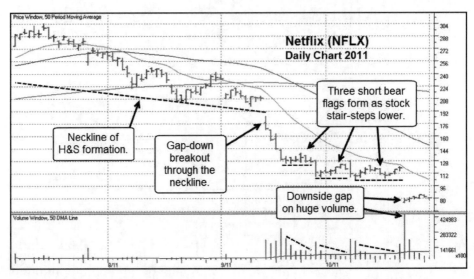

FIGURE 6.6 Netflix (NFLX) daily chart 2011. NFLX broke out to the downside and through the neckline of its prior H&S top formation.

Source: Chart courtesy of HGSI Investment Software, LLC (www.highgrowthstock.com), ©2014.

held tight for a few days along the 210 price level as it awaited its next quarterly earnings report, due to be reported after-hours on September 14.

NFLX missed on earnings and the stock gaps down the next morning, as we can see in Figure 6.6. The significant divergences discussed in the prior paragraph were a clue that earnings might miss expectations, and this was in fact the case. This gap-down move sent the stock on a downside breakout through the neckline of its prior H&S formation. The stock opened up at 169.25 but rallied sharply from there to reach an intra-day high of 185.40, so we can see that trying to short the initial gap-down move on the downside breakout would have been problematic. The trick with shorting a gap-down move is that you have to be able to determine where the intra-day high is going to be so that it can be used as a guide for an upside stop. In this manner, one treats the gap-down move in the opposite manner to how one would handle a buyable gap-up move. In a buyable gap-up, we used the intra-day low of the gap-up day as a selling guide, so this can work in reverse for a downside gap. Often, determining where the intra-day high is for a shortable gap-down move is not possible until later in the trading day. Once the 185.40 high was set, one could have attempted to short the stock as close to that high as possible, and then once the stock closed at the lows of the day at 169.25, right where it opened, the position would have been locked and loaded.

The gap-down breakout through the neckline carried all the way down to the 128 price level, and one would have been quite justified in taking a profit on any short position that had been initiated on the gap-down day. Notice, however, how NFLX was unable to rally at the end of September 2011 and formed a six-day bear flag before breaking out again to the downside. It dropped 10 percent or so and then formed a second short bear flag, shook out to the upside (where it found resistance at the lows of the prior bear flag around the 128 price level) and then moved lower again. This resulted in a third bear flag, from which the stock gapped down in late October 2011 after finding resistance at the 20-day moving average. Notice how each bear flag shows declining volume from left to right as the flag consolidates very much like the way a stock moving to the upside within a bull flag might, except in reverse. As the stock dropped lower and then moved sideways for a few days as it consolidated that prior price drop, volume dried up before the stock again broke out to the downside.

We can see that while one could have worked NFLX on the short side within each of these bear flags, the real meat of the downside move in NFLX occurred after the shortable gap-down and downside breakout through the neckline of the H&S formation. In theory, one could have shorted the moves to the high end of each bear flag's price channel with the idea of trying to catch a substantial downside breakout, but this takes several weeks to occur, and doesn't do so until the third short bear flag runs into the 20-day moving average. Had one had the foresight to short that move, the ensuing gap-down move would have produced an instant profit of 34.9 percent. The total breakdown in NFLX from the peak 304.79 in July 2011 to the December 2011 low was 79.5 percent.

■ Summary

NFLX illustrates that no matter how overvalued investors might think a stock is, and no matter how compelling some hedge fund manager's deeply thought out "bear case" against a stock is, betting against the trend is a dangerous proposition. Sure, eventually the shorts were right, but standing in the way of the stock all the way up is an expensive way to prove one's manhood (women are spared this character flaw, it appears!). Efficiency dictates that the time to short NFLX was not at hand until it began to show concrete signs of breaking down. In this case study, we see quite clearly how the stock first changed character in July 2011 on a late-stage breakout failure which then developed into an H&S topping formation. Alert short-sellers would have been able to capitalize on two early short-sale entry points at SP and SP2 in Figure 6.4, and both of these would have produced reasonable downside profits. The "fat" part of NFLX's breakdown occurred after the gap-down breakout through the neckline, resulting in a very sharp, deep, and furious collapse to the downside. This is the type of breakdown that a short-seller lives for, but it requires persistence and the ability to recognize when the pattern has reached a point of maximum "ripeness," at which point the fruit falls easily from the tree.

CHAPTER 7

Case Study #3: Keurig Green Mountain (GMCR) in 2011

Green Mountain Coffee Roasters (GMCR) was another favorite of valuation short-sellers in 2011, but the stock's persistent rally simply ground up short-sellers like so many rich, aromatic coffee beans all the way up. The company made a name for itself with its innovative Keurig single-cup coffee makers and K-Cup® format, which personalized the so-called "coffee experience." GMCR later changed its name to Keurig Green Mountain in order to emphasize its flagship products while retaining the same stock symbol. Figure 7.1 shows the latter part of the stock's indefatigable upside run, the peak in September 2011, and the ensuing downtrend that extends into 2012. We should note that GMCR's top occurred about two months after NFLX's top and price breakdown, which were discussed in Chapter 6.

What makes GMCR stand out in my mind as an interesting case study is the way it formed not one but two head-and-shoulders (H&S) patterns within the overall downtrend off of the September 2011 peak. We can see the compact, roughly 12-week H&S pattern that formed right at the top, and the wider 24-week H&S that formed between November 2011 and May 2012. Both of these H&S formations offered decent short-sale opportunities, so let's break Figure 7.1 into its smaller components on the daily charts, starting with Figure 7.2.

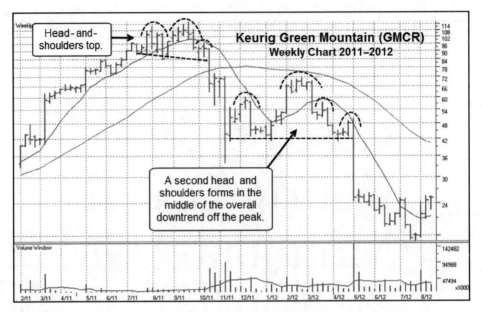

FIGURE 7.1 Keurig Green Mountain (GMCR) weekly chart 2011–2012. GMCR's top in 2011–2012 formed two head-and-shoulders patterns, one at the peak and one midway along its overall downtrend.

Source: Chart courtesy of HGSI Investment Software, LLC (www.highgrowthstock.com), ©2014.

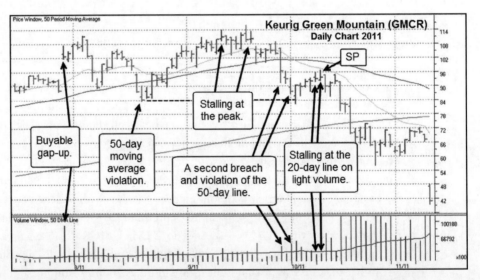

FIGURE 7.2 Keurig Green Mountain (GMCR) daily chart, 2011. It took two 50-day moving average violations to finally drive a stake through GMCR's heart and send the stock lower.

Source: Chart courtesy of HGSI Investment Software, LLC (www.highgrowthstock.com), ©2014.

GMCR's topping phase began with a buyable gap-up breakout to all-time highs in late July 2011. This buyable gap-up quickly failed as the general market ran into trouble and the NASDAQ Composite Index, shown in Figure 7.3, broke down sharply at the beginning of August. This caused GMCR to wobble a bit, and after one short bounce off of the 50-day moving average, the stock rolled over and broke through the line on a textbook violation in mid-August. However, this moving average violation turned out to be a fake out, as the stock turned back to the upside and made a marginal new, all-time high in mid-September. Had one tried to short this as a late-stage failed-base (LSFB) type of set-up, one would have been stopped out at the 20-day moving average.

As we can see on the chart, this move to new highs was met with several days of stalling around the peak, with the last stalling day as the stock attempted to move to new highs being followed by a gap-down move on heavy selling volume. This gap-down off the peak found temporary support along the 50-day line, but after drifting slightly upward over the next four days, the stock again broke down through the 50-day moving average as selling volume picked up again. Two days later, GMCR officially violated its 50-day moving average, the second such violation in the pattern after the late July buyable gap-up day. Thus, it took two stakes through the heart to kill off GMCR's rally, and the second one took the stock down to the 84 price level where it undercut a low from mid-August, which I've indicated with a dotted line on the chart. This led to a wedging rally up into the 20-day moving average that saw the stock stall on low volume right at the 20-day line. There is also some overhead

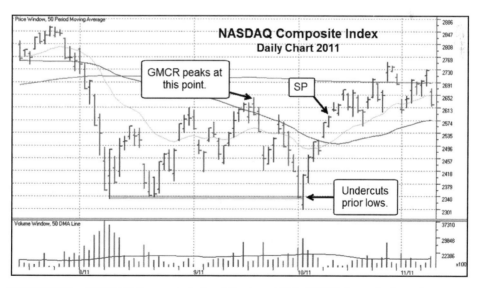

FIGURE 7.3 NASDAQ Composite Index daily chart, 2011. GMCR decouples from the NASDAQ in mid-October 2011, heading lower as the index heads higher.

Source: Chart courtesy of HGSI Investment Software, LLC (www.highgrowthstock.com), ©2014.

resistance along the September lows running along and just above the 50-day moving average. This is the first short-sale entry point, labeled SP on the chart.

Comparing Figure 7.2 and Figure 7.3, we can see that GMCR's absolute peak at around mid-September perfectly correlates to the NASDAQ's absolute peak on its first rally following the sharp downside bust in early August. Thus, we can see how the NASDAQ's actual top in late July and the early August collapse caused GMCR to begin wobbling around its highs, and as the market correction continued to build, the stock eventually began to break down. However, once the NASDAQ bottomed in early October after undercutting its mid-August lows, GMCR decoupled from the index and began to move in the opposite direction.

Based on my own observations of how short-sale target stocks tend to play out, I have found that when things work they tend to work relatively quickly and in coherent fashion. And when such stocks begin to drop, they will tend to follow the 20-day moving average as they build velocity to the downside in the short-term. Generally, when the stock stops obeying the 20-day line as it is able to move above it, the 50-day moving average becomes more relevant as an area of potential upside resistance. The bottom line is that when it is effective, making money on the short-side can feel quite easy. If you catch a stock at the right point it will tend to come apart relatively quickly, and produce what can be intoxicatingly fast profits. Often I can tell that I'm not going to make any money shorting a stock at a particular point on the chart that looks like a logical short-sale point because the stock simply does not want to cooperate. Thus, if you find yourself struggling with a stock, chances are that it is best to go away and wait for the stock to "ripen" a bit.

In Figure 7.4, we can see how well GMCR obeyed the 20-day moving average once it violated the 50-day moving average in late September. As it stalls and rallies back up towards the 50-day line, it halted at the 20-day line and rolled over quite quickly at that point. Once it broke through the 200-day moving average in the latter part of October, it rallied one day back up into the line before rolling over again and building a 12-day bear flag formation that finally came apart as the stock met up with the 20-day moving average in early November. That was a short-sale point, although one could have also entered on the one-day rally into the 200-day line as well. GMCR then blew apart and gapped to the downside on huge selling volume, but that is not a shortable gap-down move.

Figure 7.5, a longer-view daily chart of GMCR, shows why this gap-down move is not a shortable one. By the time that GMCR gapped down in early November it was already in the third leg down off the peak, and I have denoted each leg with a dotted line arrow. It is also undercutting a major low in the pattern at #4. Figure 7.5 also shows the other three areas of prior support and/or overhead resistance, which I've highlighted in gray and labeled 1–3 on the chart. You can see how the stock acted as it undercut each low, staging an undercut and rally move each time, but of varying upside magnitude. You also get a better idea of how the stock followed

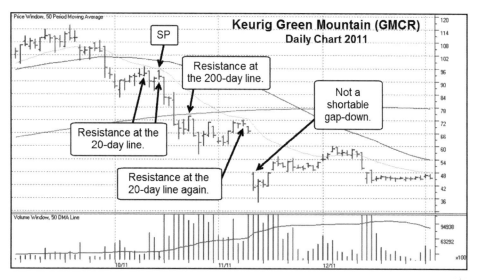

FIGURE 7.4 Keurig Green Mountain (GMCR) daily chart, 2011.

Source: Chart courtesy of HGSI Investment Software, LLC (www.highgrowthstock.com), ©2014.

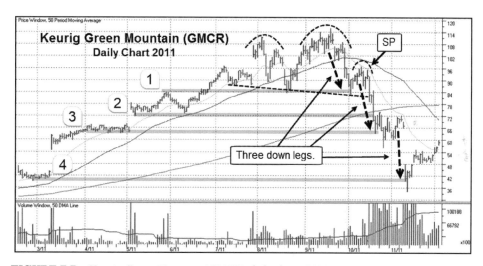

FIGURE 7.5 Keurig Green Mountain (GMCR) daily chart, 2011.

Source: Chart courtesy of HGSI Investment Software, LLC (www.highgrowthstock.com), ©2014.

the 20-day moving average on the downside as it progressed through all three downside legs.

Figure 7.6 shows the stock rallying after the massive-volume gap-down at the terminus of GMCR's third leg down. Once the stock put in its low, the general market, as represented by the NASDAQ Composite Index chart shown in Figure 7.7, bottomed 10 trading days later and began to rally to the upside, pausing for the entire month of December before continuing higher. At the same time, GMCR had

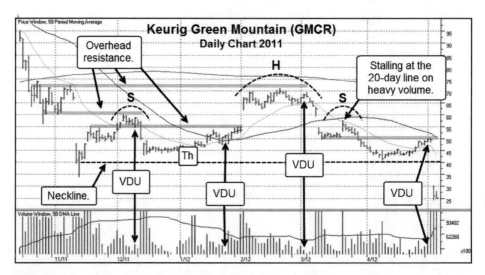

FIGURE 7.6 Keurig Green Mountain (GMCR) daily chart, 2011. GMCR forms a second H&S formation in early 2012.

Source: Chart courtesy of HGSI Investment Software, LLC (www.highgrowthstock.com), ©2014.

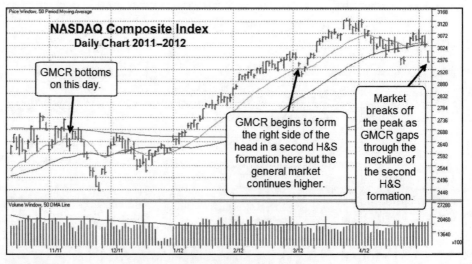

FIGURE 7.7 NASDAQ Composite Index daily chart, 2011–2012.

Source: Chart courtesy of HGSI Investment Software, LLC (www.highgrowthstock.com), ©2014.

rallied up into resistance near the 60 price level as upside volume dried up at the first VDU point on the chart. It then rolled over to the downside, and this coincided with the NASDAQ also pulling back in mid-December. Another VDU or voodoo day occurred five trading days before the end of January 2012, but the stock simply found support along the 50-day moving average and continued higher from there. Notice that at this point, the stock was not obeying the 20-day moving average, as it offered no real resistance. Meanwhile, the 50-day was decisively cleared in early February when the stock gapped up to a higher high. All of this indecisive action appears fairly normal when viewed within the context of the prior sharp, three-legged breakdown off the September 2011 peak. Outside of a quick and dirty short-sale point in early December 2011 at the first VDU as the stock rallies up into resistance, it really isn't offering anything that substantial on the short side.

As the NASDAQ continued rallying into the end of February 2012, GMCR paused to build a one-month bull flag during the same month. The peak of this February bull flag found resistance just above the 70 price level. At the start of March, the NASDAQ gapped down for two days off of the peak, which coincides with GMCR failing from its one-month bull flag and breaking to the downside. This began the formation of the right side of the head in GMCR's second H&S formation within the overall movement shown in Figure 7.1. The rally off of the early November 2011 lows was completely broken, and GMCR gapped down through its 50-day moving average on heavy selling volume. Toward the end of March 2012, the stock tried to rally back up to the 50-day line, but it stalled and churned on very heavy volume after running into resistance at the 20-day moving average. This is a short-sale point at what becomes the peak of the right shoulder, and short-sellers are now back in business on GMCR. Observe how this peak occurs a few days before the NASDAQ topped out in late March. From the right shoulder peak GMCR broke down to a point near the 40 price area which coincided with the prior low from early January and what was forming as the neckline in this second H&S formation.

As GMCR rallied up off the 40 price area, it ran into resistance at the prior lows along the 50 price level, as I've highlighted in gray on the chart, and the 50-day moving average. Two days later the stock gapped down on a bad earnings report, and this coincided with the NASDAQ gapping down sharply on the fourth day of May 2012. The comparison chart of GMCR versus the NASDAQ, shown in Figure 7.8, gives the reader a nice view of all the peaks and valleys in GMCR's decline off the September 2011 peak. While some of GMCR's movements within this macropattern occurred in synchrony with the NASDAQ, we can see that there are many areas in the pattern where the two decoupled and moved in different directions. It is interesting to note that GMCR's downside breakout through the neckline of the lower H&S formation in late April 2012 occurred in synchrony with the NASDAQ top and sharp downside break at that time. As well, throughout GMCR's bear trend that lasted from September 2011 to May 2012, the NASDAQ was actually in an overall countertrend to the upside, as Figure 7.8 clearly illustrates.

■ Summary

Keurig Green Mountain (GMCR) shows that not all leading stocks necessarily top at the same time as the market. In GMCR's case, the stock continued to make new highs

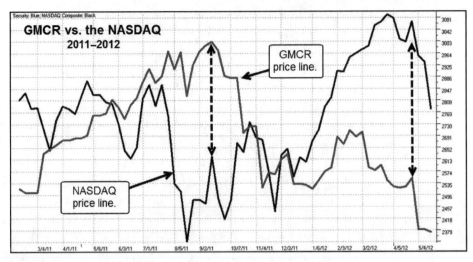

FIGURE 7.8 A comparison chart of Keurig Green Mountain (GMCR) versus the NASDAQ Composite Index daily chart, 2011–2012.

Source: Chart courtesy of HGSI Investment Software, LLC (www.highgrowthstock.com), ©2014.

even as the NASDAQ Composite Index was plunging to the downside. However, the NASDAQ's top in July 2011 sent GMCR into a bit of a wobble as it violated its 50-day moving average in early August before turning back to the upside and moving to new highs in September. This peak, which formed the top of the head in GMCR's upper H&S formation, does coincide with the NASDAQ's reaction rally peak at the same time. These are all pieces of the puzzle that short-sellers have to try and put together. Sometimes all of the pieces fit perfectly, sometimes they don't. It also illustrates the concept of knowing when to strike on the short side and when the stock needs time to digest a prior, major downside move. GMCR had to form an entirely new H&S pattern lower in its macropattern, as shown in Figure 7.1, before it was ready to break down again. In hindsight, the optimal time to get short GMCR was at point SP in Figure 7.2, and in fact our website, www.virtueofselfishinvesting.com, put out a short-sale set-up alert to our members right at that time around the 93 price level. As Figure 7.8 shows, that was where the biggest downside move in the stock began.

CHAPTER 8

Case Study #4: 3D Systems (DDD) in 2014

Nobody disputes the phenomenon of the Internet as a truly disruptive technology that has changed the way we do many things, from buying goods and services to keeping tabs on our friends and, in some cases, making new ones. For consumers and investors alike it has served as an obtuse example and demonstration of what is meant by the term *disruptive technology*. When a hitherto obscure industry like three-dimensional (3-D) printing suddenly saunters into investors' fields of vision and collective consciousness as a "disruptive technology," magic happens, as the weekly chart of 3-D printing leader 3D Systems (DDD) in Figure 8.1 shows. DDD actually came public at the end of March 1988, just a few months after Black Monday and the October 1987 Market Crash. The stock had one quick, three-month, 142 percent upside move from an IPO base in the latter half of 1989 and then sank back into obscurity for the next two decades, at one point reaching a low of 50 cents a share in 1992.

In 2012 that all changed, as 3-D printing suddenly came of age as a disruptive technology, spawning big price moves in other names that made up what became known as the 3-D printing group. In addition to DDD, this group included names like fellow "old-timer" Stratasys (SSYS), which had come public in 1994, and newer entrants like Proto Labs (PRLB), Exone Company (XONE), and Voxeljet (VJET). PRLB had come public in February 2012, XONE in February 2013, and Voxeljet

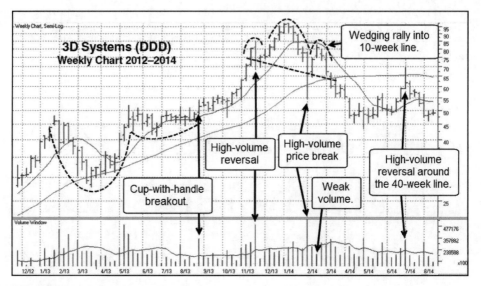

FIGURE 8.1 3D Systems (DDD) weekly chart, 2012–2014. One of the hottest 3-D printing stocks finally tops in a clearly defined H&S formation.

Source: Chart courtesy of HGSI Investment Software, LLC (www.highgrowthstock.com), ©2014.

(VJET) at the height of the 3-D printing investment craze in October 2013. All of these stocks were hot tickets in 2012–2013, as the 3-D investment craze ignited a huge group move. But as with similar group moves from the past such as, for example, the solar stocks in 2007, the 3-D printing stocks eventually topped in 2014 and became prime short-sale targets. We've already discussed SSYS and XONE in previous chapters as examples of short-sale set-ups, and so it is only fitting that we include DDD as our fourth case study.

DDD's final upside leg in its big 2012–2014 price run came after a breakout from a rather large, −41.9 percent deep cup-with-handle base in late August 2013. As we can see in Figure 8.1, this was not the type of breakout that sent the stock immediately charging to the upside. After clearing to new highs in late August, it moved sideways and shook out below its 10-week moving average in early October before embarking on a sharp 5-week move to the upside. This move ran into a high-volume reversal that formed what later became the left shoulder of the head and shoulders (H&S) top DDD formed between November 2013 and March 2014.

A high-volume price break finishes off the right side of the head in the formation, and this coincides with a test of the 40-week moving average, corresponding to the 200-day moving average on a daily chart. From there the stock rallied back up to the 10-week moving average as volume dried up right at the line to form the peak of a right shoulder. DDD then rolled over and headed back down towards the 40-week moving average and eventually through the neckline of a fully-formed H&S top. DDD then found support along the lows of the handle area from which it broke out in late August 2013 and worked its way back above the 10-week moving average before staging a sharp 3-week move into the 40-week moving average that reversed on very heavy volume.

Based on a cursory observation of the weekly chart, we can surmise that the break off the absolute peak that forms the right side of the head and the breakdown from the peak of the right shoulder and through the neckline represented the "fat" parts of the stock's breakdown from a short-selling perspective.

Figure 8.2 shows a comparison chart of DDD versus the NASDAQ Composite Index during the relevant 2013–2014 period and gives us a macro-view of how DDD's top played out relative to what was going on in the general market. Here we can see that DDD formed most of its H&S pattern while the NASDAQ was in an uptrend. The peak of the head in early January 2014 occurred a couple of weeks before the NASDAQ went into a short-term correction. As the NASDAQ bottomed and turned higher in late January DDD continued lower into the end of the month before rallying with the market. However, as the NASDAQ continued into new high price ground in early February, DDD was rallying just enough to form the peak of a right shoulder. That right shoulder peak occurred about two weeks before the NASDAQ topped and went into a more severe short-term correction in March and April. Thus, while DDD's price movement was not precisely correlated to the NASDAQ's at that time, key points in its pattern, such as the peak of the head and the peak of the right shoulder and the ensuing breakdowns from those

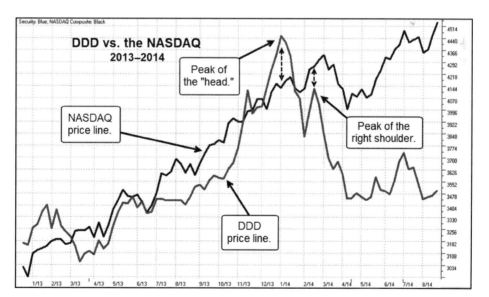

FIGURE 8.2   Comparison chart of 3D Systems (DDD) versus the NASDAQ Composite Index, 2012–2014.

Source: Chart courtesy of HGSI Investment Software, LLC (www.highgrowthstock.com), ©2014.

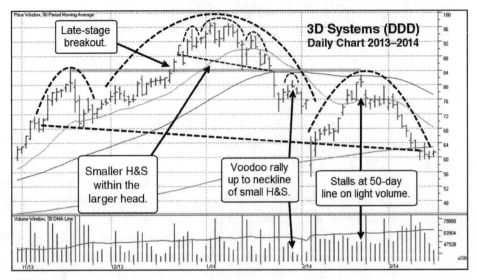

FIGURE 8.3 3D Systems (DDD) daily chart, 2013–2014. A detailed "anatomical" view of the overall H&S formation.

Source: Chart courtesy of HGSI Investment Software, LLC (www.highgrowthstock.com), ©2014.

peaks, roughly corresponded to short-term peaks and subsequent corrections in the NASDAQ in late January and early March.

Now let's break down DDD's top and price decline during 2014 into its smaller components on the daily chart. Figure 8.3 gives us a granular view of the entire H&S that DDD formed between November 2013 and March 2014. Notice that the head of this large H&S formation also contained a miniature fractal H&S within its upper half. We can even draw a short neckline to this fractal, and the stock breaks out to the downside of this neckline in the latter part of January 2014 as the NASDAQ is engaging in a short, shallow correction. This is also a late-stage breakout failure as the stock drops through the breakout point of a short cup base it formed from mid-November to roughly mid-December 2013.

A three-day voodoo rally followed from there before the stock came completely apart and gapped down to its 200-day moving average. At that point the stock was so oversold that it rallied sharply all the way back up to the 50-day moving average, where it stalled on light volume and declined all the way back to the 200-day moving average. In a nutshell, this sums up the action as it played out within the overall H&S formation itself. Figure 8.4 details the first short point that occurred after the stock broke through the neckline of the smaller fractal H&S pattern at around the 84 price level, as highlighted in gray on the chart. Notice that as the stock dropped below the miniature H&S neckline, it undercut some lows on the left side of the pattern just before the late-stage base breakout and then staged a little undercut and rally sort of move that carried up toward the 50-day moving average. The stock found

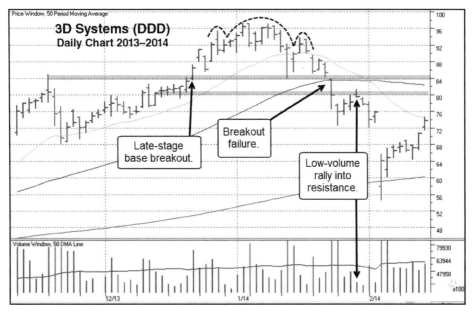

FIGURE 8.4   3D Systems (DDD) weekly chart, 2013–2014.

Source: Chart courtesy of HGSI Investment Software, LLC (www.highgrowthstock.com), ©2014.

resistance just below the 50-day line and the series of lows preceding the late-stage base breakout. We can see how despite the fact that the weekly chart in Figure 8.1 shows five straight down weeks that take the stock into its 200-day/40-week moving average, the action on the daily chart is far more subtle. And while it is impossible to determine it using the weekly chart, I consider this wedging rally into the 80 price level to be the first short-sale entry point in the pattern. While one might have waited to see if the stock could rally up to the 50-day line closer to the 83–84 price level, the giveaway here was the extreme voodoo or volume dry-up (VDU) action on the third day of the rally.

In the old *How to Make Money Selling Stocks Short* by William J. O'Neil with Gil Morales, published in 2004, we referred to the *three-day rule*, whereby a breakdown in a stock that was followed by a three-day rally back to the upside could be shorted on the third day or later. While this works a good deal of the time, it is not something written in stone, since there can be four- or five-day rallies that also fail in a similar manner. Here we see that the stock goes up exactly three days before it breaks back to the downside, and while the stock doesn't make it all the way to the 50-day line, it does get up into resistance along the lows preceding the late-stage base breakout which I've highlighted in gray in Figure 8.4.

The ensuing gap-down to the 200-day moving average occurred on a bad earnings report and did not represent a shortable gap-down move of any kind. There are a couple of good reasons why, and they are better seen on a wider view of the

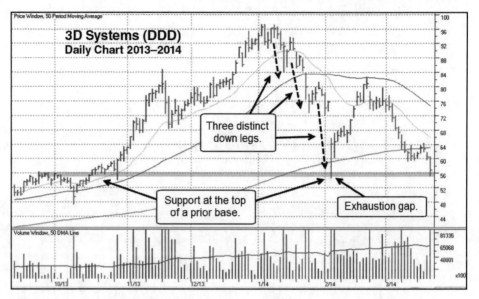

FIGURE 8.5 3D Systems (DDD) daily chart, 2013–2014.

Source: Chart courtesy of HGSI Investment Software, LLC (www.highgrowthstock.com), ©2014.

action on the daily chart shown in Figure 8.5. The first factor is that the stock has come all the way down to a prior base and logical area of support that it formed back in September through October 2013. Putting this together with the fact that we can easily discern three downside selling waves or down legs on the daily chart in Figure 8.4 tells us that DDD was likely "sold out" at this point and ready for a decent rally. As well, we could also see that the pattern had now completed a left shoulder and a head, and it was logical to assume that it would try to form at least some sort of right shoulder as it eventually completed a fully-formed H&S pattern. There were enough "clues at the scene of the crime" at this point to determine that the stock was no longer shortable and needed more time to further develop its topping pattern, if in fact that was what it was going to do.

DDD rallied sharply off of the early February 2014 lows and the 200-day moving average, and this set up the second optimal short-sale point in the pattern. In fact, we might consider this the "Mother of all Short-Sale Points" given how perfectly textbook it was. This was a very steep move that carries all the way back up to the 50-day moving average, where it ran smack into resistance right at the line, which coincided with the prior late-stage failed breakout way on the left side of the chart. In addition, this is where the first short-sale point, discussed in Figure 8.4 and labeled SP in Figure 8.6, occurred, adding another clue that this was a strong potential area of upside resistance. That certainly turned out to be the case as the stock stalled on the second day of a two-day weak-volume rally at that point and began to roll over to the downside.

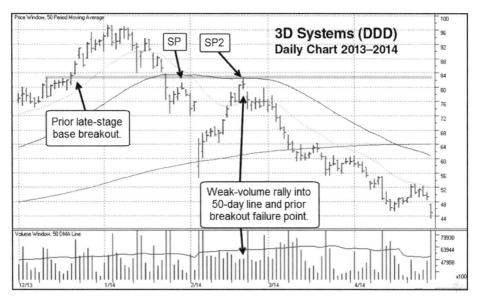

FIGURE 8.6 3D Systems (DDD) weekly chart, 2012–2014. The peak of the right shoulder forms and present the "Mother of all Short-Sale Points."

Source: Chart courtesy of HGSI Investment Software, LLC (www.highgrowthstock.com), ©2014.

The day after running into resistance right at the 50-day line at SP2, the stock moved sideways and continued to stall on any attempts to retest the 50-day line on the upside. This capped off the peak of the right shoulder in the overall H&S pattern. The stock then completed a fully-formed H&S by dropping all the way back to the 200-day moving average.

Once DDD was back below its 200-day moving average, it found support along the prior early February low, as I've highlighted in gray in Figure 8.7. This led to a short bounce back up into the 200-day line, where the stock stalled and churned right at the moving average on very weak "voodoo" volume. This is the third short-sale point in the pattern, labeled SP3 in Figure 8.7. The stock had a quick three-day break from there and then rallied back up into the prior early February low and the low it formed when it first dropped below the 200-day line in the earlier part of March, as is highlighted in gray on the chart. This highlighted area also roughly coincides with the neckline of the head-and-shoulders pattern as it is drawn in Figure 8.1, DDD's weekly chart. Thus you have several areas of potential resistance working against the stock. This then led to a final move to lower lows before the stock began tracking sideways just below its 20-day moving average.

Notice how once the stock reaches the peak of the right shoulder and the 50-day moving average at point SP2, it began to track just below the 20-day line and remained below this shorter-duration moving average all the way down. It stayed under the 20-day line throughout most of April, as the stock had a final gap-down

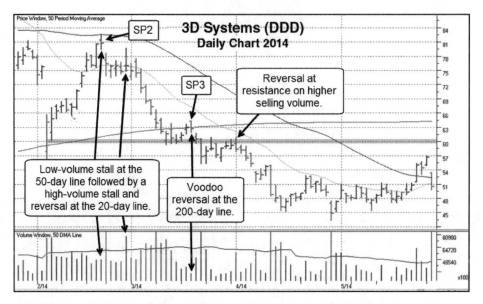

FIGURE 8.7 3D Systems (DDD) weekly chart, 2012–2014. The third short-sale entry point occurs on a rally back up into the 200-day moving average in mid-March.

Source: Chart courtesy of HGSI Investment Software, LLC (www.highgrowthstock.com), ©2014.

move that undercut the mid-April low before rallying back up into the 20-day line in early May. It tracked along just below the moving average throughout most of May before poking its head back above the line. At this point, one can get the sense that the overall top in the stock is starting to "max out."

We have previously discussed how stocks will tend to follow the 20-day moving average on the downside as they are down-trending in coherent fashion. Once that behavior ends and the stock pokes back above the 20-day line, short-sellers should be standing clear. Figure 8.8 shows how DDD was able to clamber back above the 20-day line and make a move back above the 50-day moving average as well. Note the high-volume gap-down move at the end of May, but this does not develop into anything more serious. Certainly, had one tried to short this break back below the 50-day moving average, this was a viable short-sale entry point attempt, but one would have soon been stopped out as the stock cleared the 50-day line in mid-June.

There was one final short-sale point at the very beginning of July 2014 that occurred on news of a possible buyout of the company by International Business Machine (IBM). This sent the stock scurrying past the 200-day moving average, but as the buyout rumors faded, so did the stock, and it simply stalled out at the 200-day line on heavy volume. This did offer a reasonable short-sale point at the time, using the 200-day moving average as a guide for an upside stop once the stock closed below the line and in the lower half of that big, churning price range.

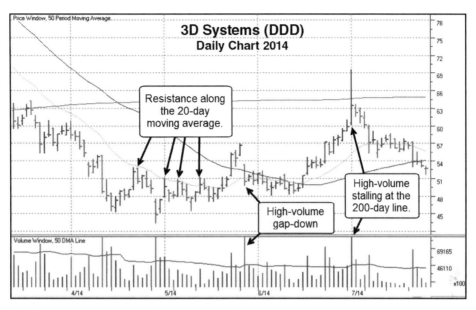

FIGURE 8.8 3D Systems (DDD) daily chart 2014. Once the stock stopped tracking below the 20-day moving average, the move was more or less played out in the short term.

Source: Chart courtesy of HGSI Investment Software, LLC (www.highgrowthstock.com), ©2014.

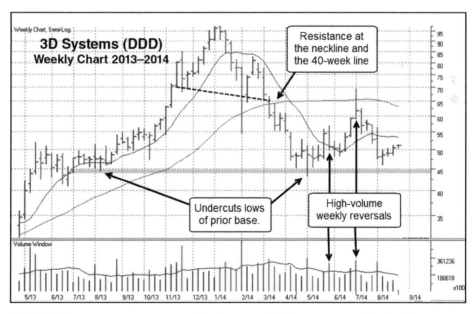

FIGURE 8.9 3D Systems (DDD) weekly chart, 2013–2014. DDD was a "textbook" H&S formation that was in fact playable using nothing but the weekly chart to guide one's short-sale decision-making process.

Source: Chart courtesy of HGSI Investment Software, LLC (www.highgrowthstock.com), ©2014.

The interesting characteristic of DDD's top is that it was one of those situations where one could have played this on the short side using nothing but the weekly chart, given how "textbook" the H&S pattern played out. In Figure 8.9, a weekly chart of DDD's overall topping phase, we can see the low-volume rally into the peak of the right shoulder in the middle of February 2014. As the stock rolled over, it broke down through the neckline of the pattern and the 40-week moving average, corresponding to the 200-day moving average on the daily charts. DDD kept dropping until it finally undercut some key lows in a base consolidation it had formed from May to August of 2013, as highlighted on the chart. From there we can see the steady rally back up through the 10-week (50-day on the daily) moving average that ended with a big churning and stalling week right at the 40-week (200-day) moving average.

■ Summary

3D Systems (DDD), in context with the examples of its group cousins, Exone Company (XONE) and Stratasys (SSYS) discussed in other chapters of this book, offers an instructive example of a dynamic group move based on a compelling investment theme or craze—in this case the "disruptive technology" of 3-D printing. And while such investment crazes can offer fantastic upside profit potential, eventually everyone who has piled into the stocks on the basis of the hype and substance of the 3-D printing investment theme starts to pile out. Short-sellers should be on the lookout for these types of "hot" group moves, as the excitement drives everyone into the stock and then sets up excellent short-sale opportunities once everyone who is going to buy the stocks has done so. The next time you see a major investment theme, whatever it is, take hold of investors' imaginations and investment dollars and understand that the "hotness" of the upside move is what creates the foundation for a subsequent meltdown that, in almost all cases, inevitably occurs.

CHAPTER 9

Case Study #5: Molycorp (MCP) in 2011

Market history is filled with examples of compelling, hot investment themes that drive huge upside moves in groups of stocks. In Chapter 8, we saw how the disruptive technology of 3-D printing created a group move in the 2012–2014 market, but before that investment craze hit the market there was another mania that arrived in the form of what were known as *rare earth metal* stocks. Rare earth metals, technically known as rare earth elements, consist of seventeen chemical elements in the periodic table. Fifteen of these names are known as the *lanthanides*; and the other two are scandium and yttrium. The lanthanides are lanthanum, cerium, praseodymium, neodymium, promethium, samarium, europium, gadolinium, terbium, dysprosium, holmium, erbium, thulium, ytterbium, and lutetium. What these metals all had in common was not that they were rare per se, but that they tended to be geologically dispersed and hence not found in concentrations great enough to make the economics of mining such metals ideal.

Because of this, they are not so much *rare* as they are *scarce*. And because they were critical to a number of industrial and technological processes and applications, they were considered to have strategic value. Throw in fears that China was attempting to control supplies of rare earth metals as they shut out the rest of the world, and you had the ingredients for a boom in rare earth metal mining stocks.

One key factor driving the upside in rare earth metals stocks in 2010 was simple supply and demand. Because there were only two viable stocks that could serve as vehicles for riding the rare earths craze, Rare Element Resources (REE) and Molycorp (MCP), there was a shortage of supply to feed investor interest in the space. As the only two stocks in the rare earth metals, these were not just rare earth plays—these stocks were themselves somewhat rare. Because it reached the highest absolute price, peaking at 79.16 in April of 2011, we will focus on MCP as our case study. While REE ran up from about $3 a share in August of 2010 to a peak of 17.92 in late December 2010, it never exceeded "teenage" price status. Thus, MCP can be considered the primary big-stock play in the rare earth metals phenomenon of 2010.

The weekly chart in Figure 9.1 shows the "superstructure" of MCP's top in late 2010, including its fast and sharp run-up after coming public in late July 2010 and its steady "round-trip" back to and well below its initial public offering price of $14 a share. In fact, at the time of this writing in 2014, MCP was selling below the $3 price level. The decimation of MCP is a brutal illustration of what a "long-term" investment mentality can do to one's portfolio. Stocks have their life-cycles, and it is important for investors to understand this. While they will be favored by investors for one or two consecutive market cycles, sometimes three, there will almost always comes a time when the music stops and the dance floor empties.

What makes MCP a bit unique among our short-sale case studies is its ascending neckline. Theoretically, an ascending neckline is not as "weak" as a flat or horizontal neckline, which in turn is not as weak as a descending or downward sloping neckline. In practice, this is mostly bunk, since we can observe for a fact that the "stronger" ascending neckline formation can lead to some very severe downside

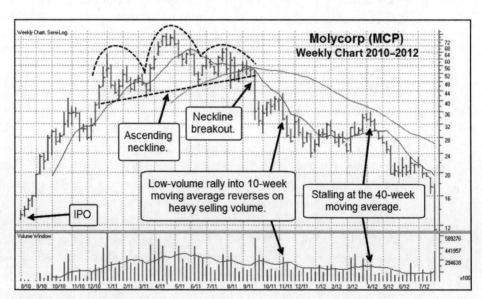

FIGURE 9.1 Molycorp (MCP) weekly chart 2010–2012.

Source: Chart courtesy of HGSI Investment Software, LLC (www.highgrowthstock.com), ©2014.

breaks and downtrends. As MCP ran up from its IPO date, it formed two reasonably well-defined bases. After breaking out and running up about 45 percent from the second base, MCP formed a short two- to three-week flag formation from which it tried to break out at the beginning of May 2011. This breakdown off the peak lasted seven weeks and took the stock down to the 40-week moving average, corresponding to the 200-day on a daily chart. At that point it became clear that the stock had completed a left shoulder and a head in a potential head and shoulders (H&S) set-up.

The entire right shoulder complex took another three months to form, and at that time the stock broke out to the downside and through the neckline at what could be considered a short-sale entry point. The only issue here is that the move through the neckline did not occur in continuous fashion; it occurred on a downside gap following its third-quarter earnings report, so the entry point is not as cut and dried as it appears on the weekly chart. From there, a rally back up into the 10-week moving average would offer another short-sale entry point, and the second rally up into the 10-week line four weeks later offered yet another entry point. As MCP continued to break down, it dropped below the 24 price level in late November 2011, and the stock chopped back and forth between that level and the 32 price area before pushing further above the 10-week line and up into the 40-week line. That represented a short-sale entry point in early April 2012, and the stock came apart from there. One more little bounce up into the 10-week line in June of 2012 ended with another cascading break that completed the stock's round-trip from a $14 IPO to a high of 79.16 and then all the way back below the original IPO price.

We can also see on the comparison chart of MCP versus the NASDAQ Composite Index throughout this time period, shown in Figure 9.2, that MCP correlated reasonably well to the NASDAQ throughout the formation of its H&S. In fact, the two appear to have formed their respective H&S patterns in synchrony, with only a few minor variations.

The left shoulder peak of MCP's formation, which was actually the start of its second base on the way up, preceded a left shoulder peak in the NASDAQ by a little over a month. MCP's breakdown and failure on the breakout attempt from the short flag formation at the absolute peak of the head correlates exactly to the NASDAQ's peak and breakdown at the same time. The peak of the right shoulder in MCP's pattern correlates to a second, slightly lower peak in the NASDAQ at the end of July 2011, which could be viewed as a sort of right shoulder as well. MCP rolled over from its right shoulder peak and completes its H&S formation just as the NASDAQ broke down sharply in late July and early August of 2011. The NASDAQ, however, bottomed in mid-August and began to trend higher, eventually running into a short term peak in mid-September that was followed by a sharp downside break in late September. This September peak and ensuing breakdown coincided with MPC's downside breakout through the neckline of its now fully-formed H&S pattern.

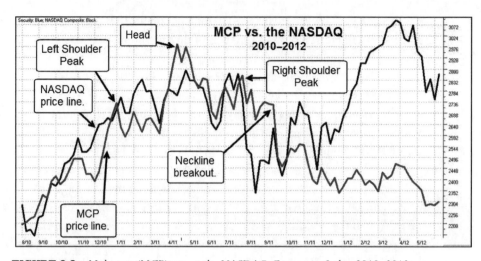

FIGURE 9.2 Molycorp (MCP) versus the NASDAQ Composite Index 2010–2012.

Source: Chart courtesy of HGSI Investment Software, LLC (www.highgrowthstock.com), ©2014.

I suppose if we wanted to, we could get away with simply showing the weekly chart of MCP and drawing arrows at the obvious short-sale points at the neckline breakout and the subsequent rallies up into the 10-week and 40-week moving averages as the stock progress through its overall downtrend. Unfortunately, there are many more details that in fact make MCP a rich example as a short-sale case study.

First, let's break this down on a close-up weekly chart view of the entire H&S complex that MCP formed around the early May 2011 peak in Figure 9.3. We can see that the right shoulder in the pattern was actually the start of a 10-week double-bottom base from which the stock broke out in late March 2011. This led to a quick four-week run-up before the stock started to consolidate in a short flag formation of two to three weeks in duration. A volume reversal off the peak marked the top of the head, and the stock dropped below the 10-week moving average. The low-volume rally back into the 10-week line was in fact your first short-sale point in the pattern, labeled SP on the chart, and occurred at the mid-point of the right side of the head. A breakdown from there to the 40-week moving average completes the right side of the head and another rally up into the 10-week line ensues before the stock drops back to the 40-week moving average. The bounce off the 40-week moving average carries beyond the 10-week line and into prior resistance at the prior peak at point SP. This is a second short-sale entry point, labeled SP2 on the chart. Notice also that point SP2 also marks the peak of a "head" within the entire right shoulder complex. That is, the entire area underneath the dotted line that arcs from late June to mid-September is itself a smaller, fractal H&S formation. The right shoulder of this mini-H&S shows stalling action at the 10-week line on weak volume, and two weeks later the stock collapses through the neckline.

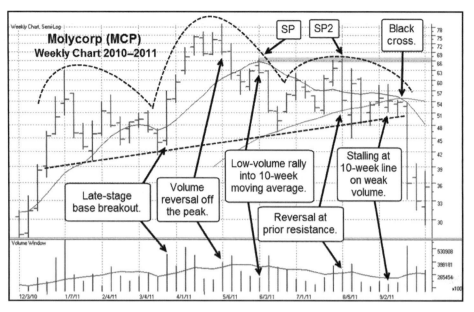

FIGURE 9.3 Molycorp (MCP) weekly chart 2010–2011. A close-up view of MCP's H&S complex.

Source: Chart courtesy of HGSI Investment Software, LLC (www.highgrowthstock.com), ©2014.

Now let's look at MCP's entire H&S complex on a daily chart, shown in Figure 9.4. We can see that the breakout from the base that the stock formed from early January 2011 to the latter part of March began with a pocket pivot buy point coming up through the 50-day moving average. That pocket pivot led to a 52 percent–plus move from the closing price of the pocket pivot day to the peak at 79.12 in early May.

The short V-shaped flag formation at the peak leads to a breakout attempt through the 76 price level, and volume looks very good on this move. However, the very next day the stock reverses on heavy selling volume, and this marks the peak of the head in MCP's overall H&S formation. Remember that in Figure 9.2, MCP's peak coincided with a sharp breakdown in the NASDAQ. In some cases, if I can correlate a possible peak in a stock on such a high-volume reversal to a similar peak in the general market, I will just short the stock right there, although this can't really be classified as a typical short-sale point.

The breakdown off the peak carried below the 50-day moving average as the stock tested the top of the prior base formed from January through March. The short bounce back up into the 50-day moving average in late May coincided with a similar bounce at the same time in the NASDAQ. At the end of March, the NASDAQ started to break down in earnest, and MCP likewise broke down below its 50-day moving average. This is the first short-sale point in the pattern, labeled

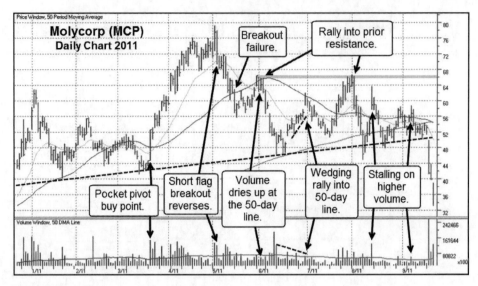

FIGURE 9.4 Molycorp (MCP) daily chart 2011. Another close-up of MCP's H&S complex at a more granular daily view.

Source: Chart courtesy of HGSI Investment Software, LLC (www.highgrowthstock.com), ©2014.

SP in Figure 9.3. There was a very sharp collapse to the 200-day moving average, which represented a cover point for any short position taken at point SP as one waited to see what the stock did from there. We can view this action in greater detail in Figure 9.5.

In the latter half of June, MCP started rallying up and off of the 200-day line in a little wedging and stalling rally that was capped off with a little "exhaustion gap" that carried right into the 50-day line, and the stock caromed back to the downside. Notice, however, that as the stock came down, selling volume dried up to the point of becoming nonexistent. Had one shorted the stock into the short-term exhaustion gap in late June, this would have been a clue to cover one's position and bank whatever profit was there to be had. This then led to a rally through the 50-day moving average, and the alert reader might notice the pocket pivot buy point as the stock came up through the 50-day line 7 days before the end of July. As we've discussed previously, this is at least a cover signal if one is still short the stock from any prior short-sale entry points.

Notice that as MCP rallied back up towards resistance around the 66 price level and the prior short-sale entry point at SP, volume dried up sharply at the peak, and then the stock reverses on heavy selling volume. This led to a sharp breakdown that carried below the 200-day moving average.

Scrolling a little further, we can now view Figure 9.6, which overlaps with Figure 9.5 to show the entire right shoulder complex from early June through the latter part of September. As we've already pointed out, MCP's right shoulder

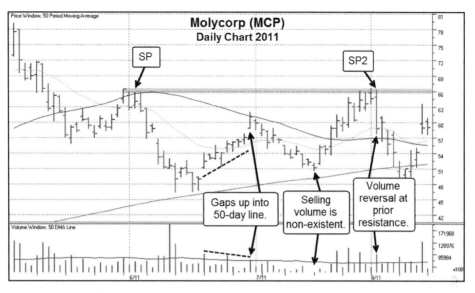

FIGURE 9.5 Molycorp (MCP) daily chart 2011. The peak of the right shoulder offers a second short-sale entry point.

Source: Chart courtesy of HGSI Investment Software, LLC (www.highgrowthstock.com), ©2014.

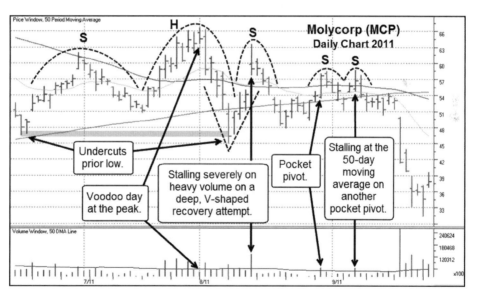

FIGURE 9.6 Molycorp (MCP) daily chart 2011. A complete view of MCP's right shoulder complex that is also a fractal H&S formation.

Source: Chart courtesy of HGSI Investment Software, LLC (www.highgrowthstock.com), ©2014.

complex was itself a smaller, fractal H&S formation, and we can now see how the short-term exhaustion gap in late June formed the right shoulder, and the rally up into the 66 price level and prior resistance at point SP in Figure 9.5 formed the head. The breakdown through the 200-day moving average undercut the prior June low, and this led to a sharp, V-shaped upside rally attempt that stalled out on heavy volume as the stock gaps above the 50-day moving average. This can be viewed as a short-term exhaustion gap of sorts, and indeed the stock dropped back below the 50-day line over the next few days.

At that point, the stock got into a little bit of a "slop and chop" phase and in fact flashed a pocket pivot buy point when it regained the 50-day moving average in late August. This pocket pivot didn't hold up, however, and the stock dropped back below the 200-day line before making another attempt to clear the 50-day line in early September on another pocket pivot. This second pocket pivot had a couple of things working against it, namely the V-shaped move from which it was occurring and the fact that it stalled and closed in the lower half of the daily range on above-average volume. Over the next two days, the stock dropped below the 200-day line and then slid sideways just underneath the line before gapping to the downside in a nasty neckline breakout.

On the day of the gap-down and neckline breakout, MCP could have easily been played as a shortable gap-down, as we can see on the daily chart in Figure 9.7. The stock opened up at 49.73, got as high as 49.91 on an intra-day basis, and

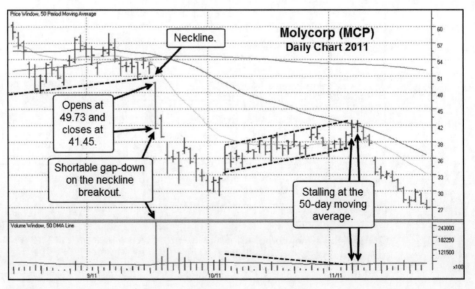

FIGURE 9.7 Molycorp (MCP) daily chart 2011. The neckline breakout occurred on a shortable gap-down move.

Source: Chart courtesy of HGSI Investment Software, LLC (www.highgrowthstock.com), ©2014.

then plummeted to an intra-day low of 41.33 before closing just a few cents higher at 41.45. Thus one was able to use the 49.91 as the high of the day for the purpose of setting an upside stop either at the 49.91 level or 3–5 percent higher, depending on one's personal risk preference and precise entry point. For example, if one had entered a short position at 48, then using the 49.91 intra-day high represents a slightly less than 4 percent stop. Obviously, entering a position on any gap-down day carries risk and is not guaranteed to work every time. The fact that this was also a neckline breakout, and the neckline was running through the 50–51 price area, which was within 2 percent of the 49.91 high of the day, also worked in its favor. Thus, the closer to the neckline one can short the stock, the better. This breakout through the neckline was the beginning of a sharp move to the downside that cut the stock down just about 45 percent by the end of September 2011.

As the stock descends, it loses downside velocity before it bottoms out and begins a slow move within a short uptrend channel that carries right into the 50-day moving average. The stock stalls here and rolls over with another gap-down move that leads to even lower lows.

Let's back up for a moment and look at a wider view of the action so far on the daily chart shown in Figure 9.8. This shows us why the low at the end of September was a good place to cover any short position taken on the neckline breakout. As the stock came down into the 30 price level, it reached a support level along the lows of the first base it formed back in the late October through mid-November 2012 time period. With a 40 percent profit-plus in the position, there was absolutely no

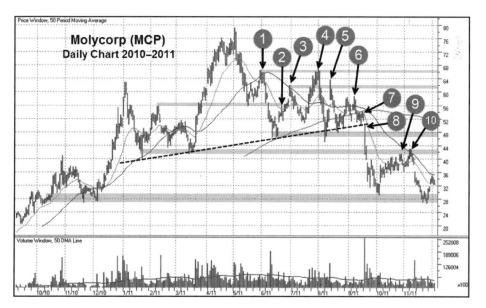

FIGURE 9.8   Molycorp (MCP) daily chart 2010–2011.

Source: Chart courtesy of HGSI Investment Software, LLC (www.highgrowthstock.com), ©2014.

reason not to take profits. If you can get a profit like this in a short-sale position within five to ten trading days, that is a gift horse that you certainly don't want to look in the mouth. This would have allowed for a potential re-short at the 50-day moving average at Point #10 in Figure 9.8.

Staying on Figure 9.8, we can also conclude that it's very easy to go back with full benefit of hindsight and pick off all the potential short-sale points. The reality, however, is that in real time, you will see a number of points at which the stock might be shortable, and you can't tell beforehand exactly how they might or might not play out. Things are always much trickier in real-time and never as cut and dried as they look in hindsight! Obviously, when we analyze these in hindsight, we can get a sense of how short-term peaks in the pattern are likely to occur. MCP was the type of short-sale set-up that could have been campaigned on the short side at several points within the right side of the pattern (everything right of the peak of the head). Note the various support areas in the pattern, including where the stock undercut lows and began to rally in logical undercut and rally moves.

At Point 1, we see the first rally into the 50-day moving average following the violation of the moving average. MCP bounced off the midpoint of the prior base and pushed just above the 50-day moving average before failing and breaking back to the downside. Point 2 represents a possible short-sale point because the stock bounced off of the 200-day moving average and retraced about 50 percent of the distance from Point 1, which also coincided with the midpoint peak of the prior base. The stock gapped down for one day before turning back to the upside and eventually gapping right into the 50-day moving average at Point 3. Keeping a tight stop at Point 2 would have avoided the more-than-10-percent move higher from there into Point 3 and would have put one in a position of coming after the stock on the short side once again.

The decline from Point 3 ended well before the stock reached the 200-day moving average, and one could get a sense that it didn't have a lot of selling thrust behind it by the volume drying up, as was seen in Figure 9.5. As well, in Figure 9.9, the weekly chart of MCP over the same period reveals that while it did not reach the 200-day moving average on the daily chart, it did reach the 40-week moving average on the weekly chart. From there the stock found support and bounced up into Point 4. In Figure 9.8, we can see that Point 4 occurred at the same price level as Point 1, which is now viewed as a point of upside resistance, and this is highlighted in gray on the chart. Point 4 led to a jagged break to the downside that broke through the 200-day moving average, but this undercut the prior low from mid-July and sparked a very sharp undercut and rally move. This move into Point 5 ran into a resistance point marked by Point 3, as is highlighted on the chart, and the stock again broke down through the 200-day line. Now, in Figure 9.8, we can see

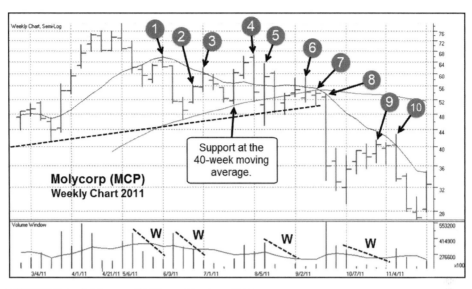

FIGURE 9.9 Molycorp (MCP) weekly chart 2011.

Source: Chart courtesy of HGSI Investment Software, LLC (www.highgrowthstock.com), ©2014.

that the stock was starting to find consistent support at the neckline of the overall head and shoulders formation. This is also evident in the weekly chart in Figure 9.9.

We can jump back and forth between the daily chart in Figure 9.8 and the weekly chart in Figure 9.9, both of which are labeled with the various short-sale points in the pattern, and compare the information that each gives us at each labeled point. This gives some insight into how the action on the weekly can be combined with the action on the daily to provide more "clues at the scene of the crime." We can see on the weekly chart that Point 6 and the week before it would represent reasonable short-sale points if one were only relying on the weekly chart. However, we already know that the peak that occurred just before the peak at Point 6 on the daily chart was also a pocket pivot buy point, so it was not until that pocket pivot began to fail that we would have discerned Point 6 as a short-sale point on the daily chart.

By the time we get to Point 7, the weekly chart is showing a black cross, as the 10-week moving average, corresponding to the 50-day moving average, was already crossing below the 40-week moving average, corresponding to the 200-day moving average on the daily chart. What we notice here is that the black cross occurred on the weekly chart before it occurred on the daily chart. Thus, by the time we reach Point 8, we might be on the alert for a major short-selling point to occur, and it did with the neckline breakout and shortable gap-down that occurred at Point 8.

Point 9 occurs at a potential overhead resistance level, as is highlighted in Figure 9.8, which means one might have reasonably viewed that as a short-sale point, but the stock continued higher into the 50-day and 10-week moving averages in both Figures 9.8 and 9.9. Notice the big weekly outside reversal at point 10 in the weekly chart as the stock plummeted to new lows.

Finally, the weekly chart in Figure 9.9 gives a very clear view of the wedging rallies (labeled with a W) that occurred as the stock moved up on declining volume into Points 1, 3, 6, and 10. Even briefly analyzing and comparing the action between Figure 9.8 and 9.9 demonstrates why one should be monitoring the stocks on their short-sale watch list in real-time on *both* daily and weekly charts. As well, it is important to study both daily and weekly charts when reviewing historical examples, and the reader will have a substantial opportunity to do that in the next chapter.

■ Summary

Molycorp (MCP) provides another strong example of a stock that had a wild upside run based on a sudden interest in its particular field, with the added benefit of favorable news flow that played upon the emotions of investors. Rare earth metals suddenly became a hot topic in 2010, and the added story of a foreign power, China, gaining control of the world's rare earth metals supplies fed investors' imaginations with the potential for rare earth miners like MCP, despite the fact that the stock was showing increasing losses in 2010 to the tune of −56 cents per share versus losses of −34 and −15 cents in 2009 and 2008, respectively. MCP did finally show a profit of $1.31 a share in 2010, but the stock topped right in the middle of all the good news. For the June 2011 quarter, MCP reported a net profit of 53 cents a share, but the stock had already topped in May 2011.

MCP was technically very playable on the upside throughout the latter part of 2010 and the first few months of 2011. The stock had two pocket pivots coming off the lows of each of its two bases that were formed on the way, and MCP had sharp upside moves following each and in short order. So the next time you're making money on the long side of a "hot" stock that is the subject of a current hot news topic, keep in mind that eventually you could be looking at an equally profitable vehicle on the short side once the stock tops.

CHAPTER 10

Templates of Doom: A Short-Selling Model Book

In November 2013, Magnus Carlsen of Norway became the second-youngest World Chess Champion in history when, at the tender age of 22, he defeated then-reigning champ Vishwanathan Anand. Carlsen began his chess career as something of a child prodigy, giving former champions and chess "giants" like Garry Kasparov (who still holds the distinction of being the youngest World Chess Champion in history) and Anatoly Karpov serious runs for their money when he was as young as 13, and attributes a large part of his success to his phenomenal memory. At the age of 7, he had memorized all the countries of the world and their respective capitals. As an adult professional chess player, he attributes his meteoric rise to the top of the chess world to his ability to memorize and retain mental images of chess board positions from games between prominent chess players of the past, both recent and long ago. He can recall these positions and the moves that followed, and this gives him an edge when faced with similar positions in his own real-time games.

In the same way, studying and memorizing the chart patterns and positions of stocks that served as outstanding short-sale targets from the past can give one an edge in recognizing when a major short-selling opportunity is at hand. We have already covered a number of real-world short-selling examples in previous chapters, but this chapter represents what I view as the real meat of the book in terms of putting everything together. We have selected 91 "templates of doom" or what one might consider models of the greatest short-selling plays in recent history. For the purposes of this book, we have focused on short-selling examples that occurred after the great bear market of 2000–2003. Readers who wish to see examples of stocks from before then should refer to *How to Make Money Selling Stocks Short*, by William J. O'Neil and Gil Morales (John Wiley & Sons, 2004), which contains its own model book of short-selling examples from as far back as the 1960s. In this book, we have intentionally stuck to more recent examples to demonstrate that the basic principles of short-selling discussed in that original 2004 work are still viable and continue to work even at the time of publication of this book that you now hold in your hands (either physically or electronically!).

In my view, there is nothing mechanistic or deterministic about short-selling. Sometimes these set-ups work beautifully, sometimes they don't, and the probabilities of success rely heavily on contextual factors. These contextual factors include the current action of the major market averages, the phase of the market, the overall national and global economic backdrop, industry developments, earnings news, and the occasional, random, and sudden positive news or rumors that trigger a bounce in an otherwise weak, down-trending stock. Relative to the long side of the market, my experience is that the short side tends to be far more volatile and fraught with uncertainty. While stocks can break down sharply, it is not uncommon for them to also bounce sharply within overall downtrends, and many of the examples shown in this chapter demonstrate that.

Despite the uncertainty and heightened risk of short-selling, the fact is that the same short-sale set-ups do show up frequently, and when they work, whether during a short-term or intermediate-term market correction or an outright bear market, they can result in significant profits. The precise techniques that we use are also quite effective from a profit-generation perspective, when they work. How these techniques are used in precise terms often varies from stock to stock depending on a variety of technical or contextual factors. Often, short-selling is all about being in the right place at the right time, and the methods we use are designed to put you in that place while also allowing for the possibility that in the stock market, one can also be in the wrong place at the wrong time. Thus risk management is a big component to longer-term success on the short side, and such risk management also entails having a keen idea of where you are in the stock's topping phase as well as the market's.

Many say that investing in the stock market is part art and part science. Short-selling is probably a little more of an art than a science as compared to the long side of the market. Recognizing patterns and how they might play out based on historical examples is part of this art, but it remains an art because while we can identify a particular short-selling pattern, we can never know for sure how it will play out in real time. A valid short-selling set-up can easily morph into a bullish formation from which the stock launches higher. Case studies and other material presented in previous chapters provide the reader with a framework of how to view the templates of doom shown in this chapter in terms of their basic technical components and how these relate to initiating and handling a short-sale position in a particular short-sale target stock.

It is important to understand that critical clues can be found on both the daily and weekly chart, and when monitoring short-sale target stocks one must keep an eye on both time frames. Sometimes what is not seen on the daily chart can be seen on the weekly chart and vice versa. A rally that looks strong and pulls back on the daily chart, for example, might show heavy-volume stalling or churning at a critical area on the weekly chart. A gap-down move on the weekly chart may not show a brief rally from the original gap-down day that is evident on the daily chart and hence potentially shortable.

Each template shows at least one weekly and one daily chart, with accompanying notes. The annotations are by no means intended to be complete, and the reader might discover certain characteristics and features on the charts that are not revealed in the annotations. As well, this is not a complete list of short-selling examples from the periods shown. Many more exist, but we have done our best to produce a healthy cross-section of the various set-ups and their permutations over more recent times. All charts shown are courtesy of HGSI Investment Software, LLC (www.highgrowthstock.com), ©2014, and we are grateful to them for allowing us to use their charts throughout this book. We also recommend HGSI Investor software as the perfect charting tool for studying the historical action and behavior of leading stocks. The system allows one to easily scroll backward to view historical price/volume data for any existing stock. It also enables one to scroll forward one price bar at a time, which is useful if one wants to see what the chart of any stock looked like at any given point in time. In this manner one can simulate the interpretation of price/volume action on the chart as it if it were occurring in real-time, and test themselves by scrolling forward one day or week at a time to see how their interpretation would have played out. In other words, have fun with it.

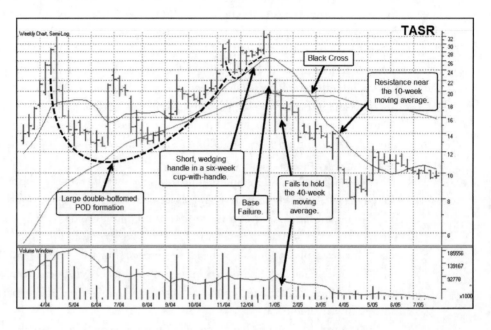

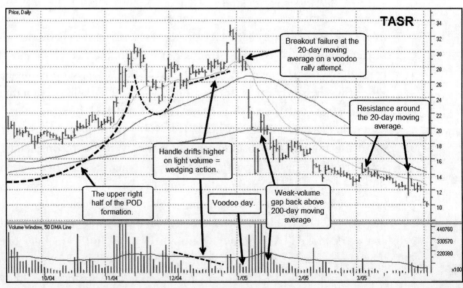

Notes: Taser International (TASR) became a "hot stock" play in the post 9/11 environment. The basic groupthink was that airlines would equip pilots with Tasers, and this would result in big sales growth for TASR. This led to a massive upside run that blew up in spectacular fashion in April 2004. The stock then bottomed and rallied all the way to a marginal new high in December 2004 to form a large punchbowl of death (POD) topping formation. The breakdown on the right side occurred after a late-stage breakout from a small cup-with-handle formation failed, resulting in what was a shortable gap-down move. Notice that as TASR trundled lower after the massive gap-down in January 2005, it followed the 20-day moving average to the downside. Both the left side and right side peaks of TASR's POD formation occurred in conjunction with general market corrections.

■ eBay (EBAY) 2004

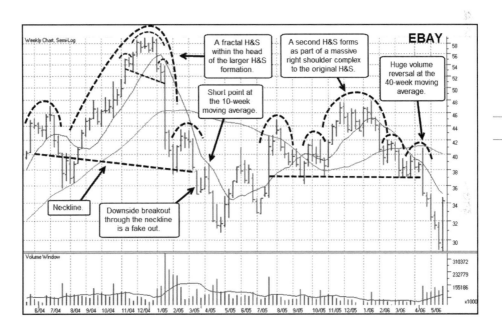

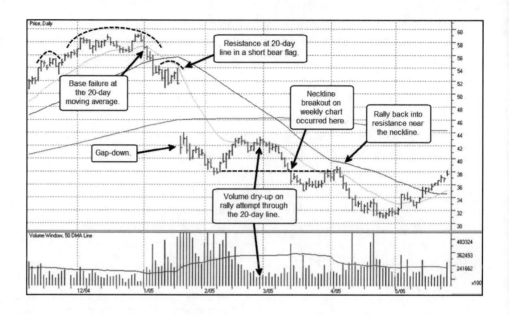

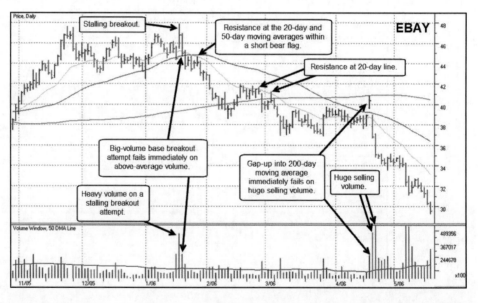

Notes: From 2004 to 2006, eBay (EBAY) set up in two different head-and-shoulders (H&S) formations that could be thought of as a primary H&S off the peak and then a secondary H&S that formed after the stock retraced a little over half of the price breakdown that occurred from January to April 2004. Two daily charts are shown here, the first of which focuses on the initial breakdown off the peak in January 2005 and the second on the breakdown off the peak of the head of the secondary H&S formation in January 2006. Note that both peaks in January 2005 and then in 2006 were late-stage failed-base (LSFB) set-ups where a breakout attempt failed once the EBAY broke below the 20-day moving average on heavy volume. Each of these peaks was associated with a short-term market correction.

■ Omnivision Technologies (OVTI) 2004

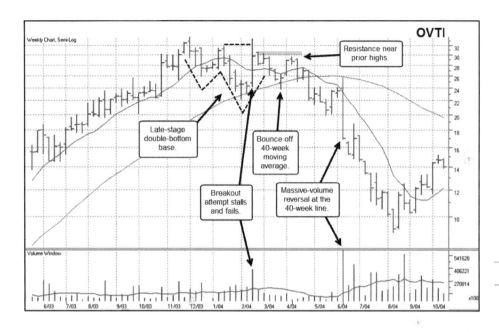

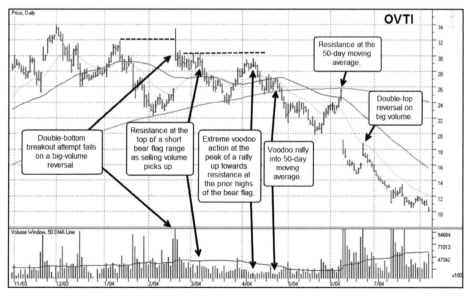

Notes: Omnivision Technologies (OVTI) made chips for the cameras that were showing up in smartphones and other handheld devices and thus became a very hot stock based on this investment theme. The stock topped with a late-stage double-bottom base that was somewhat wide and loose. The daily chart shows the exact day of the double-bottom breakout attempt that failed immediately, closing that same day near the lows of the daily trading range. It then built a short bear flag before dropping down to the 200-day moving average. Notice that the rebound off the 200-day line, which is quite logical, took the stock past both the 20-day and 50-day moving averages on the upside and right up near the highs of the prior bear flag it formed right after the failed breakout attempt. This sort of retest of prior highs just below a prior failed breakout point that also carries just beyond the 20-day and/or 50-day moving average is not uncommon in leading stocks as they just begin to fail off the peak in an LSFB type of set-up. On the weekly chart, one can make out a small head and shoulders that formed with the left-side peak of the double-bottom forming the head of this H&S pattern. The mid-point of the double-bottom W forms the peak of the right shoulder.

■ Deckers Outdoor (DECK) 2005

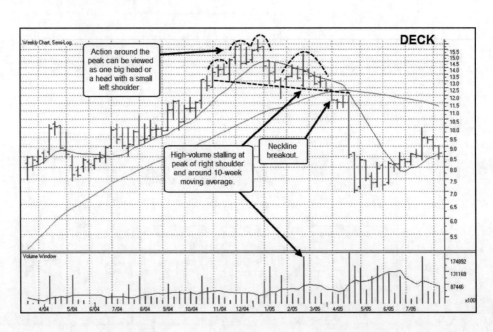

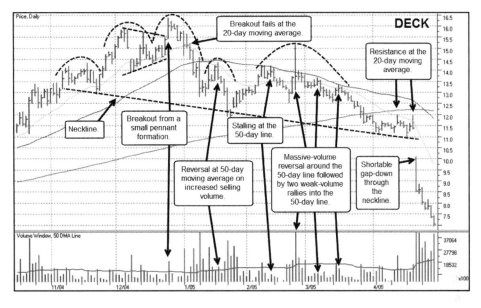

Notes: Deckers Outdoor (DECK) topped with an H&S formation that could also have been looked at as a late-stage cup-with-handle base where the handle is well in the lower half of the pattern. The peak of the right shoulder was formed by a large one-day price spike that was also a failed breakout attempt from the improper cup-with-handle that closed back below the 50-day moving average. Furthermore, notice that the right shoulder of the overall H&S formation also contains a fractal H&S where the big price spike at the peak of the right shoulder also forms the peak of the fractal H&S's head.

■ Monster Beverage (MNST) 2012

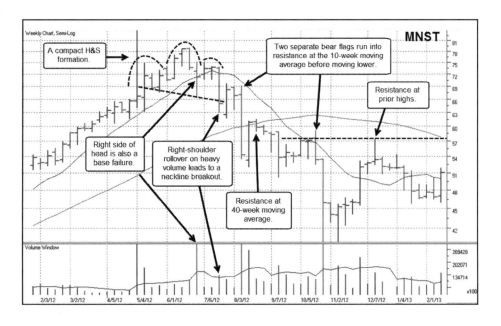

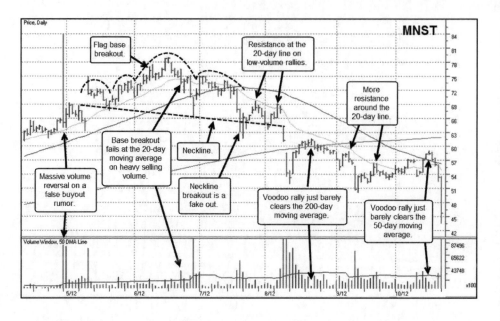

Price, Daily

MNST

Flag base breakout.

Resistance at the 20-day line on low-volume rallies.

More resistance around the 20-day line.

Base breakout fails at the 20-day moving average on heavy selling volume.

Neckline.

Massive volume reversal on a false buyout rumor.

Neckline breakout is a fake out.

Voodoo rally just barely clears the 200-day moving average.

Voodoo rally just barely clears the 50-day moving average.

Volume Window, 50 DMA Line

Notes: Monster Beverage (MNST) was formerly known as Hansen's Beverage, trading under the symbol HANS. The name change was made to emphasize its flagship Monster brand of energy drinks. The energy drink craze helped fuel strong earnings for MNST during its upside price run and rumors began to abound that Coca-Cola (KO) was going to buy the company, accounting for the huge price spike that we interpret as the right shoulder of an H&S top it formed at the peak. This, of course, assumes some interpretive license, based on the fact that the stock closed very near the lows of the weekly trading range. Just before the downside neckline breakout, the 20-day moving average came into play as it often does, serving as stiff resistance on short reaction rallies off the neckline in late July and early August 2012. The gap-down breakout through the neckline in early August 2012 was also a very playable shortable gap-down move using the intra-day high of the gap-down day as a guide for an upside stop. Interestingly, MNST topped as the general market was forming a low in June of 2012.

CBRE Group (CBG) 2007

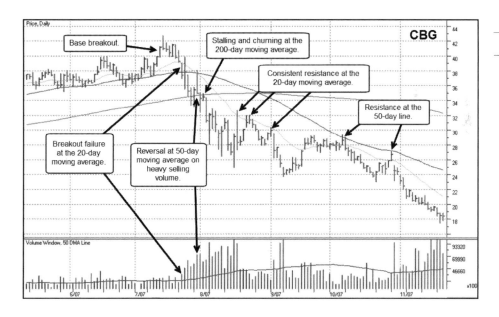

Notes: CBRE Group (CBG) was formerly known as C.B. Ellis, a real estate development company that was riding high on the real estate bubble/boom that finally ended in 2006–2007. The stock topped during a short market correction leading up to the October 2007 top after an abrupt breakout failure coming out of a late-stage cup-with-handle formation. The late-stage base was relatively well-formed, but the daily chart shows how quickly the stock came apart once it failed at the breakout point and dropped through the 20-day moving average on heavy volume. Throughout late July and August 2007, the stock followed the 20-day moving average to the downside as it slashed its way lower. As the 50-day moving average continued lower and approached the 20-day line in early October 2007, the 50-day line assumed the role of overhead resistance. The stock could have been shorted into both of the rallies it had up into the 50-day line before breaking to fresh lows in early November 2007.

■ Precision Castparts (PCP) 2007

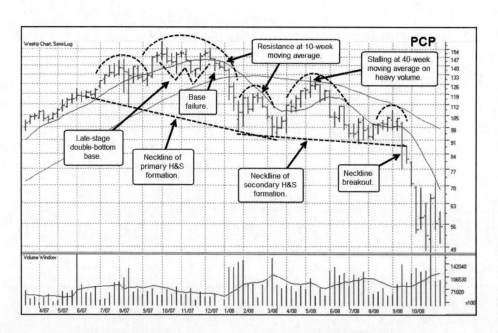

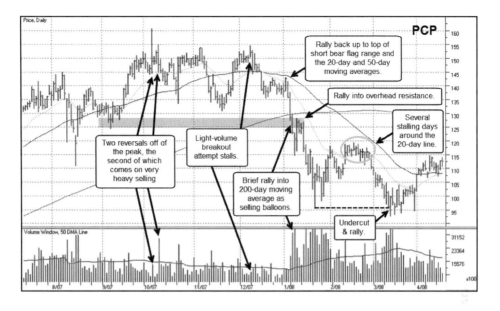

Price, Daily

PCP

Two reversals off of the peak, the second of which comes on very heavy selling

Light-volume breakout attempt stalls.

Rally back up to top of short bear flag range and the 20-day and 50-day moving averages.

Rally into overhead resistance.

Several stalling days around the 20-day line.

Brief rally into 200-day moving average as selling balloons.

Undercut & rally.

Volume Window, 50 DMA Line

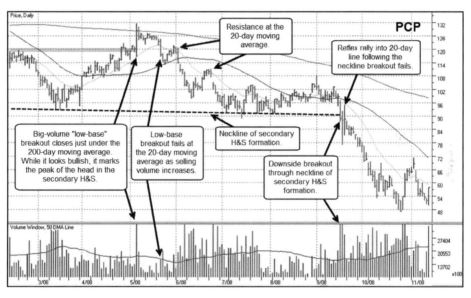

Price, Daily

PCP

Resistance at the 20-day moving average.

Reflex rally into 20-day line following the neckline breakout fails.

Big-volume "low-base" breakout closes just under the 200-day moving average. While it looks bullish, it marks the peak of the head in the secondary H&S.

Low-base breakout fails at the 20-day moving average as selling volume increases.

Neckline of secondary H&S formation.

Downside breakout through neckline of secondary H&S formation.

Volume Window, 50 DMA Line

Notes: Precision Castparts (PCP) topped in late 2007 as it formed a relatively large H&S formation. After the neckline breakout to the downside from this primary H&S formation, the stock then formed an even larger, seven-and-a-half-month-long secondary H&S formation. PCP initially topped with the general market in late 2007, and the first neckline breakout occurred during the first leg of the brutal 2007–2009 bear market. The neckline breakout from the secondary H&S formation occurred in September 2008 as the general market began the very steep second down leg of the 2007–2009 bear market.

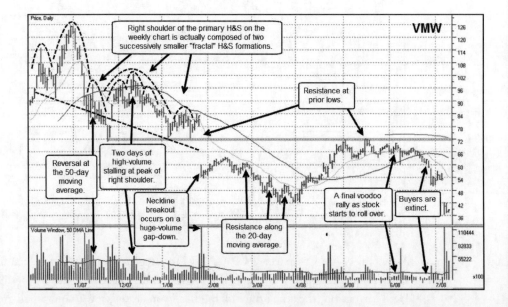

Notes: VMware (VMW) was a hot stock IPO that came public in August of 2007 and immediately ran to the upside without forming any discernible base on the weekly chart. The stock's move became somewhat climactic in late October 2007, and the stock topped in tandem with the general market peak at that time. The right shoulder of the H&S contains a small, fractal H&S formation, and the neckline breakdown occurred on a huge-volume gap-down move that could have been shorted but which would have stopped out any would-be short-sellers. The ensuing rally and "dead cat" bounce after the gap-down ran into the 20-day moving average in late February 2008, and the stock could have been shorted at that logical resistance point.

■ Baidu (BIDU) 2008

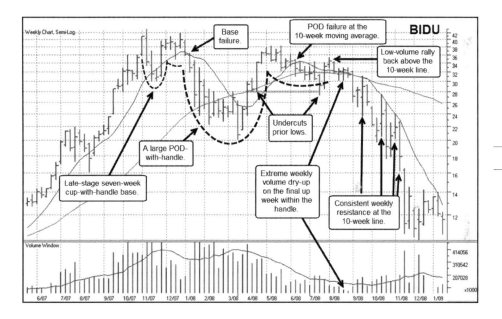

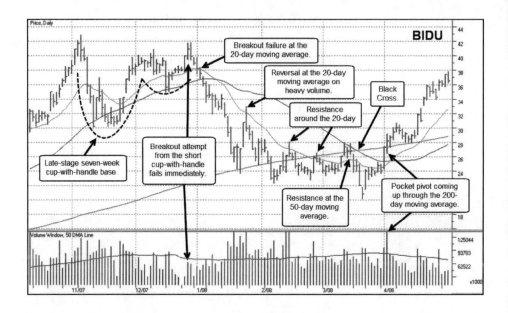

Late-stage seven-week
cup-with-handle base.

Breakout failure at the
20-day moving average.

Reversal at the 20-day
moving average on
heavy volume.

Black
Cross.

Resistance
around the 20-day

Breakout attempt
from the short
cup-with-handle
fails immediately.

Pocket pivot coming
up through the 200-
day moving average.

Resistance at the
50-day moving
average.

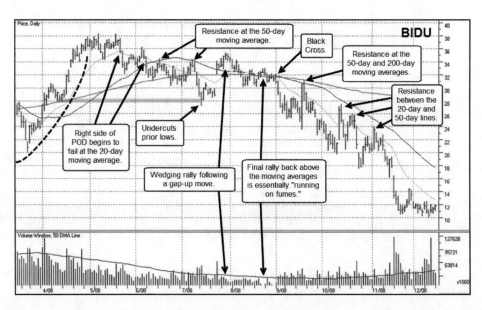

Resistance at the 50-day
moving average.

Black
Cross.

Resistance at the
50-day and 200-day
moving averages.

Resistance
between the
20-day and
50-day lines.

Right side of
POD begins to
fail at the 20-day
moving average.

Undercuts
prior lows.

Wedging rally following
a gap-up move.

Final rally back above
the moving averages
is essentially "running
on fumes."

Notes: Baidu (BIDU) topped with the general market in late 2007 after forming a short, late-stage cup-with-handle base. This late-stage base formed the left peak of what later became a big POD topping formation. BIDU broke down sharply in January 2008 after the failed cup-with-handle breakout attempt in the first daily chart, and the steep decline formed what later became the left side of the large POD formation. BIDU then rallied all the way back up to the late 2007 highs and failed from the right side peak of the POD in May 2008. The ensuing large cup-with-handle, or rather "POD-with-handle," formation took longer to break down, and is similar to the topping patterns seen in Broadcom (BRCM) in 2000, Apple (AAPL) in 2008, and First Solar (FSLR) in 2008. This POD-with-handle formed its left peak around the same time as the general market top in 2007 and its right peak at around the same time as the second leg down of the 2007–2009 bear market got going in September 2008.

■ Blackberry Limited (BBRY) 2008

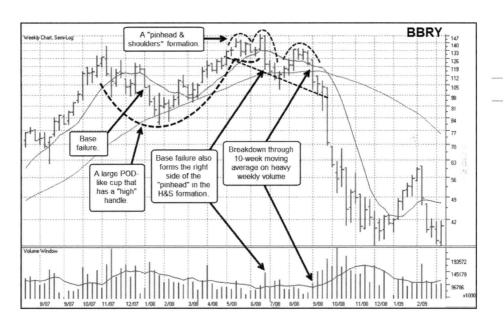

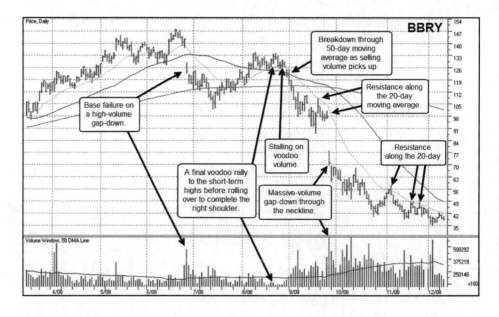

Price, Daily **BBRY**

Breakdown through 50-day moving average as selling volume picks up.

Base failure on a high-volume gap-down.

Resistance along the 20-day moving average.

Stalling on voodoo volume.

Resistance along the 20-day

A final voodoo rally to the short-term highs before rolling over to complete the right shoulder.

Massive-volume gap-down through the neckline.

Volume Window, 50 DMA Line

Notes: Blackberry Limited (BBRY) was originally known as Research in Motion (RIMM), maker of the famous Blackberry smartphone which became so popular and addictive to its users that it soon earned the nickname "Crackberry." BBRY's top is unique in that it formed a rare and unusual "pinhead and shoulders" formation on the right side of a large POD topping formation. The left side of this POD coincided with the market top in late 2007, while the right side and final breakdown from the right side and the pinhead and shoulders formation occurred in synchrony with the second down leg of the 2007–2009 bear market that began in September 2008. The neckline breakout in late September 2009 was in fact a shortable gap-down, and the stock simply followed the 20-day moving average lower from there. Notice also that the pattern that formed from late June to August of 2008 looks like a cup-with-handle, and the handle failure at the end of August would have provided a much earlier short-sale point, as the stock broke down below the 50-day moving average on expanding selling volume.

Crocs (CROX) 2007

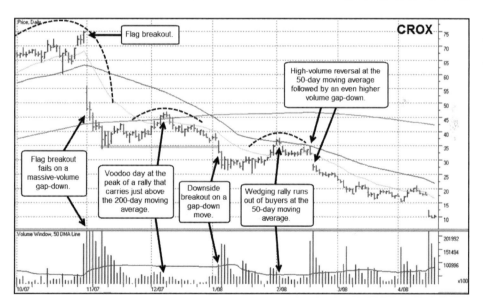

Right side of the "head" in H&S formation is also a late-stage flag failure.

Resistance at 40-week moving average.

Resistance at 10-week moving average.

Flag breakout.

High-volume reversal at the 50-day moving average followed by an even higher volume gap-down.

Flag breakout fails on a massive-volume gap-down.

Voodoo day at the peak of a rally that carries just above the 200-day moving average.

Downside breakout on a gap-down move.

Wedging rally runs out of buyers at the 50-day moving average.

Notes: In our first book we described Crocs (CROX) as the "poster child" of H&S topping formations. The big H&S formation it formed when it topped in October 2007, at the same time as the general market began the 2007–2009 bear market, has all of the textbook features of a classic H&S. The only problem is that such textbook H&S formations are more the exception than the rule. Nevertheless, CROX's 2007 H&S top provides a clear example of the basic, identifying features of an H&S formation. It was also a hot stock recent IPO with a hot product, namely the rubberized Crocs shoes that were hailed for their comfort and utility. Crocs also created Jibbitz™, shoe "charms" with which kids could decorate their shoes, adding to the Crocs craze. Crocs also found favor among certain professionals like doctors and nurses, who found the shoes to be very comfortable to wear while on long hospital shifts. The initial break off the peak occurred in late October 2007 on a bad earnings report, just as the general market was starting to top. This break came in the form of a massive-volume gap-down that was in fact a shortable gap-down, as it never again got back above the intra-day high of that gap-down day, as the daily chart clearly shows.

■ First Solar (FSLR) 2008

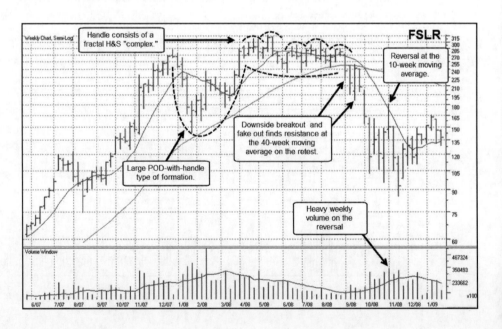

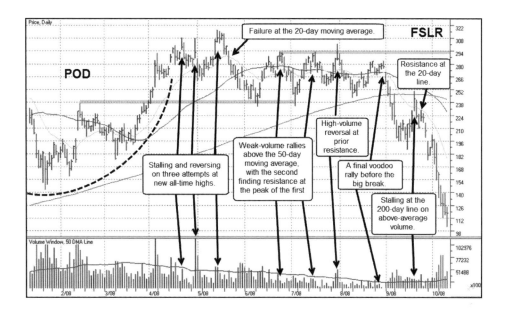

Price, Daily

POD

FSLR

Failure at the 20-day moving average.

Resistance at the 20-day line.

Stalling and reversing on three attempts at new all-time highs.

Weak-volume rallies above the 50-day moving average, with the second finding resistance at the peak of the first

High-volume reversal at prior resistance.

A final voodoo rally before the big break.

Stalling at the 200-day line on above-average volume.

Volume Window, 50 DMA Line

2/08   3/08   4/08   5/08   6/08   7/08   8/08   9/08   10/08

Notes: Solar stocks were a hot group in 2007. First Solar (FSLR) was one of the primary big-stock leaders of that group phenomenon, and it took a long time to form a complete and final top. The first top in the stock occurred after the initial October 2007 market top and formed the left side of a large POD formation. This evolved into a POD-with-handle formation that is similar to the patterns seen in Broadcom (BRCM) in 2000, Apple in 2008, and Baidu (BIDU) in 2008. Notice that the handle part of the POD-with-handle is also a fractal H&S formation that also has the look of a "rolling top." There were three rallies on the right side of this fractal H&S that formed the right shoulders and that found resistance right around the prior failed breakout point from mid-May 2008. The final breakdown occurred in synchrony with the second down leg in the 2007–2009 bear market that got going in September 2008.

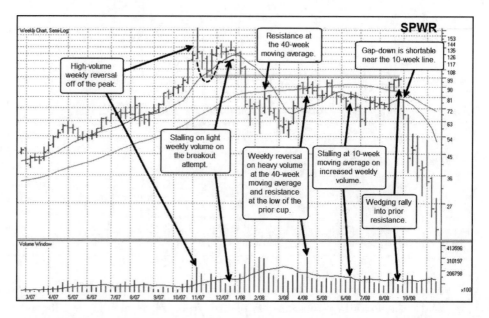

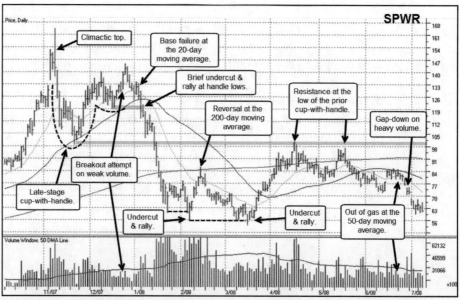

Notes: Sunpower (SPWR) was another one of the big-stock names in the "hot stock" solar group in 2007, and its meteoric rise ended in a classic climax top. This led to a sharp decline down to the 50-day/10-week moving averages and the ensuing bounce off the moving averages formed a late-stage cup-with-handle base. A breakout attempt from this cup-with-handle formation occurred in late December 2007 but immediately failed, as the stock broke back down below the initial breakout point and the 20-day moving average on heavy volume. That breakdown briefly found support at the 50-day moving average before the stock completely blew apart, dropping a total of –67.7 percent from its October 2007 peak. The stock then spent the next six months chopping back and forth but finding consistent resistance around the 100 price level. It finally failed after a final wedging rally into prior resistance before plummeting again to the downside in synchrony with the second down leg of the 2007–2009 bear market that started in September 2008.

■ JA Solar (JASO) 2008

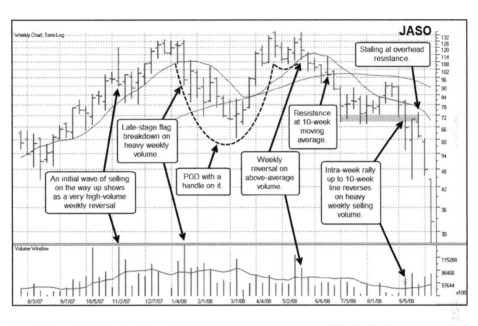

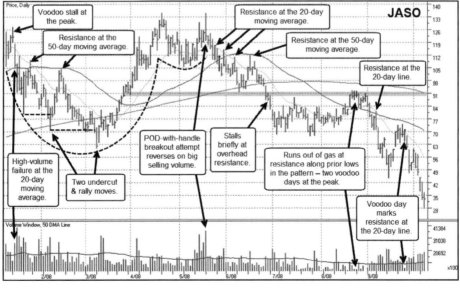

Notes: JA Solar (JASO) was a smaller "hot stock" name in the solar stock craze of 2007 and came public in February 2007. The stock very quickly launched to the upside, going on a very steep run before peaking roughly two months after the general market top of October 2007. The breakdown in January 2008 formed the left side of a narrow 15-week POD. The POD built a short handle along its right side peak before a breakout attempt in mid-May failed and reversed sharply to the downside, sending the stock through its 20-day moving average on heavy selling volume. Two short rallies as the stock began trending lower from the breakout point found resistance at the 20-day line before the stock bounced off the 200-day moving average. This bounce carried up into the 50-day moving average where it ran into stiff resistance and reversed back to the downside, slicing through the 200-day line before finding support roughly along the lows of the prior POD formation. After a brief rally that carried up into the early June 2008 low, JASO broke back down through the 50-day line and plummeted to the downside in synchrony with the second down leg of the 2007–2009 bear market that began in September 2008.

◼ U.S. Steel (X) 2008

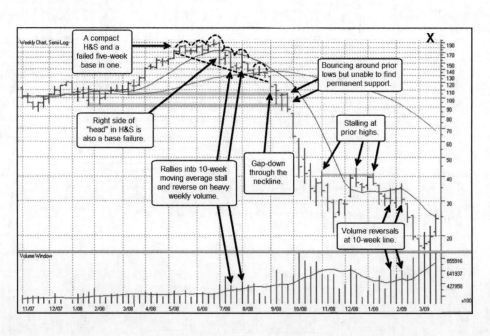

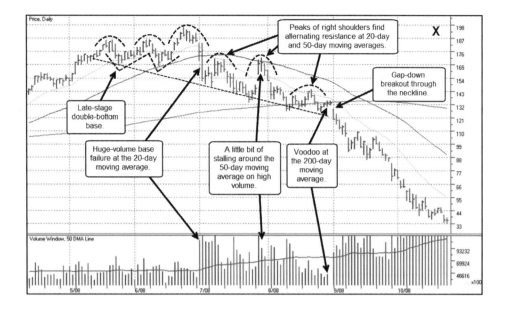

Notes: Sharply rising commodities prices, from gold and copper to oil and agricultural products like wheat and rice, gave rise to the big move in what we dubbed "stuff stocks," stocks of companies that handle the "stuff" from which other finished products are made. In addition, the need for a commodity like steel as a global building boom took hold sent steel stocks like the granddaddy of all steels, U.S. Steel (X), rocketing higher. Interestingly, X did not top with the market in late 2007, but instead continued moving higher and did not reach its final zenith until early July 2008, two months before the brutal 2007–2009 bear market began its second down leg in September. X provides a good example of leading stocks that continue moving higher even after the general market tops, but which eventually form their final top at around the same time a second or third down leg within an overall bear market takes hold. While X topped in the manner of an H&S top, it also formed an LSFB right at the peak, as is evident on the daily chart. The head of the H&S formed right at the point where the final late-stage base breakout attempt failed, gapping down through the 20-day moving average on heavy selling volume. This would have provided an early short-sale entry point. Once X began to "live" under its 50-day moving average, it formed a second, fractal H&S formation. The gap-down breakout through the neckline of this fractal H&S, which also coincided with the neckline of the overall H&S, was very shortable as the stock plummeted to the downside with the general market in September 2008.

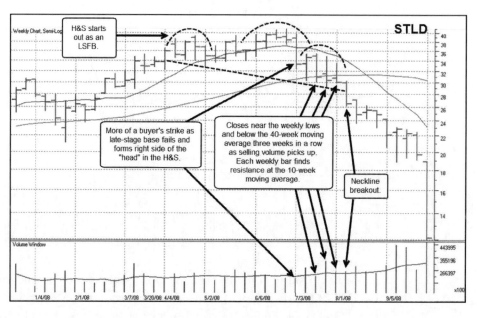

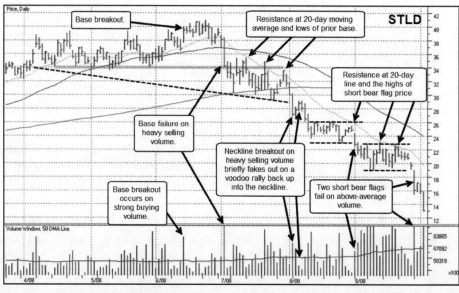

Notes: Steel Dynamics (STLD) was another steel stock moving to the upside during the stuff stock craze, and it broke down very similarly to X. While it formed an H&S top before breaking down, the daily chart, as with X, shows that the actual peak occurred on a late-stage base breakout failure. That breakout failure occurred on a massive volume breach of both the 20-day and 50-day moving averages. A notable feature on the weekly chart is the three weeks in late July and early August 2008 where the stock closed right at the lows of the long weekly ranges on above-average weekly volume. Each week found resistance just underneath the 10-week moving average on the weekly chart, but we can see that the more granular view provided by the daily chart reveals that each of these weeks found resistance at the 20-day moving average. Notice that in late June, the stock had one final little bounce back up through the 20-day line on a churning and stalling voodoo day. Like X, STLD then came completely apart as the general market came apart in September 2008.

◼ Freeport McMoRan Copper & Gold (FCX)

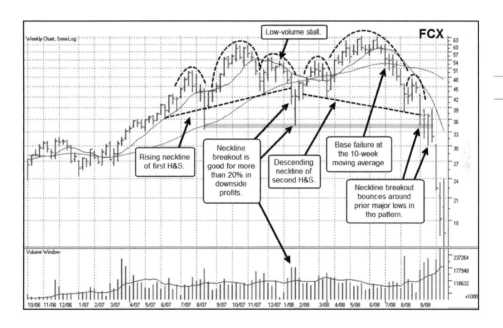

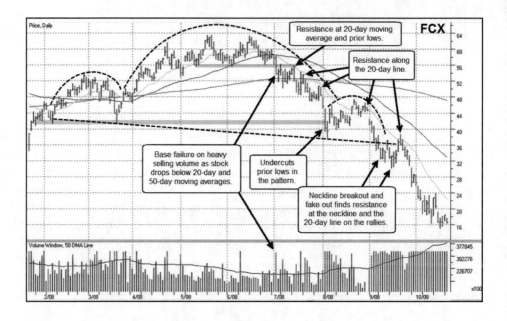

Price, Daily

FCX

Resistance at 20-day moving average and prior lows.

Resistance along the 20-day line.

Base failure on heavy selling volume as stock drops below 20-day and 50-day moving averages.

Undercuts prior lows in the pattern.

Neckline breakout and fake out finds resistance at the neckline and the 20-day line on the rallies.

Volume Window, 50 DMA Line

377845
302276
226707
x100

2/08 3/08 4/08 5/08 6/08 7/08 8/08 9/08 10/08

Notes: Freeport McMoRan (FCX) was primarily a copper stock play during the stuff stock craze of 2007. Like steel stocks, it also benefitted from the global building boom of the day. FCX is unusual for its dual H&S formations, where the peak of the head of the first H&S coincided with the general market top in October 2007 and the peak of the head of the second H&S formed a couple of months before the 2007–2009 bear market's second down leg, which began in September 2008. The first H&S formation has an ascending base, and one could have made some money shorting the neckline breakout in January 2008. Even more optimally, the stalling rally back up into the 10-week moving average in late December 2007 also offered a decent short-sale entry point. Once FCX began to break down in late June 2008, it followed the 20-day moving average all the way down to the descending neckline of the second, higher H&S formation. The final breakdown through the second H&S neckline occurred in synchrony with the 2007–2009 bear market's second down leg in September 2008.

▪ Peabody Energy (BTU) 2008

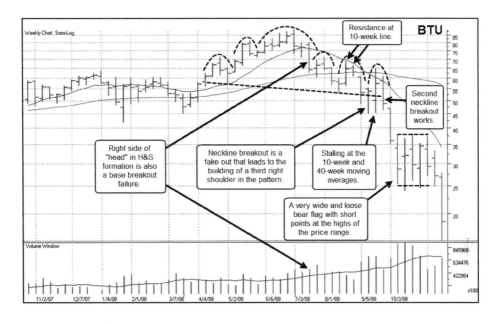

Weekly Chart, Semi-Log.

BTU

Resistance at 10-week line.

Right side of "head" in H&S formation is also a base breakout failure.

Neckline breakout is a fake out that leads to the building of a third right shoulder in the pattern.

Stalling at the 10-week and 40-week moving averages.

Second neckline breakout works.

A very wide and loose bear flag with short points at the highs of the price range.

Volume Window

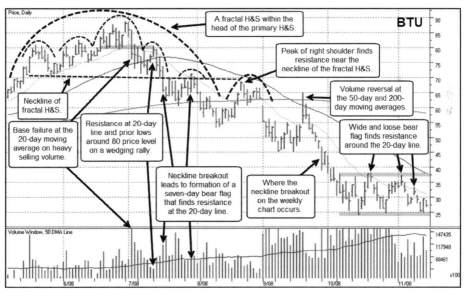

Price, Daily

BTU

A fractal H&S within the head of the primary H&S.

Peak of right shoulder finds resistance near the neckline of the fractal H&S

Volume reversal at the 50-day and 200-day moving averages.

Neckline of fractal H&S.

Wide and loose bear flag finds resistance around the 20-day line.

Base failure at the 20-day moving average on heavy selling volume.

Resistance at 20-day line and prior lows around 80 price level on a wedging rally.

Neckline breakout leads to formation of a seven-day bear flag that finds resistance at the 20-day line.

Where the neckline breakout on the weekly chart occurs.

Volume Window, 50 DMA Line

Notes: Since coal is a particular type of "stuff" that is not only used as a source of energy but also in other industrial processes, such as steel and cement manufacturing, coal stocks were also players in the stuff stock move of 2007. Among these, Peabody Energy (BTU) was a major coal play that topped out after it formed a six-month H&S pattern, but the actual peak in the stock occurred on a late-stage base breakout failure in early July 2008. One could have entered a short position as the stock rallied up into the 20-day moving average in mid-July. As well, the head of the larger H&S formation contained a smaller, fractal H&S pattern, and the neckline breakout in mid-July was also shortable. The ensuing rally back up into the neckline and the 20-day line in late July was also a reasonable short-sale entry point. One final rally up into the 50-day and 200-day moving averages in mid-September that stalled on heavy volume provided a final short-sale point before the stock blew through the neckline of the larger head and shoulders formation in synchrony with the second down leg in the 2007–2009 bear market.

■ Consolidated Energy (CNX) 2008

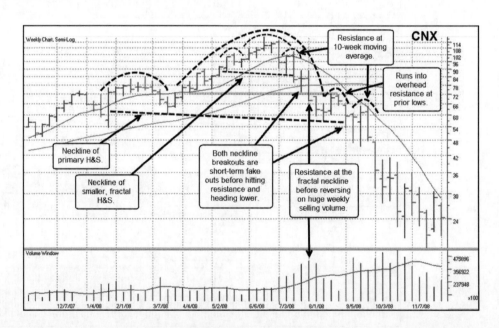

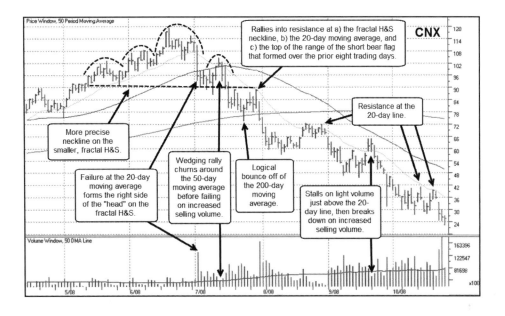

Notes: Consolidated Energy (CNX) was another leader among the coal-related names that participated in the stuff stock rally of 2007. The stock formed a massive eight-month H&S formation, but from a practical standpoint it actually became shortable within the fractal H&S that formed inside the head of the primary H&S pattern. Shorting the fractal neckline breakout in mid-July would have been a reasonable entry point. Notice the Black Cross that occurred in late August 2008 as the 10-week moving average crossed below the 40-week moving average. Once CNX broke the 10-week line in July, it never traded back above the line throughout its downside break in the latter part of 2008.

▪ Cliffs Natural Resources (CLF) 2008

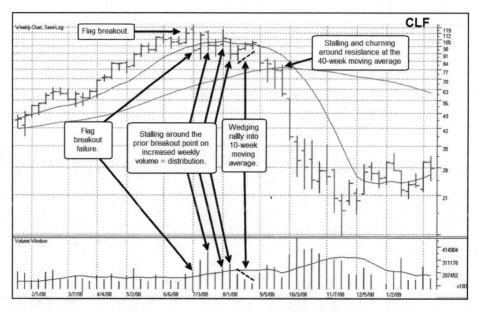

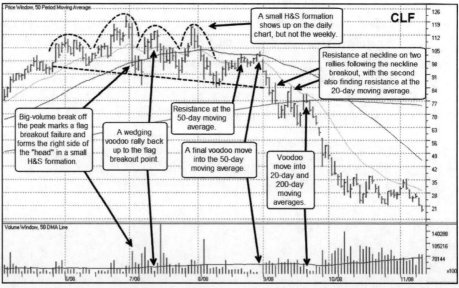

Notes: Cliffs Natural Resources (CLF) provided a combination play on metals and coal as a major iron ore producer and a significant producer of high- and low-volatile metallurgical coal. The stock began to wobble around its peak in July 2008 as the weekly price ranges began to widen. On the daily chart, notice the improper double-bottom it tried to break out of July 2008 and failed miserably right at that point. One final, wedging rally into the 10-week and 50-day moving averages on the weekly and daily charts, respectively, in late August provided short-sellers with a reasonably optimal entry point given the voodoo rally evident on the daily chart. The stock essentially blew apart from there.

Rio Tinto Plc (RIO) 2008

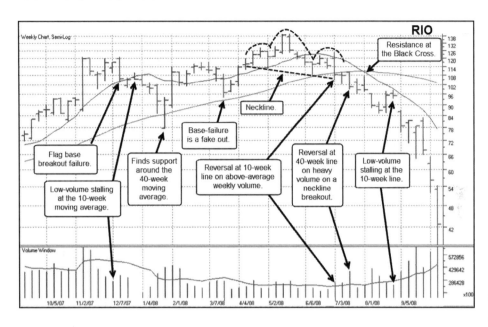

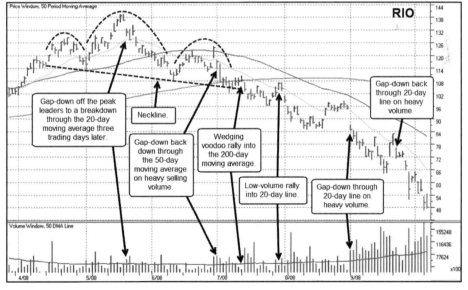

Notes: Rio Tinto PLC was another producer of various ores, including aluminum, copper, and iron, that performed similarly to CLF in the great stuff stock boom of 2007. RIO corrected 35.9 off of its peak during the initial general market top in October 2007, but like CLF, it recovered and broke out to new highs in April 2008.

That breakout lasted all of four weeks before the stock topped in June in an initial LSFB set-up. This eventually evolved into an H&S top that finally split wide open with the general market when the second leg of the 2007–2009 bear market took hold in September 2008.

■ Union Pacific (UNP) 2008

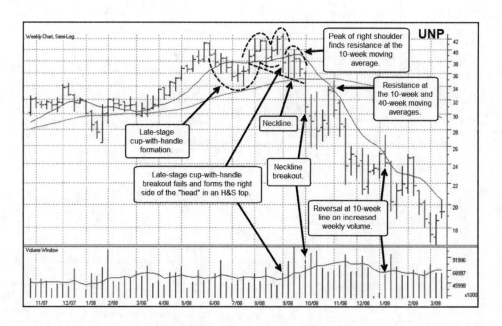

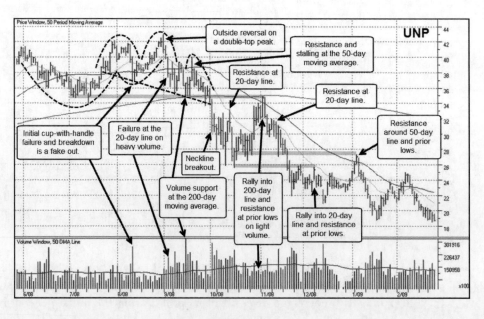

Notes: As stuff stocks were moving in 2007, so were the stocks of companies that moved stuff, such as the railroads. Union Pacific (UNP) was a big-stock railroad leader during this period, and it bucked the general market top in October 2007 as it continued to make new highs until finally topping in the first week of September 2008 as the second leg of the 2007–2009 bear market was beginning. UNP topped after forming a late-stage cup-with-handle and failing on a big outside reversal week to the downside, as can be seen on the weekly chart. This later evolved into a big H&S formation, but note that the action around the handle of the late-stage cup-with-handle formed a smaller, fractal H&S formation that provided earlier reference points for short-sale entries. In fact, the fractal neckline breakout provided a very profitable move to the downside for short-sellers.

◼ CSX Corporation (CSX) 2008

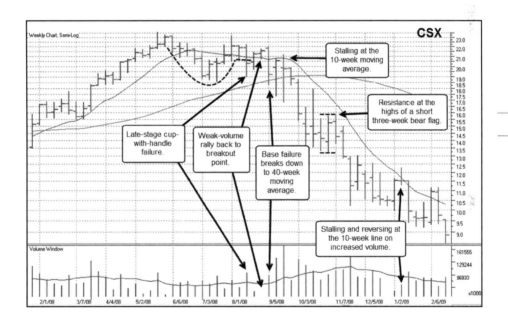

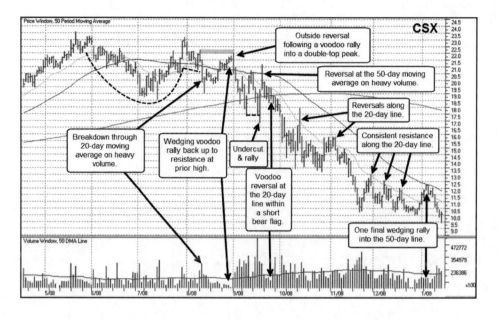

Notes: Railroad stock CNX Corp. (CNX) was another stuff stock rally participant, and had a role in the coal boom as well given its exposure to coal-producing areas in the Eastern United States. It topped in similar fashion to UNP, making new highs after the general market top in October 2007. The stock rolled over off of the peak in early September 2008 at the same time as UNP and the start of the second down leg in the 2007–2009 bear market. CSX had formed a late-stage cup-with-handle, and topped with a big outside reversal week exactly as UNP did. Notice the rally in late August 2008 that carried right up to the prior breakout point before reversing hard on heavy volume. This is a common retest of a breakout point that is often seen in LSFB set-ups.

Diana Shipping (DSX) 2008

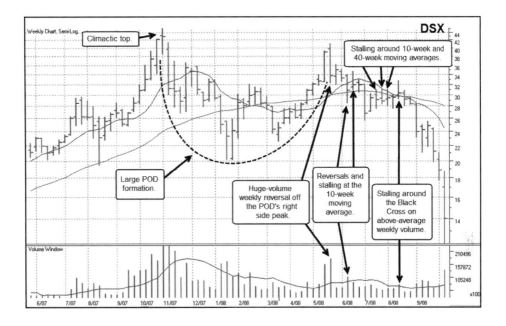

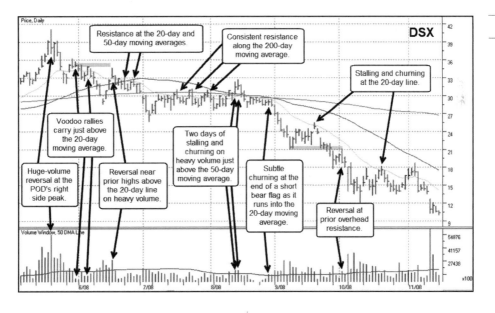

Notes: Railroads weren't the only movers of "stuff" that had big price moves during the stuff stock craze of 2007. In addition to the need to move stuff over land via rails, stuff also had to be moved over the oceans, and oceangoing shippers like Diana Shipping (DSX) had phenomenal upside moves in 2007. DSX initially topped with the market in October 2007 and broke down with a great deal of downside velocity, diving –55.4 percent below its November 2007 high before turning back to the upside and coming within 11 percent of that high by May 2008 to form a 28-week-long POD topping formation. Notice how the POD formed logically within the context of what was going on in the general market. The left side peak of the POD coincided with the market top in October 2007 while the right side peak and eventual breakdown coincided with the start of the second leg of the 2007–2009 bear market in September 2008.

■ Dryships (DRYS) 2008

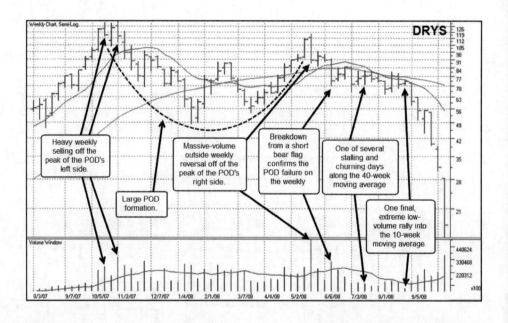

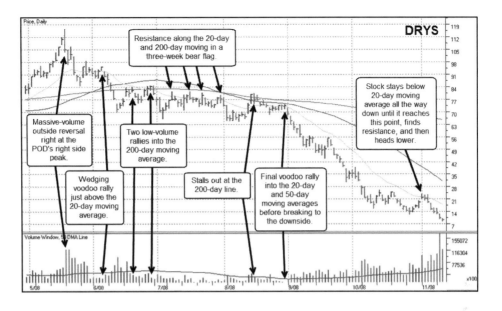

Notes: Dryships (DRYS) joined DSX in the stuff stock shipper rally, and you could not find better proof that stocks tend to move in packs. DRYS topped in POD fashion exactly as DSX did, forming a 29-week POD where the left side was formed in sync with October 2007 general market top and the right side was formed as the market was beginning to break down again in late summer 2008 on the second leg of the 2007–2009 bear market.

Potash Saskatchewan (POT) 2008

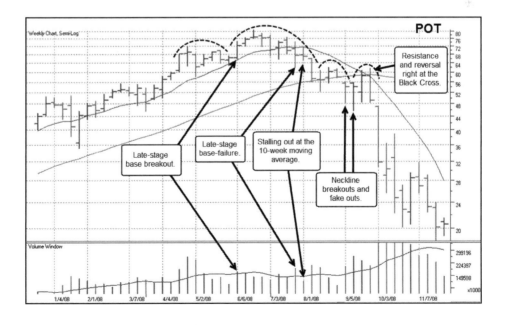

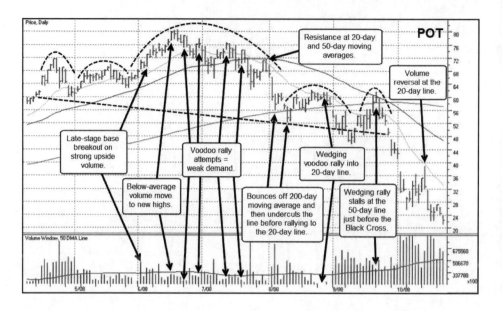

Notes: With commodities on the move during the stuff stock rally of 2007, the upside trends in agricultural commodities led to increases in the prices of products that helped grow those commodities, namely stocks of companies that produced fertilizer components. Nitrogen, phosphorus, and potassium are the three main ingredients in fertilizer, and Potash Saskatchewan was a major miner and manufacturer of potash, essentially a mined or manufactured form of water-soluble potassium. POT started out as an LSFB set-up and later evolved into a five-month-long H&S formation that finally blew apart with the market in September 2008. One last wedging rally into the 50-day moving average in late September provided an optimal short-sale entry point, and the stock plummeted from there.

■ Agrium (AGU) 2008

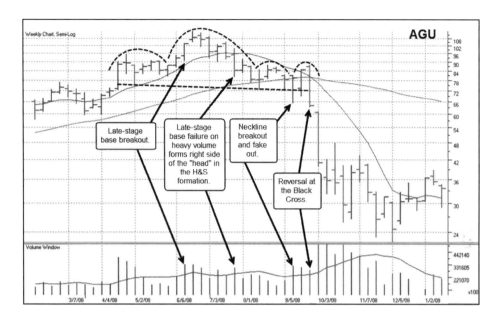

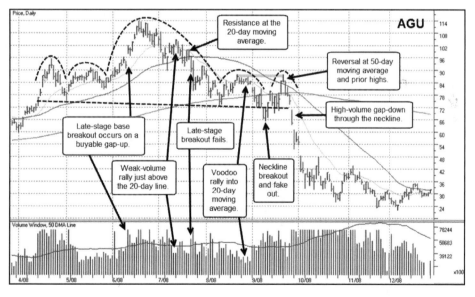

Notes: Agrium (AGU) was another big-stock fertilizer play in 2007, and its business covered most of the bases when it came to fertilizer production. AGU manufactured nitrogen, phosphate, and potassium as well as "crop protection products," and was also a major supplier of crop production services. It topped in similar fashion to POT, topping initially as an LSFB and then evolving into a larger, roughly five-month H&S formation. The gap-down neckline breakout was in fact a very manageable shortable gap-down move, and the stock blew apart from that point as the second leg of the 2007–2009 bear market took hold in September.

■ CF Industries (CF) 2008

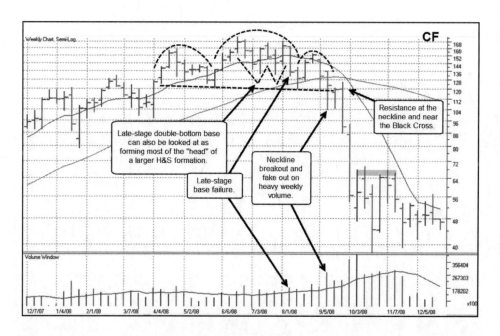

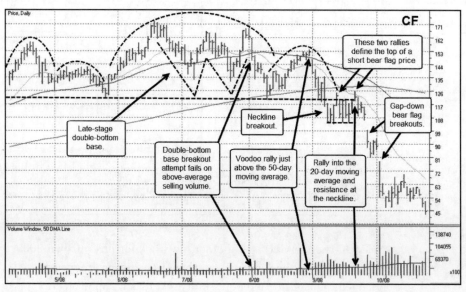

Notes: CF Industries (CF), as a producer of nitrogen, was the third of the big-stock fertilizer plays in 2007, and it topped in similar fashion to POT and AGU. A slight wrinkle occurred here in that the stock topped after a failed double-bottom breakout attempt, as is evident in the daily chart. One last voodoo rally in late August formed the peak of the right shoulder in the five-month H&S pattern before the neckline breakout in early September 2008. Following the neckline breakout, CF formed a short, two-week bear flag and then gapped down through the lows of the flag on heavy volume as the stock blew apart with the general market.

■ Mosaic Company (MOS) 2008

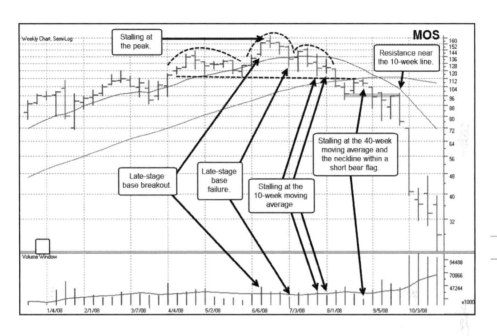

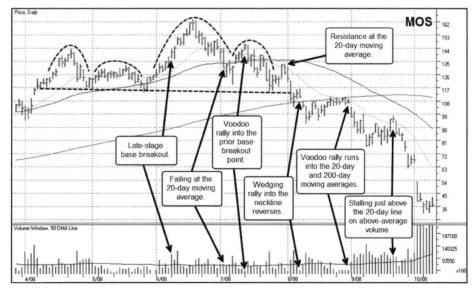

Notes: The fourth and final 2007 big-stock fertilizer leader was Mosaic Company (MOS), the world's largest combined producer of phosphates and potash. It topped in similar fashion to the other fertilizer names in mid-June 2008, starting out as an LSFB and later evolving into a five-month H&S formation. An interesting point here is that one can actually draw a neckline on the daily chart that is higher than the neckline on the weekly chart. The neckline breakout on the daily chart occurred in early August, while the neckline breakout on the weekly chart occurred in early September. There was one last voodoo rally into the 20-day and 200-day moving averages before the stock blew apart with the general market in September 2008.

■ Goldman Sachs (GS) 2008

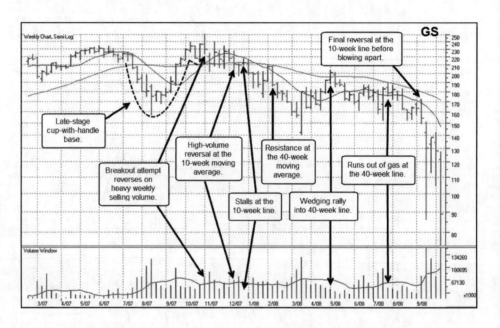

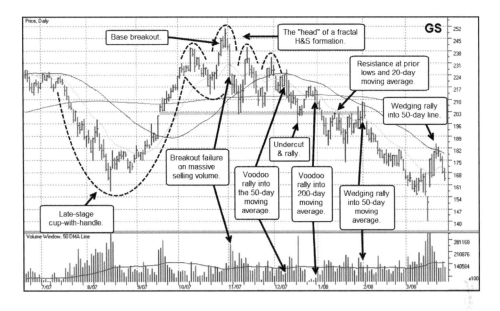

Notes: The bear market of 2007–2009 was all about the great financial crisis of 2008, and many financial stocks were hammered during this bear market. These names were difficult to play on the short side because of the extreme volatility and highly news-oriented moves they had. Goldman Sachs (GS), certainly one of the biggest of the big-stock leaders in the 2007 bull market, is a reasonable example of this phenomenon. GS topped after forming a large, late-stage cup-with-handle. The daily chart shows a great deal of volatility around the cup-with-handle breakout point, all of which served to form a very jagged, fractal H&S formation. As the stock zig-zagged lower, there were a number of undercut and rally moves, and each rally following an undercut of a prior low in the pattern eventually ran into resistance and reversed. GS's downtrend began to plummet in a fairly uniform move throughout February 2008, and the short-term low occurred at the time that Bear Stearns (formerly BSC) went bankrupt. This created something of a short-term panic low for the stock and the general market at the time as the first leg of the 2007–2009 bear market came to a conclusion.

Apple (AAPL) 2008

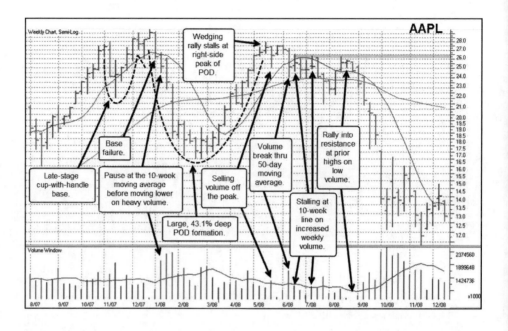

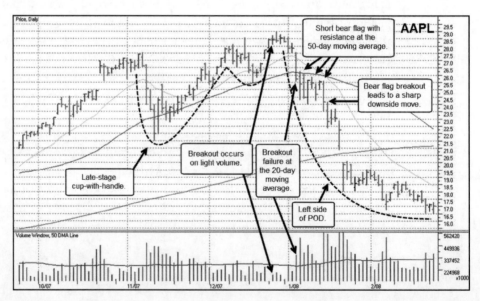

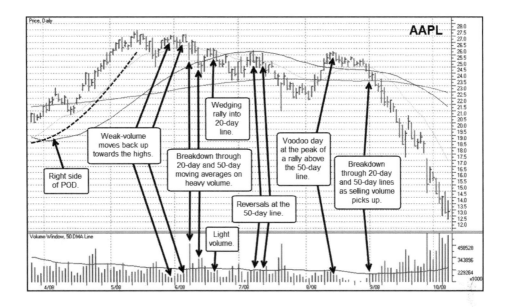

Notes: In Chapter 5 we discussed Apple's (AAPL) top in 2012, but the stock also put in a major top during the 2007–2009 bear market. After the general market topped in October 2007, AAPL continued moving higher into the end of December as it broke out from a late-stage cup-with-handle formation. That breakdown coincided with the first major leg down in the general market and resulted in an AAPL decline of −43.1 percent from the peak. The stock then turned back to the upside and in May 2008 came within 5.5 percent of its prior December 2007 high to form a large POD topping formation. The first daily chart shows the left side of the POD, the second shows the right side of the POD. The breakdown off the right side peak took time to develop and eventually split wide open in September 2008 as the general market began its second down leg in the 2007–2009 bear market. This is a rich example that illustrates how a long-term big-stock leader like AAPL can have periods where it becomes a very profitable short-sale target, even in the midst of a longer-term upside price run over many years.

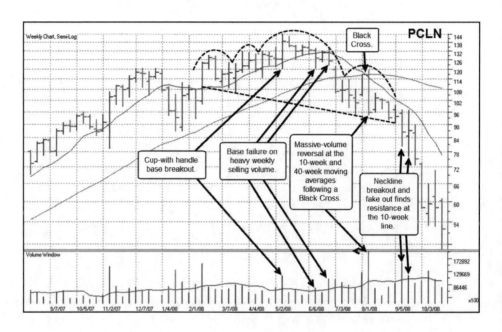

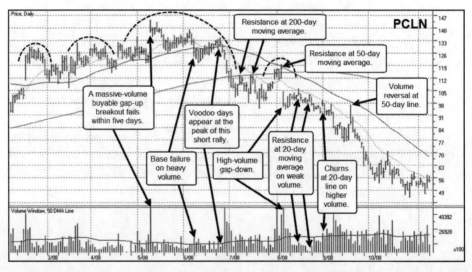

Notes: By the time September 2008 rolled around and the bear market of 2007–2009 was embarking on its second major down leg, leaders of all stripes were pummeled. Big-stock NASDAQ leader Priceline.com (PCLN) was no exception. It topped after a cup-with-handle breakout that was also a buyable gap-up in early May 2008 failed and evolved into a five-month H&S formation. In early August 2008, the stock gapped down from the 50-day moving average and then followed the 20-day line all the way down to the November 2008 bottom.

■ Amazon.com (AMZN) 2008

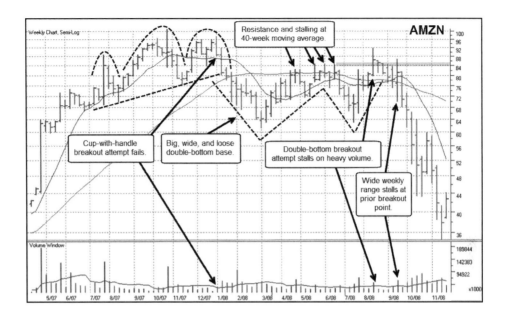

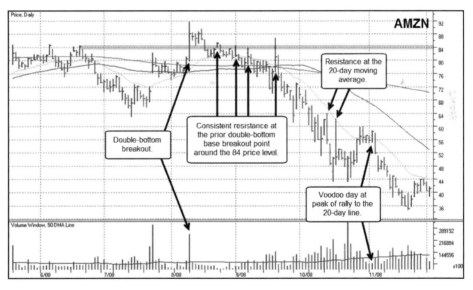

Notes: Amazon.com (AMZN) also did not escape the wrath of the September 2008 market break, and an early August breakout attempt from a big, ugly, late-stage double-bottom base failed in short order at the beginning of September. The weekly chart also shows that the left side of this big double-bottom formation was formed by a breakdown from a late-stage cup-with-handle breakout failure in January 2008. Notice how the left side of that cup coincided with the October 2007 market top. Like AAPL at that time, AMZN tried to make a comeback but could not quite make it to new price highs; it broke hard to the downside throughout January and February of 2008 as the market staged its first major leg down in the 2007–2009 bear market. AMZN blew apart along with everything else on the second major leg down that carried into November 2008.

■ Salesforce.com (CRM) 2008

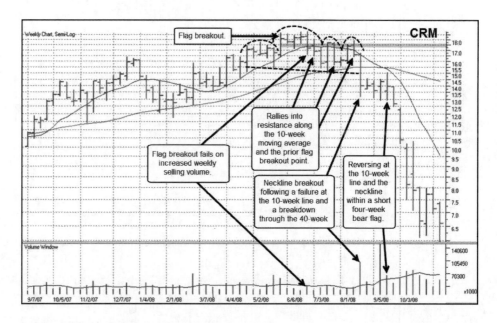

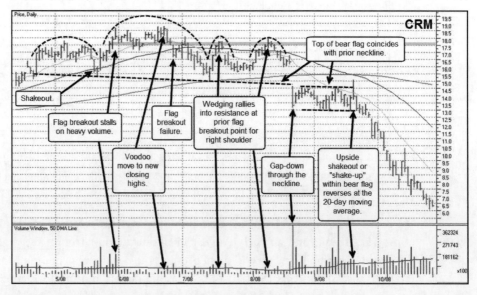

Notes: Salesforce.com (CRM) was one of the first hot "cloud" stocks to hit the market after its IPO debut in 2004. It had a relatively shallow price run in 2007, but it topped with the same velocity that any number of big leading stocks did in September 2008. After forming something of a "squat" H&S formation, CRM gapped down in the latter half of August 2008 and worked its way sideways in a four-week bear flag before splitting wide open in late September. The rallies into the highs of the bear flag and the 20-day moving average in early September provided reasonable short-sale entry points.

■ Molycorp (MCP) 2010

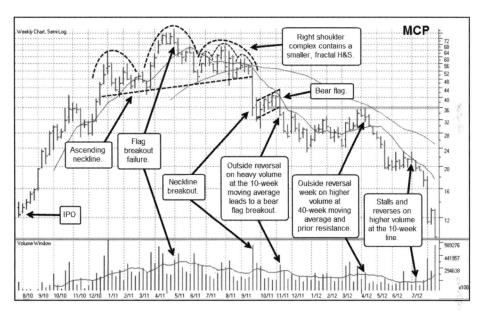

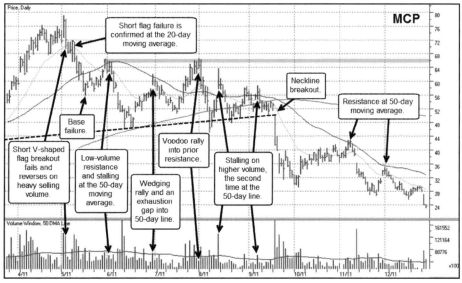

Notes: Molycorp (MCP) is discussed in detail in the Chapter 9 Case Study.

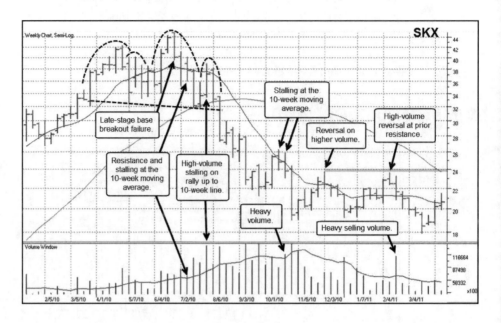

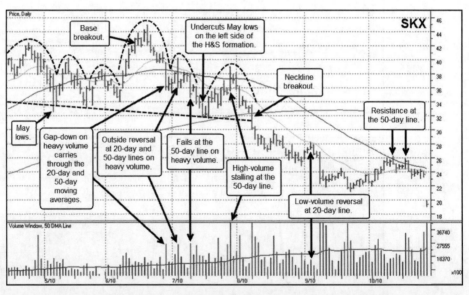

Notes: Shoemaker Skechers USA (SKX) had a big price run off the April 2009 market lows and finally topped during the summer 2010 market correction that began with the Flash Crash in May. SKX tried to break out of a wide and loose late-stage base in late June 2010, and as the general market began to bottom and turn back to the upside, SKX diverged and headed lower. As the market began to bottom in the latter part of August 2010, SKX broke out through the neckline of a roughly four-month

H&S formation. The neckline breakout came on heavy volume and coincided with a breach of the 40-week and 200-day moving averages on the weekly and daily charts, respectively.

◼ Blackberry Limited (BBRY) 2011

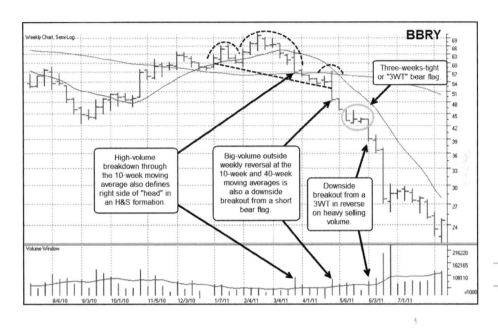

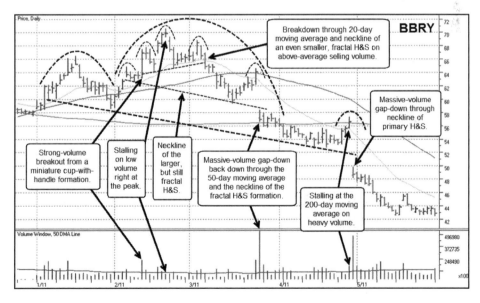

Notes: After its initial major top in 2008, Blackberry Limited (BBRY), formerly known as Research in Motion (RIMM), bottomed out in March of 2009, rallied, and then retested the 2009 low in late 2010. That retest down to 42.53 held well above the 35.05 March 2009 low, and the stock then embarked on a 65.8 percent upside price run from there. This six-month price run ended in February 2010, and the stock formed a short, three-month H&S formation. The gap-down through the neckline of the fractal H&S in late March 2011 was a shortable gap-down. The stock then descended below the 200-day moving average, and one last stalling rally up into the 200-day line resulted in a second gap-down neckline breakout in late April, this time through the neckline of the larger H&S formation. From there the stock never really looked back as it plummeted all the way down to a low of 6.22, more than a 90-percent decline off the 70.54 peak of the H&S formation that formed during the first quarter of 2011. This is a good example of a company that is coming under serious brand pressure as its products are displaced by newer, faster, and better ones made by other companies, and how it can have a final, highly profitable short-selling wave as its obsolescence destroys earnings and sales. This in turn results in a final "extinction" selling wave that decimates the stock price.

■ Rovi Corp. (ROVI) 2011

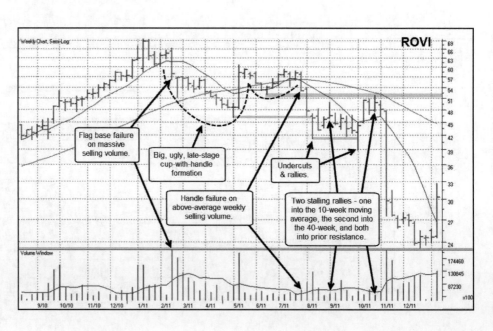

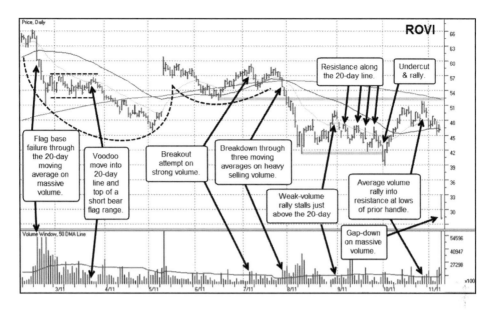

Notes: The boom in digital entertainment in the New Millennium gave rise to the need to find, organize, and record such content and created a business opportunity for companies like Rovi Corp. (ROVI). The company provided software for updating and maintaining media libraries and interactive program guides that help users find, sort, select, schedule for viewing, and record specific digital entertainment content. Bottoming in November 2008 before the market low of March 2009, ROVI had a big price run throughout 2009 and 2010, and topped in February 2011 after a late-stage flag breakout attempt failed on heavy selling volume. That led to a -33.8 percent decline off the peak before the stock bottomed and began building what became a big, ugly, and improper cup-with-handle base. That base failed in late July 2011, leading to a decline that finally saw the stock bottom nearly 12 months later at 9.91, a decline of over 85 percent from its January 2011 high of 69.50.

■ Akamai Technologies (AKAM) 2011

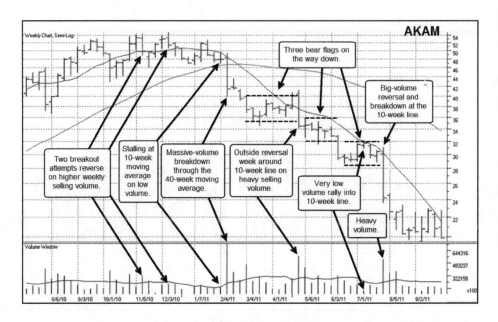

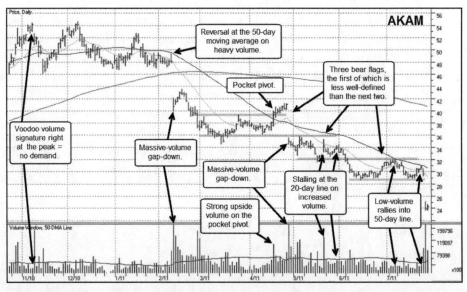

Notes: While the term *cloud computing* might conjure up images of applications and data floating in the air, the reality is that the cloud, for all practical purposes, exists on remote servers that are networked together. Akamai (AKAM) became a play on the cloud-computing theme in 2009–2010, if not part of the cloud itself, with its global network of computer servers. The stock eventually topped out in a very nondescript way, falling out of bed, so to speak, from a choppy four-month triple-bottom sort of structure in early 2011. Once it gapped down through its

200-day moving average in early February 2011, it was in play on the short side. This gap-down move occurred less than two weeks before a short-term general market correction took place. While the "dead-cat" bounce after the early February gap-down could have been shorted into on the fourth-day of the bounce, the only other practical places to attempt to short the stock would be on moves up to the top of the three bear flags it formed after the February gap-down.

■ F5 Networks (FFIV) 2011

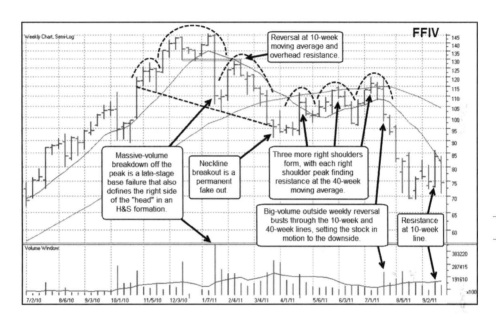

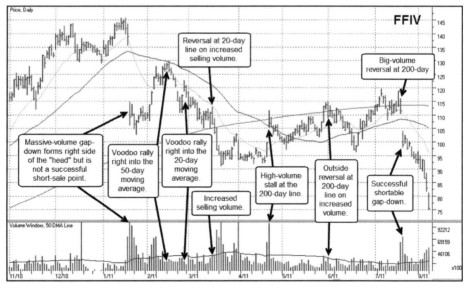

Notes: F5 Networks (FFIV) was another cloud play that had a huge price run from late 2009 into early 2011. The breakdown off the peak in January 2011 occurred on a huge-volume gap-down following a poor earnings report. That move was not shortable, as it turned out, but the ensuing rally right back into the 50-day moving average that formed the right shoulder of a H&S topping formation offered a very optimal textbook short-sale entry point. The rally itself ended with a voodoo upside day followed by an outside reversal right at the 50-day moving average, as can be seen in the daily chart.

■ Netflix (NFLX) 2011

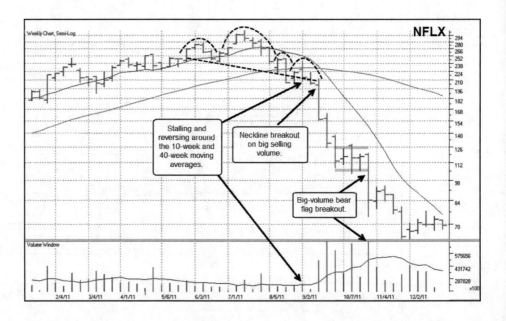

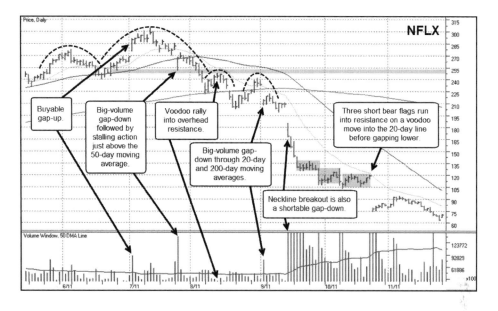

Notes: Netflix (NFLX) and its 2011 top are discussed in detail in the Chapter 6 Case Study.

■ Keurig Green Mountain (GMCR) 2011

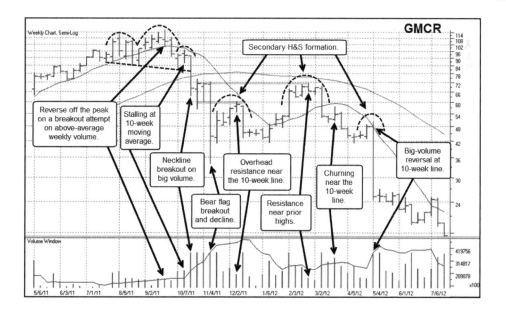

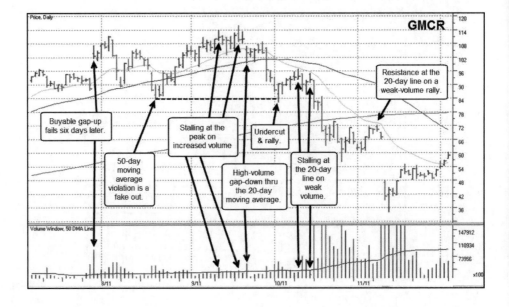

Notes: Keurig Green Mountain (GMCR) and its 2011 top are discussed in detail in the Chapter 7 Case Study.

■ Omnivision Technologies (OVTI) 2011

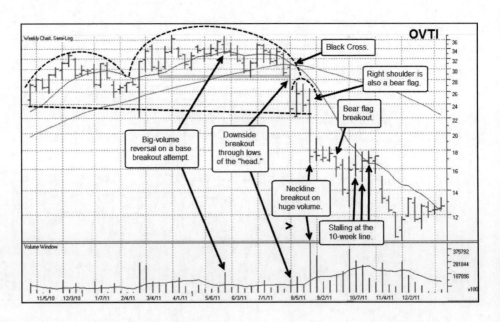

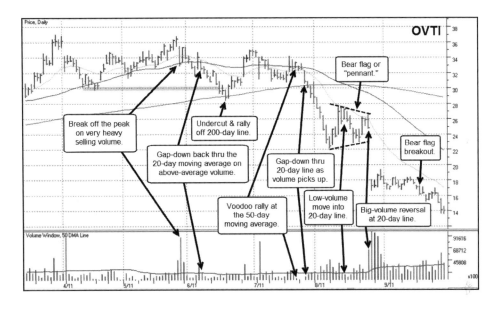

Notes: Since Omnivision Technologies (OVTI) began trading as a public company in year 2000, it has had something of a jagged past, with two massive price runs and three major tops. We looked at OVTI's 2004 top earlier in this section of the book, and OVTI's other major top occurred in 2006, but after a lesser upside price run where the stock "only" tripled off the lows. The stock topped from a long, rolling five-month base that formed a sort of head in a big H&S formation. However, the critical short point occurred as the stock "fell out of bed" from the five-month base in July of 2011. There was a very uniform, almost "slow motion" breakdown as the stock steadily descended through the 200-day moving average and just kept going. A short bear flag or "pennant" formed in the middle of August 2011; the highs of this pennant formation found resistance along the 20-day moving average. OVTI then gapped down from the 20-day line and well below the lows of the pennant in late August.

◼ Riverbed Technology (RVBD) 2011

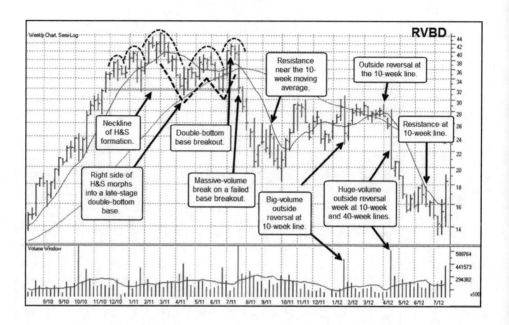

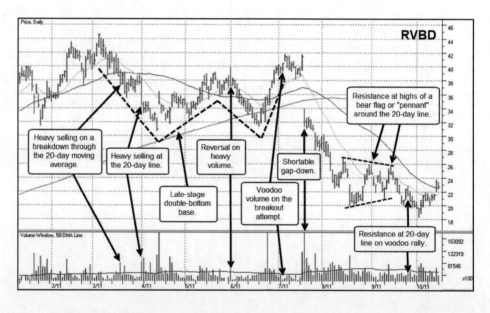

Notes: Riverbed Technology (RVBD) was another cloud networking company that had a huge price run throughout most of 2010 and into early 2011. The stock topped in March 2011 and formed a clear H&S top, but eventually was able to break out above the highs of the first right shoulder to form a second, higher right shoulder. However, another way to look at this is as a late-stage double-bottom base, where the second low of the double-bottom W did not undercut the first low. RVBD briefly moved up through the middle of the W on a standard-issue double-bottom breakout attempt in early July 2011. That breakout attempt failed on a massive-volume gap-down at that time that blew right through the 200-day moving average and which was quite shortable. The stock continued lower from there, finding resistance along the 20-day moving average as it moved lower.

■ Jinko Solar (JKS) 2011

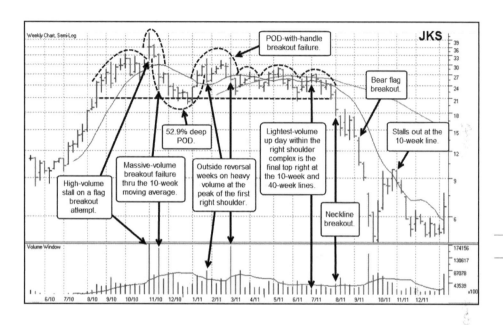

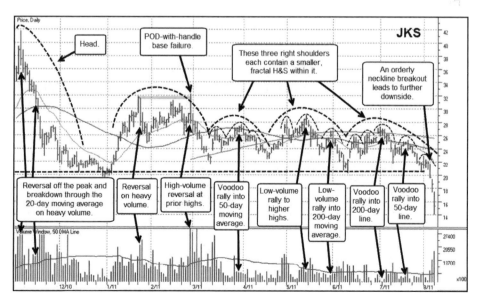

Notes: Jinko Solar (JKS) missed the solar stock boom of 2007, but it came public in May of 2010 at $11 a share and had a sharp 279-percent upside move from there to a peak of 41.75 in November 2010. The stock broke out of what could be considered a late-stage flag formation in November and immediately failed. That breakout failure is shown at the extreme left of the daily chart. The stock could have been shorted as it blew through the 20-day moving average right after the breakout failure, and this would have led to some very sharp downside gains over the next four weeks. The stock slowed its descent, then started back to the upside, forming a large, late-stage cup-with-handle formation, as can be seen in the weekly chart. A breakout attempt from that formation occurred in early March 2011, then the stock simply rolled sideways for the next five months. JKS is an unusual example, because it started with a failed flag breakout, stabilized, and set up in a cup-with-handle, tried to break out again and failed, then morphed into a "pinhead and shoulders" formation with four right shoulders. The final three right shoulders formed their own fractal H&S, and the stock eventually blew apart in August 2011 during a sharp market correction. It also came under pressure with the rest of the stocks in the solar group, as the next example will show.

■ First Solar (FSLR) 2011

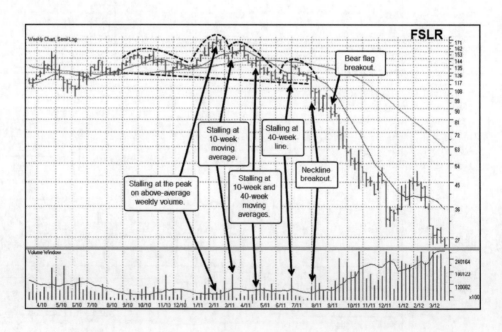

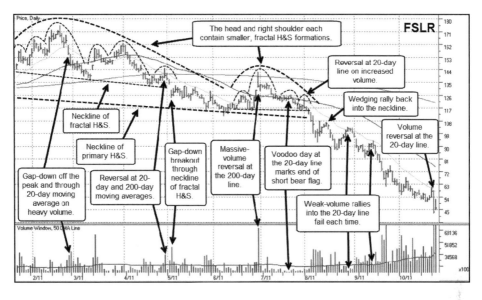

Notes: First Solar (FSLR) put in a major top in 2008, which we looked at earlier in this section of the book. The breakdown from the 2008 peak formed the first down leg of what became a long-term price decline that saw the stock decline from a peak of 317 in 2008 to a low of 11.43 in 2012. The second down leg of this long-term decline began in in early 2011 with a long, rolling H&S top that broke apart in August 2011 during a severe market correction and an overall breakdown in the solar stock group. On the daily chart, two fractal H&S formations can be seen, and there were two key short-sale entry points where the stock rallied into resistance at the 200-day moving average within these fractal H&S patterns.

▪ NXP Semiconductor (NXPI) 2011

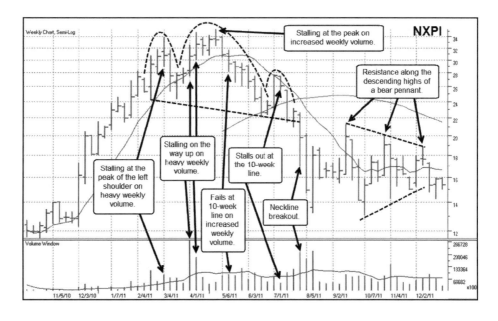

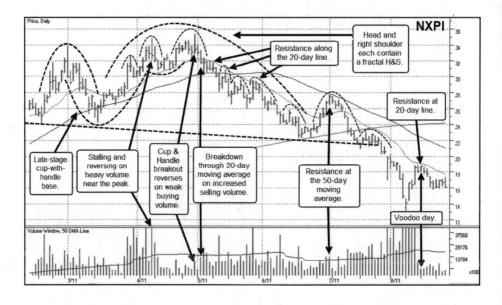

Price, Daily   **NXPI**

Resistance along the 20-day line.

Head and right shoulder each contain a fractal H&S.

Resistance at 20-day line.

Late-stage cup-with-handle base.

Stalling and reversing on heavy volume near the peak.

Cup & Handle breakout reverses on weak buying volume.

Breakdown through 20-day moving average on increased selling volume.

Resistance at the 50-day moving average.

Voodoo day.

Volume Window, 50 DMA Line

Notes: Fabless semiconductor company NXP Semiconductor (NXPI) was a hot IPO in August 2010 that spent 16 weeks building a cup-with-handle base right out of the gate. It then broke out of this base formation and set off on a quick 152-percent upside run. The stock's glory was brief, however, and finally topped after breaking out of a V-shaped cup-with-handle formation in April 2011. As can be seen on the daily chart, that breakout failed in late April. Once the stock failed, it broke below the 20-day moving average and followed the line all the way down until it met up with its 200-day moving average in mid-June. This breakdown formed the right side of the head in what later became a full-blown H&S top. The mid-June low at the 200-day line provided the third point along which the neckline was formed, and the ensuing bounce off the 200-day line ran into resistance right at the 50-day moving average. That then led to a breakdown through the 200-day moving average as well as the H&S neckline. From there the stock never looked back. Overall this was a very straightforward, textbook breakdown with simple entry points along the way that worked in very neat fashion. If only all short-sale target stocks behaved this well on the downside!

Aruba Networks (ARUN) 2011

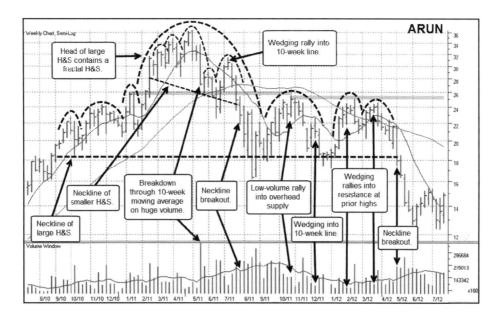

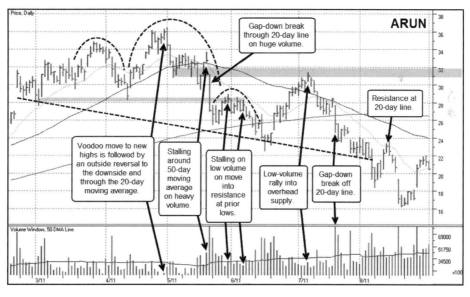

Notes: On August 29, 2010, on a very warm summer day in New York City, I was sitting on the live television stage of Fox Business News spewing my market views to anchors Liz Claman and Cheryl Casone. I was actually constructive on the market at that time, as both I and Chris Kacher were seeing a number of stocks that were acting well. One of these was Aruba Networks (ARUN), a hot new mobile networking company that had just broken out of a short flag formation at around $18 a share. The stock went on to double from there before topping out at 36.40 in early May 2011. The absolute peak occurred as the stock was moving to all-time highs on a very low-volume voodoo day, as can be seen on the daily chart. As the stock broke down from there, it moved along the 20-day and 50-day moving averages in a short bear flag and was shortable along the highs of this formation. Eventually the stock broke down through its 200-day moving average in mid-June 2011, and then rallied back above the 50-day line in early July but right into a short congestion area defined by the lows of the bear flag that formed right after the breakdown off the peak. From there, the stock broke back down to the neckline of a now fully-formed H&S formation. There was one neckline breakout and fake out, but the stock was quite shortable on the bounce back up through the neckline once it ran into the 20-day line in early August. The stock finally came apart in sync with the severe August 2011 general market correction.

■ Tata Motors (TTM) 2011

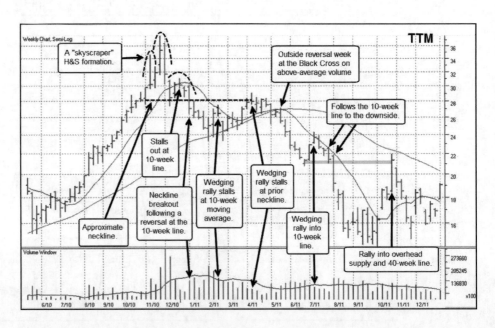

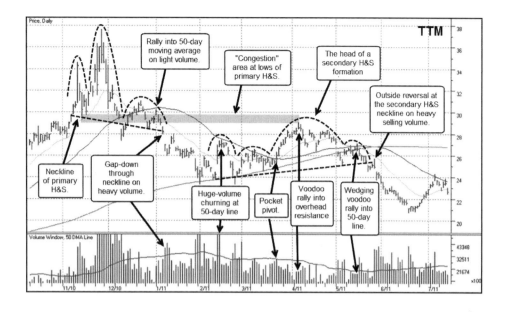

Notes: In 2001, the term *BRIC* led to a hot investment theme, as investors were lured to the strong economic growth of newly developing countries Brazil, Russia, India, and China. As the largest automobile manufacturer in India, Tata Motors (TTM) was a clear BRIC play and had a big upside move off of the 2009 market lows. The stock topped after a climactic run to new highs led to another spastic sort of move to new highs with wide, volatile, daily price ranges in late November 2010. The breakdown off the absolute peak was very severe and formed the right side of the head of a small H&S formation. The ensuing rally back to the upside and just above both the 20-day and 50-day moving averages was shortable and served to form the right shoulder in the narrow H&S pattern. A gap-down through the neckline rallied one time back up into the neckline before splitting wide open all the way down to the 200-day moving average. This was a very profitable move for short-sellers, and it occurred during a general market uptrend. Three months later, as the stock rolled back down through the 200-day moving average, the stock's ensuing breakdown correlated to a sharp general market correction that began in late July 2011.

Intermune (ITMN) 2011

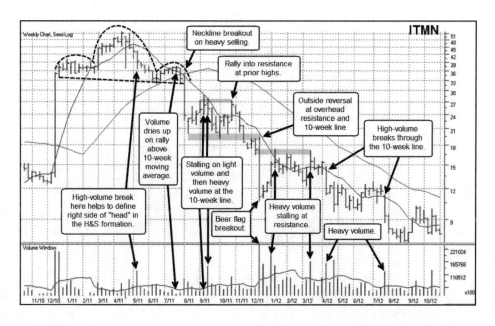

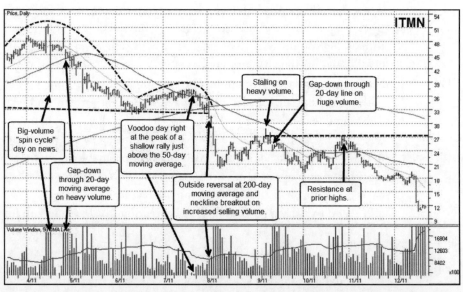

Notes: Intermune (ITMN) in 2011 is an interesting example of a volatile bio-tech that had huge news-related gap moves in both directions in 2010. This sort of action is not uncommon for bio-tech stocks, particularly those that are highly speculative and dependent on the development of a hot new drug. ITMN's first gap move was a "two-stage" gap-up in March of 2010 that took the stock from 14.61 to a high of

39.50 in three days. The stock then based for about five weeks before gapping to the downside on a massive price break that took the stock from 45.44 to 11.38 in one day. On December 17, 2010, the stock then gapped up on a blast from 14.27 to 34.89. This gap move shows up as the long price bar on the left side of the weekly chart. The stock then went on to build a very uniform H&S formation. The breakdown off the peak of the head in the pattern was a volatile affair, but eventually it gapped below the 20-day moving average and stayed there. This then led to a steady decline that remained well below the 20-day line until the stock undercut the lows of the left shoulder in the pattern. This led to a wedging rally that drifted just above the 50-day moving average and which ended on a final voodoo day right at the peak of the rally. The ensuing neckline breakout was also very "clean" in that the stock quickly dropped −35 percent over the next four days in more or less a straight line. This neckline breakout correlated to the sharp August 2011 market correction. The stock then went on to form a 15-week bear flag with one shortable rally up to the top of the bear flag range before the stock broke out through the lows and descended further.

■ Deckers Outdoor (DECK) 2011

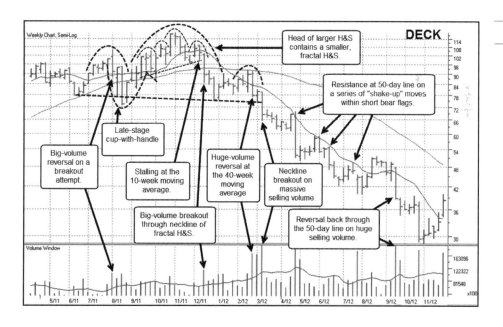

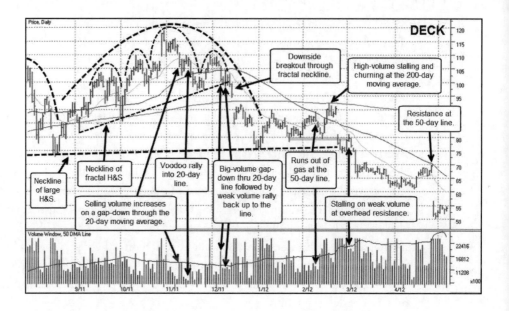

Price, Daily   DECK

Downside breakout through fractal neckline.

High-volume stalling and churning at the 200-day moving average.

Resistance at the 50-day line.

Neckline of fractal H&S.

Voodoo rally into 20-day line.

Big-volume gap-down thru 20-day line followed by weak volume rally back up to the line.

Runs out of gas at the 50-day line.

Neckline of large H&S.

Selling volume increases on a gap-down through the 20-day moving average.

Stalling on weak volume at overhead resistance.

Volume Window, 50 DMA Line

Notes: Shoemaker Deckers Outdoor (DECK) started out looking as a potential LSFB topping formation in August 2011, as it failed on a late-stage breakout attempt in synchrony with the sharp market correction that occurred at that time. The stock broke −31.2 percent off its peak before bottoming and recovering to form a sloppy cup-with-handle formation, from which it attempted to break out in late October. That breakout failed as well and formed the peak of what became the head in a developing H&S top. The initial neckline breakout from the fractal H&S that made up the head of the larger H&S formation was a very profitable downside move. This led to a price break all the way down to the lows of the left shoulder, at which point the stock began to rally and build what eventually became the right shoulder in the larger H&S. The early March 2012 breakout through the neckline of the larger H&S was also profitable. Notice, however, that the late February rally into the 200-day moving average also formed the highs of a bear flag range. The lows of this bear flag ran along the neckline of the larger H&S. From the 200-day line the stock gapped down to the neckline in late February, briefly tried to rally above the neckline, and then sharply broke back to the downside.

Rockwood Holdings (ROC) 2011

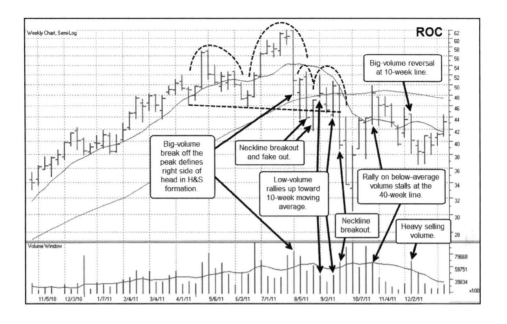

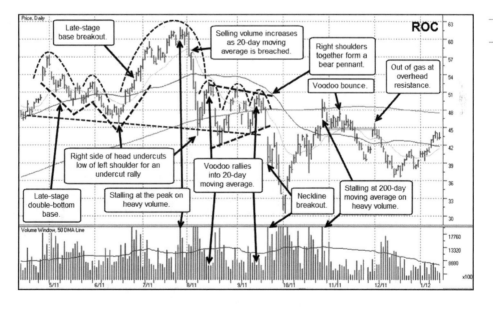

Notes: The absolute peak in chemical name Rockwood Holdings (ROC) occurred at the same time as the sharp August 2011 general market correction. This was a late-stage breakout failure that sent the stock crashing through its 20-day moving average right off the peak and formed the right side of what became the head in a H&S topping formation. The right shoulder complex could also be seen as a bear flag or "pennant" that then broke out to the downside and through the H&S neckline in late September 2011, as the market correction continued to run its course. Notice the voodoo rallies in each of the right shoulder rallies that moved up into the top of a bear pennant and the 50-day moving average.

■ Illumina (ILMN) 2011

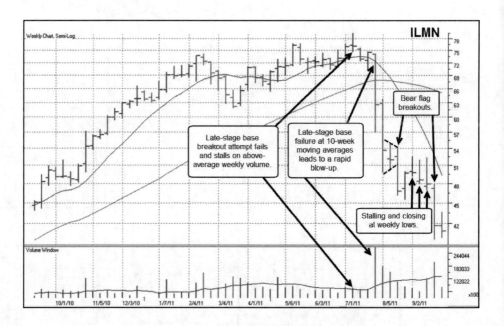

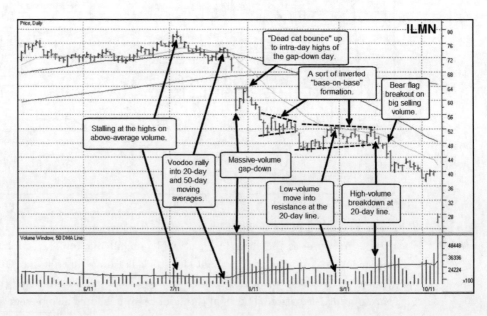

Notes: Illumina (ILMN) makes "life science" tools and systems used in the analysis of genetic variation and function, and so has been a DNA-related biotech/medical leader throughout the New Millennium since it came public in year 2000. The stock had long run from its 85-cent low in 2003 to a peak 47.87 in July of 2008, and then broke down with the rest of the market in September 2008. It then set up again and had another strong price move in 2010 into 2011. In early September 2011, the stock attempted to break out from a seven-week late-stage base and failed. After drifting along the 50-day moving average for two more weeks, the stock began a steady and rapid descent, forming a couple of bear flags on the way down. The second bear flag shows up as three straight weeks where the stock closes at the lows of the weekly range in September 2011. This can be seen as the inverse of weekly supporting action, where instead of closing at the peak of a long weekly range, generally bullish action, the stock closes at the lows of the long weekly ranges in very bearish fashion. Putting this clue on the weekly chart together with the clues provided on the daily, where a clear bear flag can be seen to be forming, would have put short-sellers on "high alert" and ready for a possible downside breakout through the lows of the bear flag.

■ Arch Coal (ACI) 2011

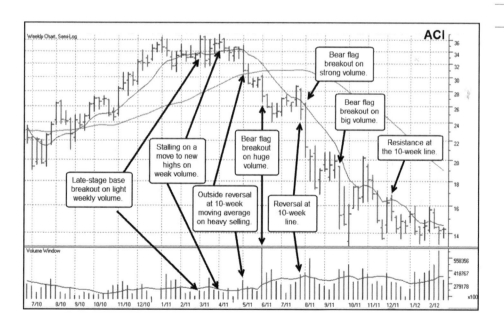

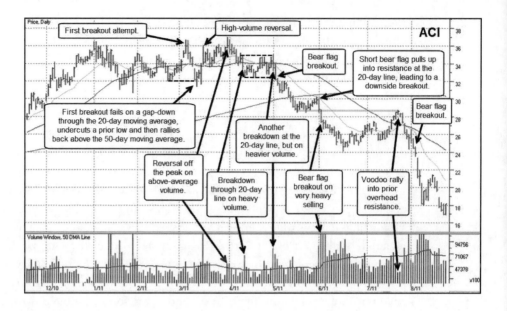

Price, Daily

First breakout attempt.

High-volume reversal.

ACI

Bear flag breakout.

Short bear flag pulls up into resistance at the 20-day line, leading to a downside breakout.

First breakout fails on a gap-down through the 20-day moving average, undercuts a prior low and then rallies back above the 50-day moving average.

Another breakdown at the 20-day line, but on heavier volume.

Bear flag breakout.

Reversal off the peak on above-average volume.

Breakdown through 20-day line on heavy volume.

Bear flag breakout on very heavy selling

Voodoo rally into prior overhead resistance.

Volume Window, 50 DMA Line

Notes: A number of the stuff stocks that broke down in the financial crisis bear market of 2007–2009 recovered after the bottom in March 2009 and had strong recovery moves from there. Many of these moves were quite playable on the upside, and eventually led to shortable tops. Arch Coal (ACI) formed an LSFB top in March and April of 2011 and then broke down in fairly uniform fashion after a failed breakout attempt in late March. This failed breakout could also be seen as the tiny head of a small fractal head and shoulders, although this can be understood and interpreted as an LSFB set-up first. The early April breakdown coincided with a general market correction that began in late April 2011. Once ACI broke down decisively through the 50-day moving average in late April 2011, ACI went on to form a series of bear flags as it stair-stepped its way lower. A voodoo rally in late July 2011 ended at what became the high end of a bear flag range that formed between early June and late July. The sharp breakdown through the 50-day moving average in late July led to a very rapid descent to new lows.

■ Peabody Energy (BTU) 2011

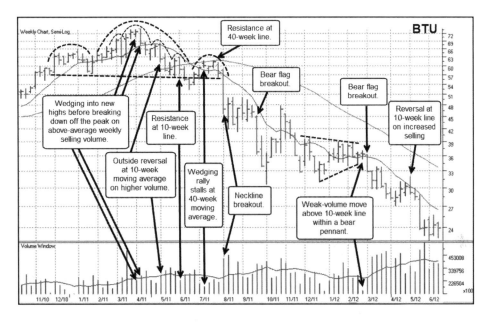

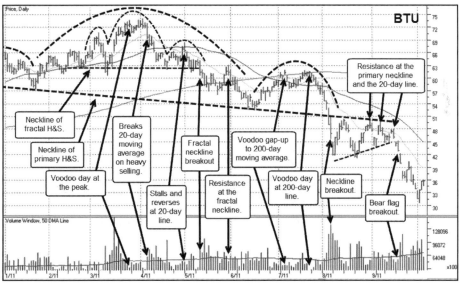

Notes: Peabody Energy was another coal-related stuff stock leader that had a comeback move after the lows of the 2007–2009 bear market. BTU topped at about the same time as ACI, and built a topping formation that is more discernible as an H&S pattern. The head of the larger, overall H&S also contained a smaller, fractal H&S. The fractal neckline was pierced in early May 2011, and three rallies over the next two and a half months all ran into resistance at that neckline. The last two of those rallies also found resistance around the 200-day moving average and together formed the right shoulder of the larger H&S. The breakout through the neckline of the larger H&S led to a decline of about –20 percent before staging a series of rallies back up into the neckline that formed a sort of "ascending triangle" bear pennant. The gap-down through the rising lows of this ascending triangle led to a sharp downside price break.

■ Walter Energy (WLT) 2011

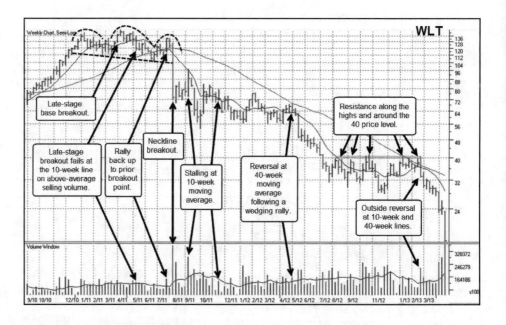

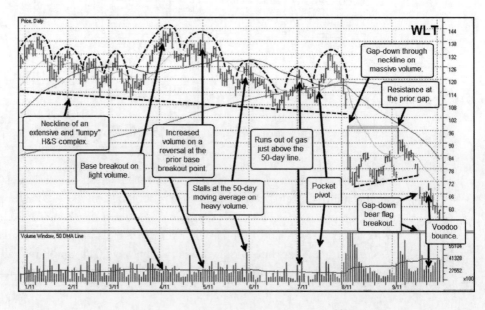

Notes: Walter Energy (WLT) was a third coal-related name that had a comeback rally after the bear market low of March 2009. WLT was unique in that this recovery rally actually took the stock to new highs, well above the 2008 peak it had reached in the prior stuff stock bull market. BTU came within 17 percent of its 2008 high, while ACI only retraced half of its 2008 bear market decline. BTU tried to break out of a late-stage base in early April 2011, but that breakout failed, chopping its way down through the 200-day moving average by late June. At this point WLT almost started to look like it was rounding out a new base as it came back up to the April breakout point, flashing a pocket pivot buy point as it came up the right side of the structure. This rally, however, gave out at the April breakout point and formed the final right shoulder in an overall H&S top. The stock broke out through the neckline of this H&S pattern and plummeted lower during the severe August 2011 general market correction. What is interesting to note here is that the end of this rally in late July 2011 started to pull back off the peak on low volume, giving the pullback a benign, orderly appearance. Once it busted through the 200-day line in early August 2011, however, volume picked up and all bullish bets on the stock at that time were off! The cascading descent included a gap-down neckline breakout that was shortable in early August, and then a second rally in early September right back up to the intra-day highs of the gap-down day. This rally stalled on heavy volume, whereupon the stock simply started losing altitude and tumbled to new lows.

▇ Jones Long LaSalle (JLL) 2011

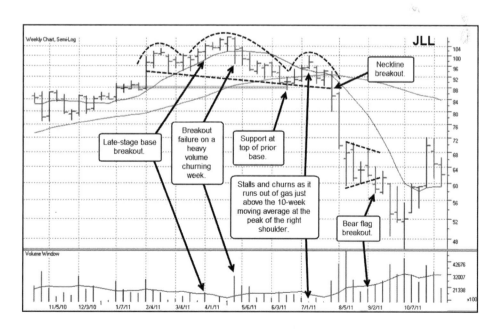

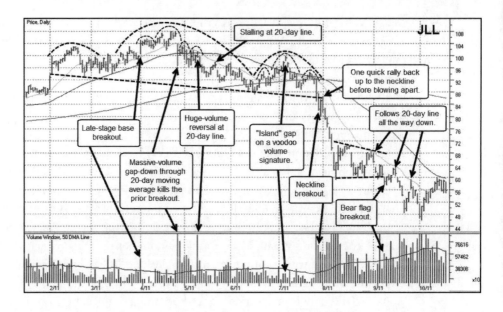

Notes: Jones Long LaSalle (JLL) was a real-estate developer and operator that had a long recovery rally off of the March 2009 lows of the brutal 2007–2009 bear market. As a real-estate-related company, it suffered mightily at the hands of the great financial crisis of that period but was able to recover in 2009 into early 2011 well enough to come within 14 percent of its 2007 peak. JLL failed on an April 2011 late-stage base breakout attempt, gapping below the 20-day moving average in late April on very heavy selling volume. This breakout failure and the subsequent decline to just below the 200-day moving average formed the right side of a head in a large H&S formation. This head also has a smaller, fractal H&S within. The rally off of the 200-day line in June carried beyond the 50-day moving average but ended with an "island gap" voodoo day right at the peak. This formed the top of the right shoulder in the larger H&S but also the head of a fractal H&S that formed inside the right shoulder. Once JLL slashed through the 200-day moving average in late July 2011, selling volume jacked higher as a sharp general market correction took hold. JLL had one brief bounce back into the neckline, and at the outset of August began a steady slide to the downside that accelerated into a final exhaustion gap-down low in early August. It then set up in a one-month bear flag and broke out to fresh lows in mid-September 2011. Note how the stock "obeys" the 20-day moving average all the way down in September.

Kraton Performance Poly (KRA) 2011

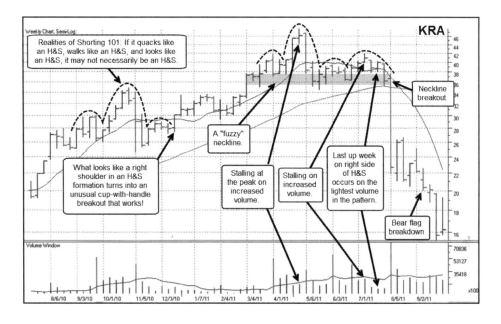

Weekly Chart, Semi-Log

KRA

Realities of Shorting 101: If it quacks like an H&S, walks like an H&S, and looks like an H&S, it may not necessarily be an H&S.

A "fuzzy" neckline.

Neckline breakout.

What looks like a right shoulder in an H&S formation turns into an unusual cup-with-handle breakout that works!

Stalling at the peak on increased volume.

Stalling on increased volume.

Last up week on right side of H&S occurs on the lightest volume in the pattern.

Bear flag breakdown

Volume Window

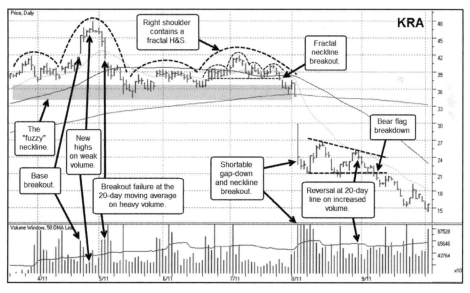

Price, Daily

KRA

Right shoulder contains a fractal H&S.

Fractal neckline breakout.

The "fuzzy" neckline.

New highs on weak volume.

Base breakout.

Breakout failure at the 20-day moving average on heavy volume.

Bear flag breakdown

Shortable gap-down and neckline breakout.

Reversal at 20-day line on increased volume.

Volume Window, 50 DMA Line

Notes: Chemical company Kraton Poly Performance (KRA) came public in December 2010 at $13.60 a share and then set up in a seven-week flat base. It then broke out in early March 2011 and took off on a 210 percent upside ramble before topping out in late April 2011. KRA's top came in the form of a steep late-stage flag breakout failure that also formed a "pinhead" in what became an H&S type topping formation. The second right shoulder of this H&S formation contains within it a smaller, fractal H&S, and the breakout through the fractal neckline in late July 2011 was shortable. The stock then formed a four-day bear flag right above the 200-day moving average and in early August gapped down through the neckline of the larger "pinhead & shoulders" formation. This led to the formation of a "descending triangle" bear flag or pennant, from which it broke out on the downside in early September on massive volume. Note how the stock "obeys" the 20-day moving average on the downside throughout September. Another very interesting point to note is that JLL's bear flag and the action following the bear flag breakout in August and September 2011 are very similar to KRA's, despite the fact that JLL is a real-estate operations and development concern while KRA is a chemical concern making polymers and other compounds for industrial use.

■ Finisar (FNSR) 2011

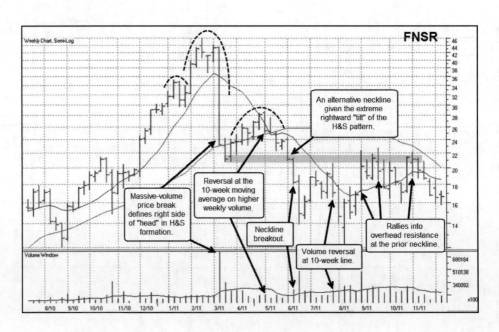

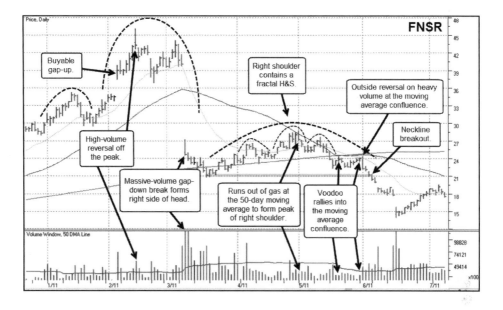

Price, Daily

FNSR

Buyable gap-up.

High-volume reversal off the peak.

Right shoulder contains a fractal H&S.

Outside reversal on heavy volume at the moving average confluence.

Neckline breakout.

Massive-volume gap-down break forms right side of head.

Runs out of gas at the 50-day moving average to form peak of right shoulder.

Voodoo rallies into the moving average confluence.

Volume Window, 50 DMA Line

Notes: Fiber optics maker Finisar (FNSR) had a brief but glorious upside move in early 2011 that ended in a climactic type of top. The daily chart shows that on the final run to the top, the stock was up 12 out of 14 days in a row and the 8th day of the 14-day price run was a buyable gap-up move. FNSR stalled at the peak on heavy volume and then tried to build a short three-week flag formation but failed on a massive gap-down through the 20-day and 50-day moving averages after a poor earnings report in early March 2011. This price break took the stock down to the top of a prior V-shaped cup-with-handle structure it had formed in October and November of 2010, as can be seen on the weekly chart. This led to a rally up into the 50-day moving average in early May 2011 that formed the peak of the right shoulder in a "poster child" H&S formation that resembles the one formed by Crocs (CROX) in 2007–2008, shown previously in this chapter. This right shoulder also contained a smaller, fractal H&S within it, and the downside breakout through the fractal neckline coincided with a breach of the 200-day moving average in the latter half of May. The larger H&S neckline breakout occurred in early June and sent the stock sharply lower over the next two weeks, culminating in a final exhaustion gap-down low in June.

Stratasys (SSYS) 2011

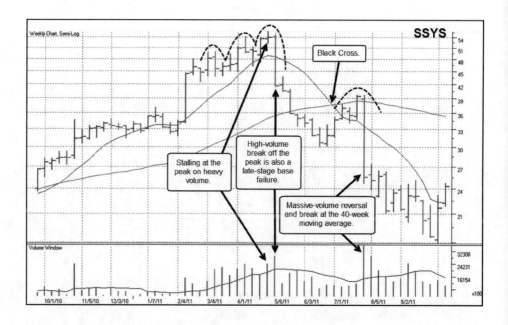

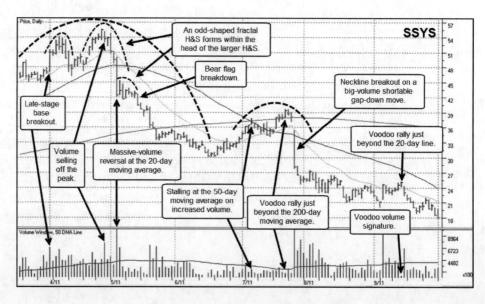

Notes: Three-dimensional (3-D) printing name Stratasys (SSYS) is a unique situation that topped after trying to break out from what is known as an ascending base. On the weekly chart, the last two of the three peaks of this ascending base are indicated with a dotted line showing them as two left shoulders in an overall H&S top. An ascending base is generally characterized as an ascending price channel, where there are three peaks followed by three pullbacks that did not exceed the prior pullback low. The pattern is said to be 9–16 weeks in duration. The first peak in the ascending base occurred in mid-February, and one can easily see how the pattern rolls higher from there with a second peak and pullback in March and a third in April. The breakout from this ascending base in late April failed very quickly as the stock collapsed through the 20-day moving average in early May 2011. The stock descended about 20 percent or so from its peak in three days, formed a six-day bear flag, then continued on down through the 200-day moving average. Downside momentum was lost as the stock bottomed and turned back up through the 20-day line in late June, first finding resistance at the black cross in early July where the 50-day line crossed below the 200-day moving average. SSYS was able to push beyond the 50-day line where it encountered resistance just beyond the 200-day line on a final voodoo up day. From there it gapped back to the downside on a shortable gap-down move in late July and then "limped" lower as it tracks below the 20-day moving average. SSYS's peak in May 2011 correlated to the start of a short-term market correction, and its gap-down through the neckline in late July occurred three months later.

▮ Sina Corp. (SINA) 2011

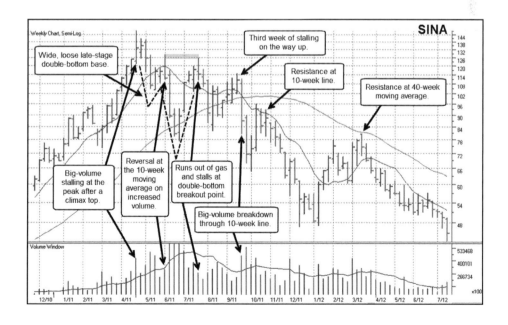

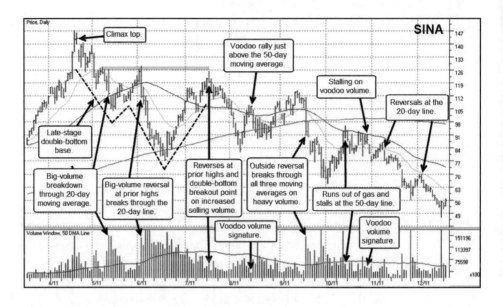

Notes: Chinese Internet names had a decent period of upside price performance that lasted from late 2010 into mid-2011. One of the strongest of these was Sina Corp. (SINA), which peaked in April 2011 on a clear climax top, as can be seen on the daily chart. This led to a sharp decline that led to the first leg down in a massive, wide, loose, late-stage double-bottom base, but the practical reality here is that the stock could have been campaigned on the short side not too long after the April climax top. The midpoint of the big double-bottom W in mid-June 2011 runs into resistance right around a series of peaks that formed around the 20-day moving average in early May. The stock reversed from there on massive volume that sent it knifing through the 50-day and 20-day moving averages. The stock finally bottomed in the latter part of June after undercutting the 200-day moving average and set off on a rally that formed the second leg up in the W pattern. This rally carried right up near to the midpoint of the W and prior resistance where it failed and dropped back below the 200-day line. The weekly chart shows the big stalling reversal weeks at the mid-point and right side peak of the late-stage W formation, and the ensuing breakdown correlates to the severe August 2011 general market correction. SINA's overall top was a very volatile affair that offered many sharp rallies into which one could initiate a short position followed by equally sharp price breaks to the downside. While the long-term downside trend was far from being smooth and orderly, and hence far from anything one might be able to sit through, the overall topping formation was ripe with numerous "swing trade" short-sale opportunities.

Sohu.com (SOHU) 2011

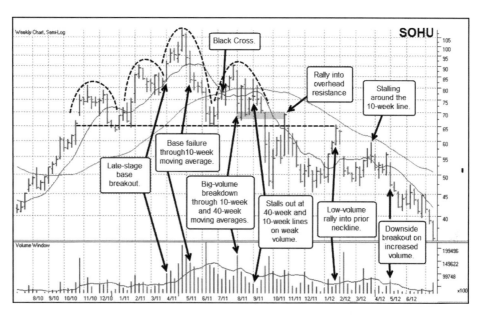

Weekly Chart, Semi-Log

SOHU

Black Cross.

Rally into overhead resistance

Stalling around the 10-week line.

Base failure through 10-week moving average.

Late-stage base breakout.

Big-volume breakdown through 10-week and 40-week moving averages.

Stalls out at 40-week and 10-week lines on weak volume.

Low-volume rally into prior neckline.

Downside breakout on increased volume.

Volume Window

8/10 9/10 10/10 11/10 12/10 1/11 2/11 3/11 4/11 5/11 6/11 7/11 8/11 9/11 10/11 11/11 12/11 1/12 2/12 3/12 4/12 5/12 6/12

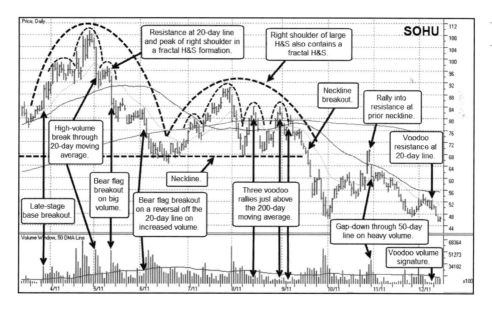

Price, Daily

SOHU

Resistance at 20-day line and peak of right shoulder in a fractal H&S formation.

Right shoulder of large H&S also contains a fractal H&S.

Neckline breakout.

Rally into resistance at prior neckline.

High-volume break through 20-day moving average.

Voodoo resistance at 20-day line.

Bear flag breakout on big volume.

Neckline.

Three voodoo rallies just above the 200-day moving average.

Late-stage base breakout.

Bear flag breakout on a reversal off the 20-day line on increased volume.

Gap-down through 50-day line on heavy volume.

Voodoo volume signature.

Volume Window, 50 DMA Line

4/11 5/11 6/11 7/11 8/11 9/11 10/11 11/11 12/11

Notes: Chinese Internet play Sohu.com (SOHU) also had a strong upside price move during the same period that SINA did, and topped at the same time as SINA in late April 2011. The breakdown off the peak in early May formed what later became the head of a large H&S formation that extended from October 2010 to September 2011. However, the head of this large H&S pattern also contained a smaller, fractal H&D that formed around the peak, as can be seen in the daily chart. The fractal neckline breakout also pierced the 50-day moving average in early May, leading to a sharp downside break. A short bear flag formed from which SINA broke out to the downside before reaching the lows defined by the left shoulders in the larger H&S formation. This led to a rally back up to the neckline of the fractal H&S in late July 2011 that ran into resistance just below the 92 price level and formed the peak of the right shoulder in the larger H&S formation. This right shoulder, however, also contained a fractal H&S within it, and the two fractal right shoulders in this formation were each formed by voodoo rallies back above the 200-day line in August. The final breakdown through the large H&S neckline occurred in mid-September during a general market correction.

■ Ctrip.com (CTRP) 2011

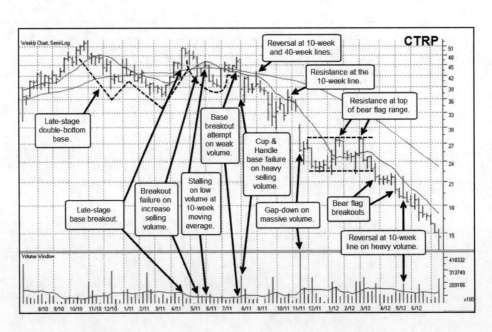

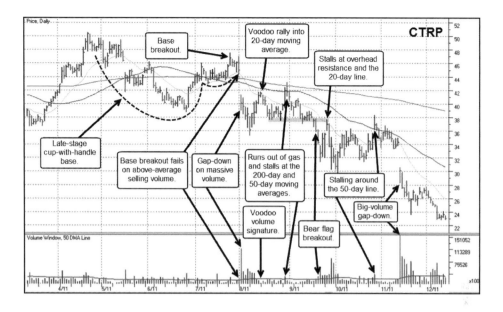

Notes: Chinese Internet travel concern Ctrip.com (CTRP) was a weaker Chinese Internet play in 2010–2011, but its breakdown in 2011 provided many profitable short-sale opportunities. Initially, CTRP began to play out as a late-stage double-bottom base breakout failure, but the stock founds its feet in late June 2011 and attempted to come up the right side of a small cup-with-handle formation, which can be seen on both the daily and weekly charts. The late July breakout attempt from this cup-with-handle base failed quickly, and the stock gapped down through its 20-day, 50-day and 200-day moving averages in early August 2011 just as a sharp general market correction was getting started. The stock rallied back up into the 50-day and 200-day lines in late August before reversing back below the 50-day line and moving to new lows. CTRP's final demise came after it formed a bear flag in October 2011, rallied to the highs of this bear flag range and the 50-day line in late October, and then gapped down as it broke out through the lows of the bear flag in mid-November.

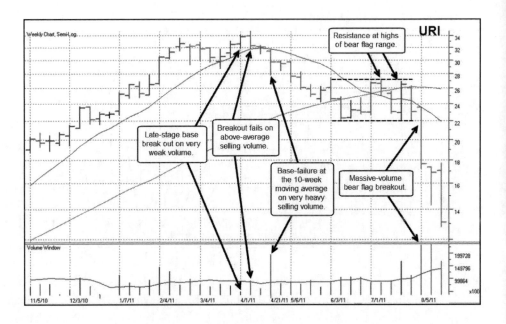

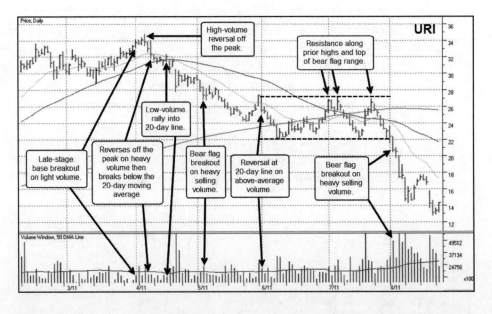

Notes: The rental business might not appear to be the type of dynamic industry context that generally drives big price moves in stocks, but United Rentals (URI) had a strong price move in the latter part of 2010 into the first quarter of 2011. It topped after a late-stage base breakout failed in early April 2011, and once the stock broke down through the 20-day moving average right after the breakout failure, it descended in orderly fashion down to its 200-day moving average over the next two months. From there the stock zigged and zagged back and forth as it built a wide and loose bear flag throughout June and most of July 2011. The downside breakout through the lows of this bear flag occurred in synchrony with the severe general market correction at that time and sent the stock moving sharply to the downside.

■ Youko Tuduo (YOKU) 2011

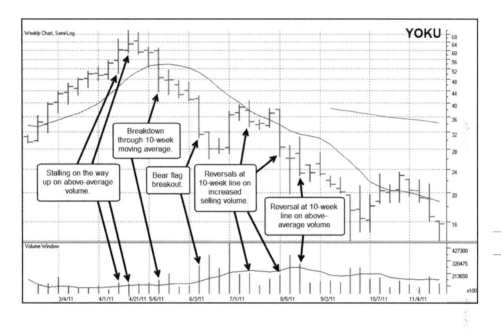

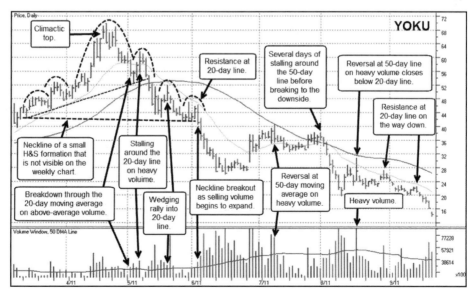

Notes: Youku Tudou (YOKU) was a hot Chinese Internet content IPO in December 2010 that had a brief but brilliant run after forming an "improper" double-bottom IPO base. The run was not quite eight weeks in duration before the stock topped in April 2011, and YOKU completely reversed that upside move and more over the next eight weeks, eventually dropping all the way to within a dollar of its $12.80 December 2010 IPO price by September 2011. On the weekly chart, one cannot outline an H&S formation, since there are no up weeks in the downtrend from late April to late June 2011. On the daily chart, however, we can see a smaller, fractal H&S form. The breakdown through the 50-day moving average can also be seen as a neckline breakout through an alternative ascending fractal neckline, the thinner of the two dotted necklines on the chart, and the stock could have been shorted at that point. The breakout through the lower neckline is also shortable, and leads to a quick 35.6-percent spill over the next nine days. The decline off of the late April peak to the mid-June low was the "fat" part of YOKU's decline, and occurred during a general market correction that covered the exact same time period.

■ Goldman Sachs (GS) 2011

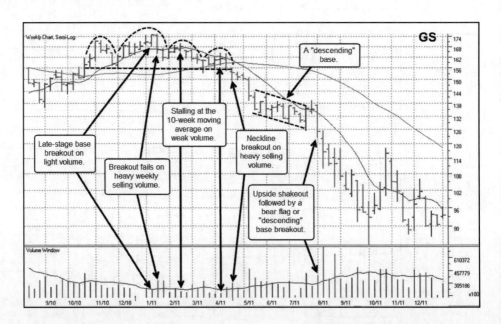

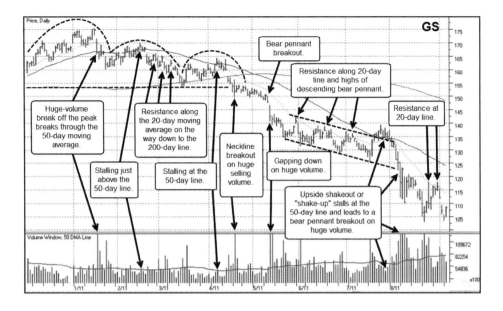

Price, Daily

GS

Huge-volume break off the peak breaks through the 50-day moving average.

Resistance along the 20-day moving average on the way down to the 200-day line.

Bear pennant breakout.

Resistance along 20-day line and highs of descending bear pennant.

Resistance at 20-day line.

Stalling just above the 50-day line.

Stalling at the 50-day line.

Neckline breakout on huge selling volume.

Gapping down on huge volume.

Upside shakeout or "shake-up" stalls at the 50-day line and leads to a bear pennant breakout on huge volume.

Volume Window, 50 DMA Line

Notes: Big-stock financial Goldman Sachs (GS) had a steady price decline during 2011 that wasn't preceded by a big upside run. In fact, the stock simply dropped out of a long, 18-month cup-with-handle formation where the handle of this long base formed as a head and shoulders pattern. A late-stage breakout attempt in mid-January 2011 started the stock out on its downward journey, and once the stock gapped down through the 200-day moving average in mid-April 2011, the descent began to accelerate. Another gap-down in the early part of May took the stock through the lows of a short bear pennant, and the stock then meandered lower in what looks like the inverse of an ascending base, which we should probably dub a *descending bear base*. An upside shakeout or shake-up in late July took the stock just above the 50-day moving average before it reversed and plummeted to the downside at the same time as the severe general market correction at that time.

■ Mellanox Technologies (MLNX) 2012

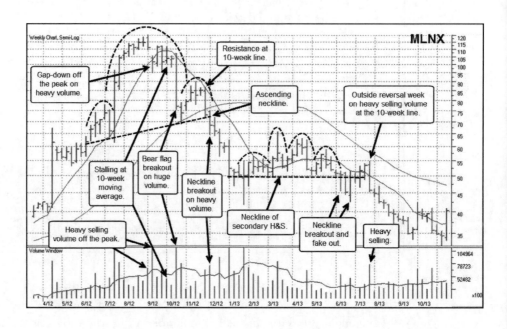

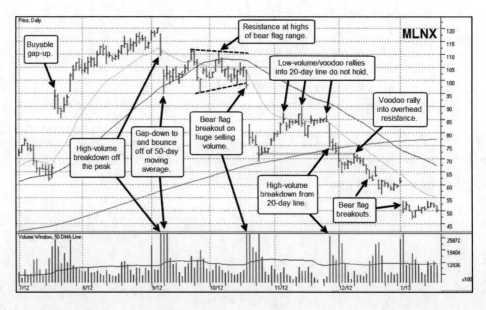

Notes: Israel-based Mellanox Technologies (MLNX) was strong leading fabless semiconductor play in 2012. The company produced chips based on the InfiniBand architecture that sped up the transmission of data throughout the cloud. Its sharp upside price move was brief by most standards, extending from April to early September 2012. The breakdown off the peak occurred on a high-volume drop through the 20-day moving average in early September. After establishing a short-term low around the 50-day moving average the stock meandered up and down to form a four-week bear flag below the 10-week moving average. MLNX then broke out through the lows of this bear flag, and the following day gapped down on a rapid descent to the 200-day moving average. A bounce off of the 200-day line found resistance along the 20-day moving average, and this served to form the peak of the right shoulder in what had evolved into a large H&S formation with an ascending neckline. The reversal along the 20-day line in late November 2012 was an optimal short-sale entry point, and the stock set off on a steady downside descent that undercut the late October low. This led to a very short undercut and rally move back up into overhead resistance, and from there the stock descended to new lows as it remained below the 20-day line.

▨ Broadvision (BVSN) 2012

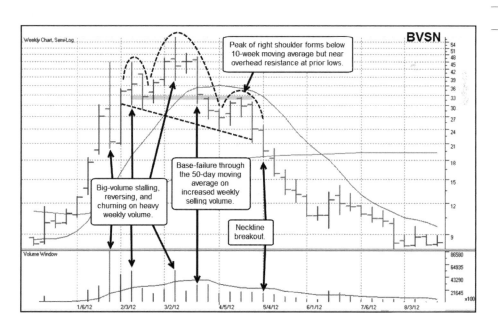

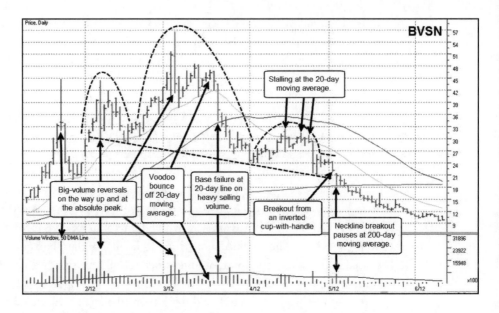

Price, Daily — BVSN

Stalling at the 20-day moving average.

Big-volume reversals on the way up and at the absolute peak.

Voodoo bounce off 20-day moving average.

Base failure at 20-day line on heavy selling volume.

Breakout from an inverted cup-with-handle

Neckline breakout pauses at 200-day moving average.

Volume Window, 50 DMA Line

Notes: Internet software maker Broadvision (BVSN) was an interesting "flameout" type of short-sale play in 2012 that had a quick nine-week run before topping out in a short H&S formation. The entire descent off of the peak was not as rapid as the prior ascent, but it was as complete, as it erased all of BVSN's upside move and then some. The high-volume reversal off the peak in March 2012 was the first sign of trouble, and this was eventually confirmed later in the month when the stock slashed through its 20-day moving average on heavy selling volume. This descent continued through the 50-day moving average, and BVSN eventually found support along the 24 price level before rallying up to the 20-day line. Three days of stalling along the 20-day line ensued before the stock collapsed down to what was now the neckline of a fully-formed H&S formation. The neckline breakout that occurred in synchrony with a general market correction in May 2012 then led to a steady downtrend that eventually took the stock to an all-time low at 7.80.

Vivus (VVUS) 2012

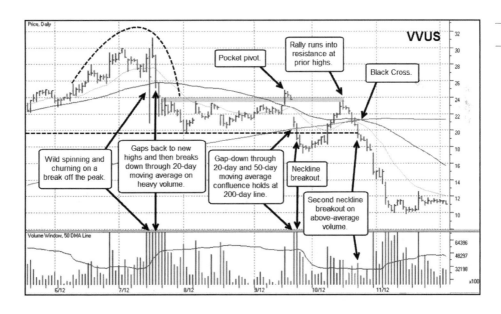

Notes: Biotech company Vivus (VVUS) was a big erectile-dysfunction play in the 1990s, but the development of therapies for obesity and sleep apnea helped drive a second price run in 2012. A big news-related gap-up in late February 2012 sent the stock doubling overnight from just over 10 to just over 20, and the ensuing trek higher eventually topped out at 31.21 in mid-July 2012. The initial breakdown off the peak was a volatile affair, but eventually the stock collapsed after a breakout attempt from a short flag formation in mid-July gave way. The stock found support in early August along the lows of a prior flag base it had formed in March 2012, and this helped to define an initial neckline for an evolving H&S top. A pocket pivot buy point in mid-September 2012 did not last long, as the stock then gapped back down to the neckline and then staged a neckline breakout and fake out as it turned back to the upside to test the mid-September high. This rally then failed as the stock dropped below the 50-daily and 200-day moving averages on higher selling volume. Notice also that shortly after this breach of the two moving averages, a black cross formed where the 50-day line moves below the 200-day line. This led to a second neckline breakout that worked, and VVUS collapsed to new lows.

◼ Chipotle Mexican Grill (CMG) 2012

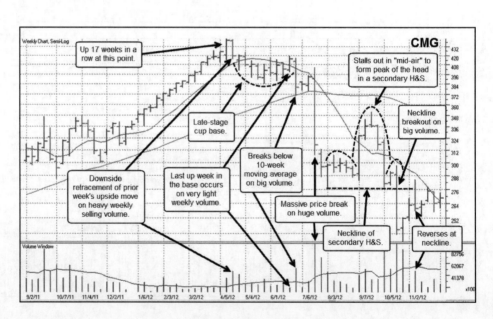

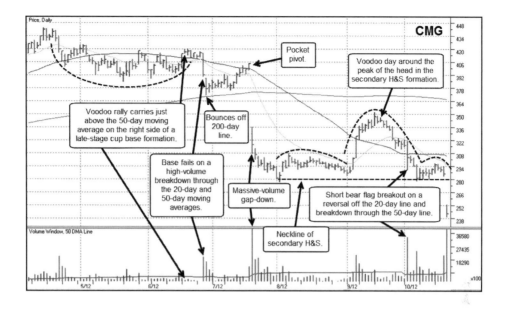

Notes: Mexican "healthy" fast-food restaurant Chipotle Mexican Grill (CMG) had a steady upside price move in 2012. The stock was looking quite powerful by early April 2012 after closing up for 17 weeks in a row. That 17-week run reversed on heavy volume right off the peak, and the stock corrected in what was looking like a normal but potentially late-stage "cup-like" base in June. CMG was tracking tight along its 50-day line at that time, but a sudden high-volume break below the 50-day and 20-day moving averages sent the stock through the lows of the cup base and down to the 200-day moving average. That engendered a logical upside bounce right up to the 50-day line where a pocket pivot buy point can be seen on the daily chart. This was abruptly slammed on a massive-volume downside gap following a bad earnings report. This gap-down could have been shorted for a relatively small amount of further downside play, but CMG quickly found its feet and began to work its way back up through the 50-day moving average. Buying interest soon waned near the peak of what became the head of a secondary H&S formation that formed from August to October 2012 and below the prior failed cup base. Once CMG dropped back below the 20-day line in late September 2012, it formed a three-day bear flag before breaking out to the downside and through the 50-day line. Another short bear flag formed in October that also made up the right shoulder of the secondary H&S. CMG then gapped down through the neckline and on to lower lows.

■ Select Comfort (SCSS) 2012

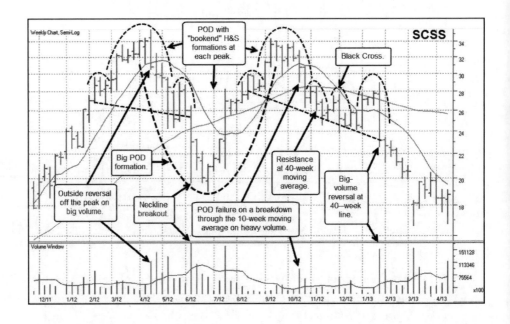

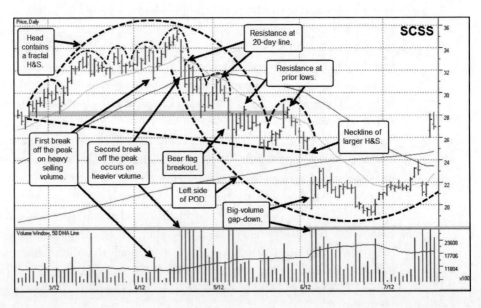

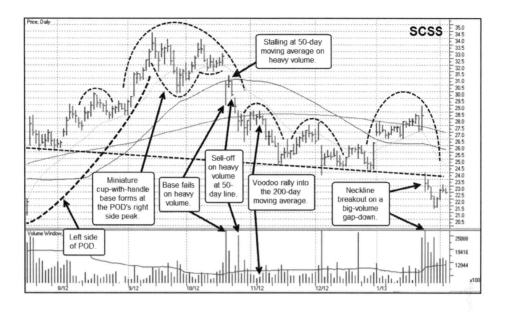

Price, Daily

Stalling at 50-day moving average on heavy volume.

Sell-off on heavy volume at 50-day line.

Miniature cup-with-handle base forms at the POD's right side peak.

Base fails on heavy volume.

Voodoo rally into the 200-day moving average.

Neckline breakout on a big-volume gap-down.

Volume Window.

Left side of POD.

Notes: Mattress retailer Select Comfort (SCSS) was a big POD top in 2012 that could have been shorted at both ends. The left side of the POD formed as an LSBF in mid-April 2012, and once the stock dropped below the 20-day moving average, it actually continued to descend along the moving average all the way down to its late June 2012 lows. Thus rallies into the 20-day line provided potential short-sale entry points as the downtrend developed. As SCSS descended below the 50-day moving average, it began to evolve into an H&S top, gapping down through the neckline in early June 2012. However, this neckline breakout did not lead to very much in the way of further downside, and SCSS started up the right side of what would become a completed POD topping formation by October 2012. The right side peak of the POD came in the form of a short, late-stage cup-with-handle base failure when CMG gapped below its 20-day and 50-day moving averages in the latter part of October 2012. A stalling day right at the 50-day line provided a short-sale entry point, and the stock descended below the 200-day moving average from there. An undercut of the 200-day line led to a voodoo-rally into the 200-day line and three right shoulders began to form in what evolved into an H&S topping pattern. A final gap-down through the neckline of that H&S sent SCSS to new lows.

■ Apple (AAPL) 2012

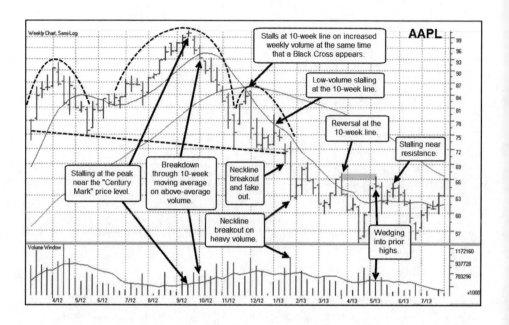

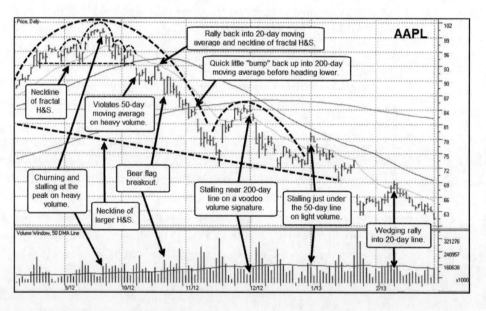

Notes: This example of Apple (AAPL) in 2012 was discussed in detail in the Chapter 5 Case Study.

Cirrus Logic (CRUS) 2012

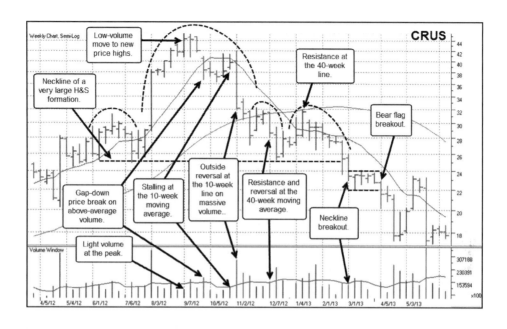

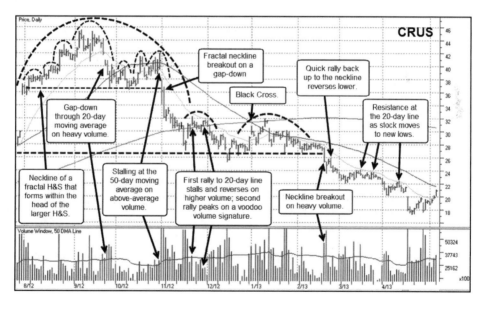

Notes: As a supplier to Apple (AAPL), Cirrus Logic (CRUS) often correlated to price movements in AAPL. When AAPL was in an uptrend, so was CRUS, and when AAPL topped in late 2012, so did CRUS. In early September 2012, CRUS was making new highs on light weekly volume, and toward the end of the month it failed and broke down through its 20-day and 50-day moving averages. A series of rallies into and just above the 50-day line in October formed the right shoulders of a smaller, fractal H&S formation that made up the head of what later became a larger H&S formation. The downside breakout through the fractal neckline in early November sent CRUS tumbling through its 200-day moving average, leading to the formation of a nearly three-month long bear flag that also forms the right shoulders in the larger H&S. A final rally up into the 200-day line marked the highs of this bear flag range and the peak of the second right shoulder, and occurred just after a black cross. The breakout through the neckline of the large H&S led to a steady descent from there that tracks just below the 20-day line.

◼ Lululemon Athletica (LULU) 2013

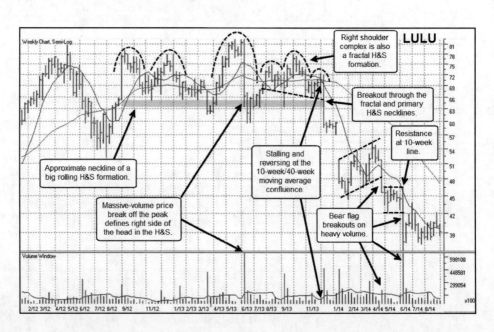

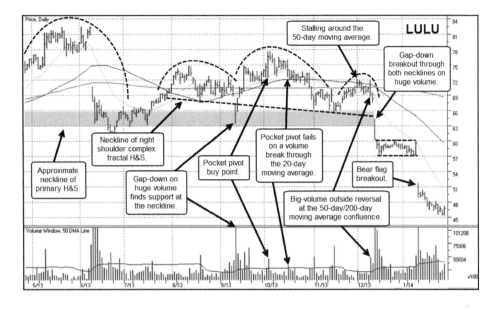

Notes: Lululemon Athletica (LULU) is discussed in detail in Chapter 4.

■ LinkedIn (LNKD) 2013

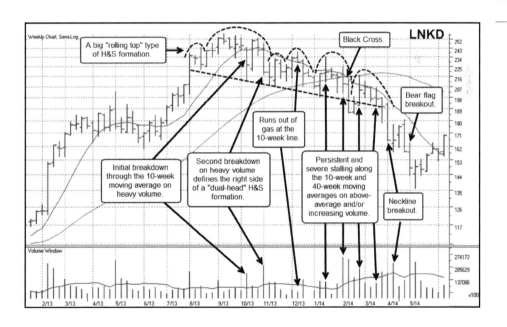

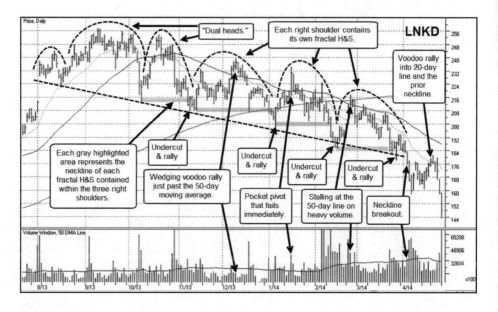

Notes: Business-oriented social-media name LinkedIn (LNKD) was a hot IPO in May 2011 that turned out to be rather cold. LNKD came public at $45 a share on May 20, 2011 and immediately launched to a high of 122.70 on its first day of trading. From there, however, the stock went nowhere as it dropped to a low of 55.98 by early December. Eventually, the stock completed a long, wide-ranging post-IPO consolidation and eventually broke out in February 2013 at 125.50. This led to a price move that carried as high as 257.60 before the stock lost momentum and built a long, rolling top that can be seen as a "mountain range" type of H&S pattern. This slow, rolling descent off the peak also looks like a downside trend channel where the lows of the channel formed a descending neckline to the H&S formation. The best way to play this descent, as it turned out, was to short LNKD into the rallies that carried up to the highs of the descending price channel. Eventually LNKD broke out through its neckline in early April 2014, broke to lower lows, and then "voodoo'd" its way back up into the neckline and the 20-day moving average before finding resistance and turning back to the downside and lower lows.

Nationstar Mortgage Holdings (NSM) 2013

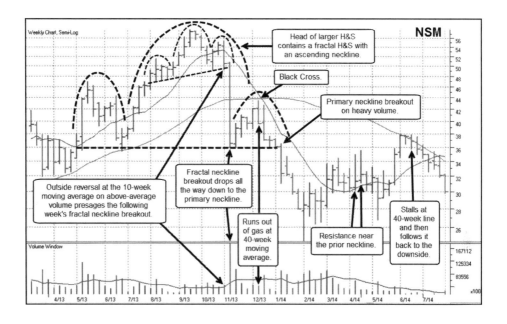

Weekly Chart, Semi-Log

NSM

Head of larger H&S contains a fractal H&S with an ascending neckline.

Black Cross.

Primary neckline breakout on heavy volume.

Outside reversal at the 10-week moving average on above-average volume presages the following week's fractal neckline breakout.

Fractal neckline breakout drops all the way down to the primary neckline.

Runs out of gas at 40-week moving average.

Resistance near the prior neckline.

Stalls at 40-week line and then follows it back to the downside.

Volume Window

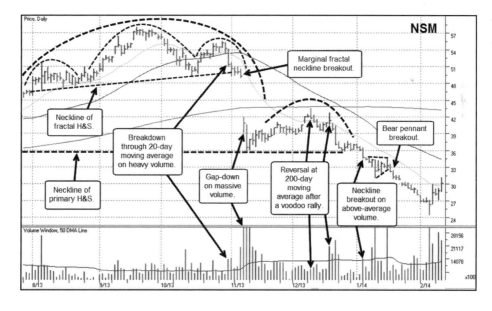

Price, Daily

NSM

Marginal fractal neckline breakout.

Neckline of fractal H&S.

Breakdown through 20-day moving average on heavy volume.

Bear pennant breakout.

Gap-down on massive volume.

Reversal at 200-day moving average after a voodoo rally.

Neckline breakout on above-average volume.

Neckline of primary H&S.

Volume Window, 50 DMA Line

Notes: As the great financial crisis of 2008 sorted itself out following massive injections of liquidity, otherwise known as *quantitative easing* or *QE* for short, from the Fed that began in late 2009, mortgage-servicing stocks became hot plays in 2012 and 2013. Nationstar Mortgage (NSM) was one of the big-stock leaders in the group, and after it came public in March 2012 at $13 a share it formed an eight-week flat base and then launched on a strong upside price run. NSM eventually topped in September 2013 at 57.95 after failing from a short five-week base in late October as it broke below the 20-day and 50-day moving averages on heavy selling volume. This led to the formation of a fractal H&S pattern that formed inside of what later became the head of a larger H&S. A gap-down below the 200-day moving average in early November found support along the lows of a base the stock had formed in May and June of 2013, and the ensuing rally formed the right shoulder in a very large H&S topping formation. The peak of the right shoulder found ready resistance at the 200-day line and the stock dropped back down to the larger H&S neckline, formed a short six-day bear flag, and then broke out through the neckline and the short bear flag. This breakdown occurred just before a short-term general market correction in late January 2014.

■ Ocwen Financial (OCN) 2013

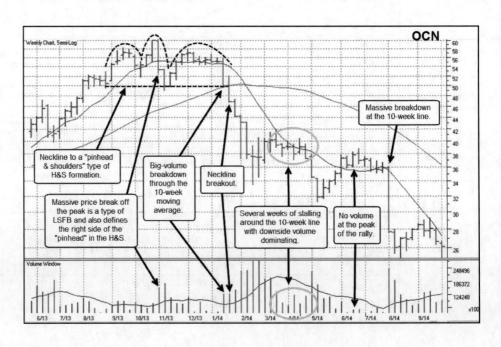

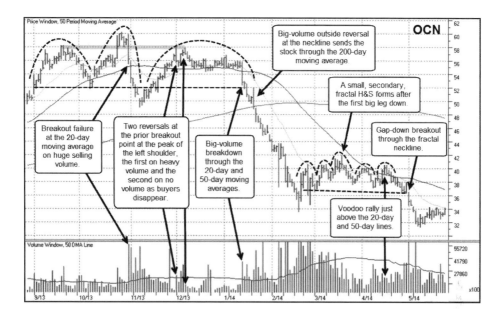

Notes: Ocwen Financial (OCN) was another big-stock mortgage-servicing play, but having come public way back in 1996 it was not a "hot IPO" play in the group. It did, however, have a big price run in 2012 and 2013 as the group caught fire. OCN topped in late October 2013 at the same time as NSM after a breakout attempt at that time failed when the stock broke below the 20-day and 50-day moving averages on heavy volume. This breakdown off the peak undercut the early October lows and then rallied right back up to the prior failed breakout point, as can be seen in the daily chart. This rally served to form a right shoulder in what had by then developed into an H&S top. The high-volume breakdown through the 50-day line in January 2014 sent the stock collapsing through the neckline and well beyond its 200-day moving average before it finally found a low in late February and began rallying up into the 20-day and 50-day lines. The neckline breakout correlated to a short-term general market correction in January 2013. As it ran into the 50-day line in April, it was forming the right shoulders of a small, fractal H&S formation. The ensuing downside breakout through this fractal neckline sent the stock to lower lows, and at the time of this writing [October 2014], the stock is continuing to make fresh lows below the 20 price level.

Angie's List (ANGI) 2013

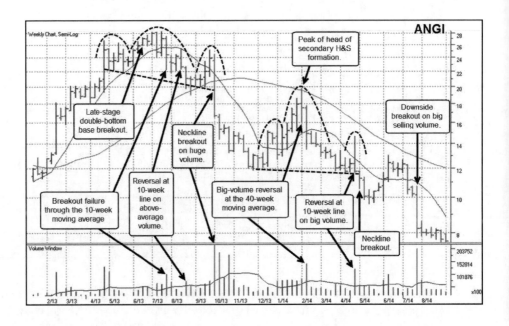

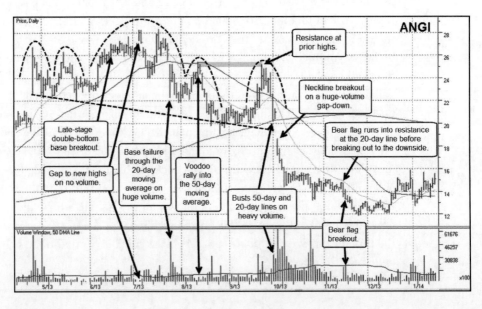

Notes: Online customer review sites caught investors' attention in 2013, as names like Yelp (YELP) and Angie's List (ANGI) had strong runs. In this example, we see one of the weaker names in the group, ANGI, as it topped in July 2013 and then broke down from an H&S formation in early October. While the stock didn't really have what one could call a big upside price run, the ensuing decline off the peak did eventually exceed –75 percent, and in our view that qualifies as a shortable downtrend! The peak in early July occurred after the late-stage double-bottom base breakout attempt failed. There was one "re-breakout" attempt in the latter part of the month, but once the stock gapped down below the 50-day moving average in late July, that price level served as strong upside resistance on ensuing rallies. The rally in early August failed right at the 50-day line, sending the stock to lower lows where it temporarily bottomed to form the neckline of an evolving H&S pattern. The final rally back up through the 50-day line in late September found resistance at the prior base-failure point and forms the second right shoulder in the H&S pattern. A high-volume reversal at that point carried through the 50-day moving average and led to a gap-down neckline breakout in early October. The stock then formed two short bear flags in October and November, what you might call a "base-under-base," and then broke out to new lows in mid-November. ANGI's overall top and price breakdown in 2013 did not correlate to the general market action. The peak price in the rally occurred as the general market was in fact coming off the lows of a short-term correction.

■ Rackspace Holdings (RAX) 2013

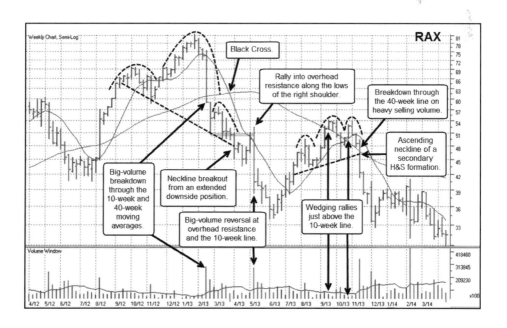

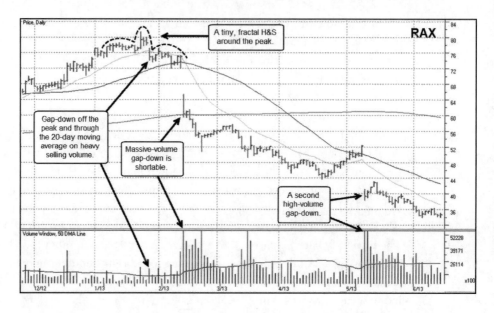

Notes: Rackspace Hosting (RAX) was a big cloud play in 2013 as a provider of managed hosting services. In other words, RAX rented out space on its cloud-based data centers to companies that didn't want to build the hardware and software infrastructure necessary for cloud-based operations. RAX had a stellar price run from the initial first-stage breakout at 11.67 in May 2008 to its 81.36 price peak in January 2013. At the peak, the general market was still rallying, but RAX failed on a breakout attempt from a short flag formation, gapping below its 20-day moving average in late January. The stock tracked along the space between the 20-day and 50-day moving averages before gapping down in the earlier half of February on heavy volume. This gap-down could have been shorted, as the stock never came close to the intra-day high of that gap-down day. It quickly dropped below the 200-day moving average and was not able to mount any kind of rally until late April 2013. That resulted in a pocket pivot buy point coming up through the 50-day line in early May that failed the next day on a massive-volume gap-down. Note that once RAX went into the steady downtrends that characterized the action from mid-February to late April, and then from early May and beyond on the daily chart, the 20-day moving average would have provided a very effective upside guide for a moving trailing stop.

Solar Winds (SWI) 2013

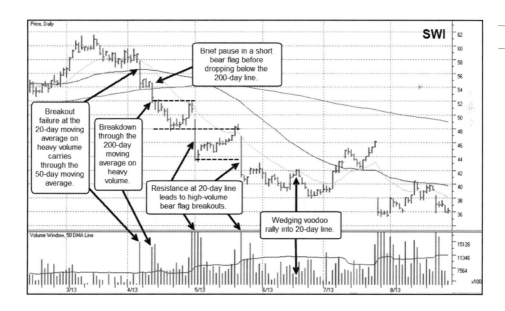

Notes: Solar Winds (SWI) had a strong price run that began in late 2011 and continued until early 2013. As a provider of network management software, SWI was another cloud play during that period. SWI started out as a big, ugly, wide, and loose late-stage cup-with-handle base failure. SWI broke down through the lows of its handle and the 50-day moving average in early April 2013, triggering an orderly price decline that formed several bear flags on the way down. After busting through the 50-day line, SWI formed a short three-day flag right on top of the 200-day moving average and then broke out to the downside, formed another bear flag that ran into resistance at the 20-day moving average, broke out to the downside again, and formed yet another bear flag that found resistance around the 20-day line. SWI then broke out through the lows of that final bear flag and then limped lower, following the 20-day line to new price lows before it was able to turn back above the line in early July 2013. Certain price breaks within SWI's overall downtrend occurred in synchrony with short-term general market corrections in 2013, but during its entire decline it moved lower as the general market moved higher.

◼ Ruckus Wireless (RKUS) 2013

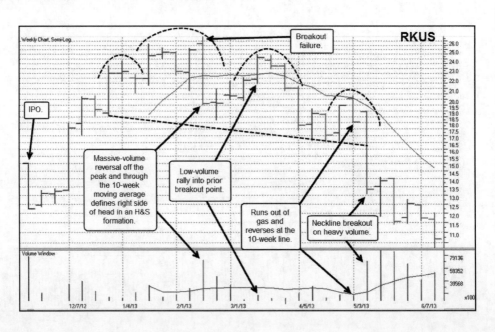

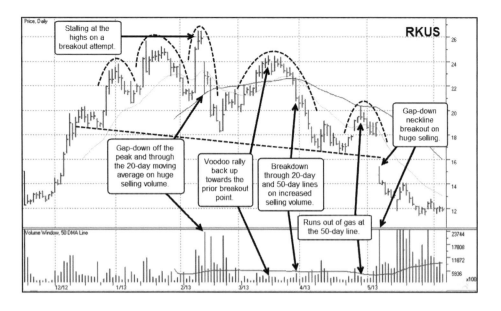

Notes: Ruckus Wireless (RKUS) was another one of these "flameout" IPOs that had a quick run after it came public in November 2012 and quickly doubled over the next 13 weeks. RKUS was another cloud-variant play, but its life span was brief. A breakout attempt from a volatile flag formation in February 2013 failed on a high-volume gap-down through the 20-day moving average that sent the stock through the 50-day moving average over the next two days. That descent came to an end as the stock found support along the lows of a short flag pattern it had formed in December 2012. A rally from there ran out of gas in late March near the prior failed breakout point as buying volume dried up in voodoo fashion. RKUS then rolled over to complete the peak of a right shoulder in a developing head and shoulders top. That descent back down through the 50-day line saw the stock close down for 14 days in a row before it finally sputtered back up towards the 50-day line in late April 2013. A reversal at the line took RKUS back below its 20-day moving average. A couple of days later the stock gapped-down through the neckline of its H&S topping formation and on to lower lows.

▪ Intuitive Surgical (ISRG) 2013

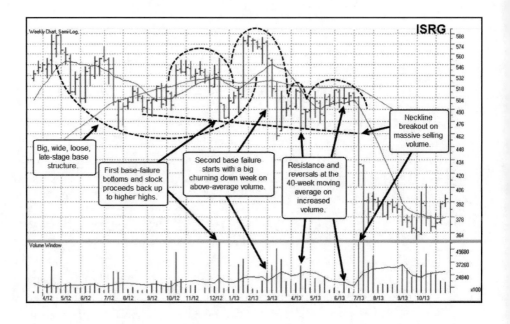

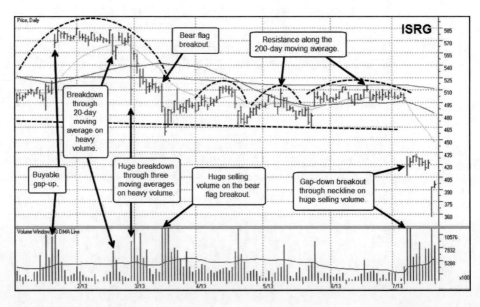

Notes: Intuitive Surgical (ISRG) is best known for its Da Vinci® robotic surgery devices, and had a big recovery move to all-time highs following the early 2009 lows of the prior 2007–2009 bear market. In early 2013, ISRG finally began to show signs of a top when it failed from a late-stage base in February. The break off the peak started with a huge-volume downside break in late February that saw the stock gap-up the very next day where it found resistance at the 20-day moving average and then reversed course, moving to lower lows over the next two weeks. ISRG then undercut the lows of the big, ugly base structure that was formed between May 2012 and February 2013. This led to the formation of a series of right shoulders within a developing H&S top. These right shoulders also have the look of a single, long bear flag formation that runs along the underside of the 40-week and 200-day moving averages on the weekly and daily charts, respectively. A gap-down breakout through the neckline of the H&S and the lows of the right shoulder complex/bear flag was a shortable gap-down move that saw the stock move to lower lows. Interestingly, this neckline/bear flag breakout occurred as the general market moved to new highs.

■ Cree (CREE) 2014

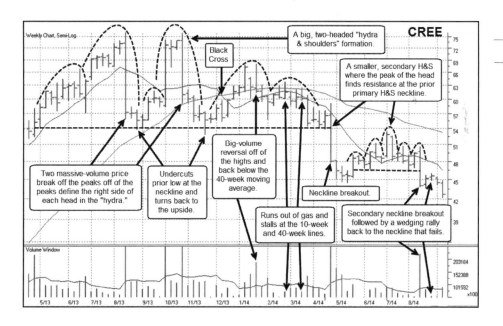

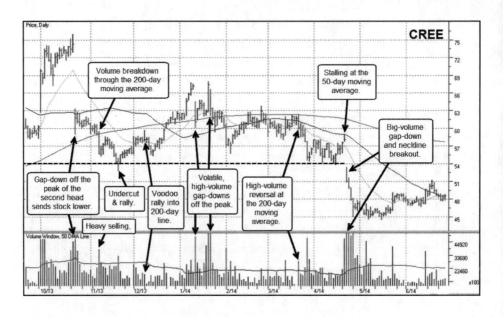

Price, Daily

CREE

Volume breakdown
through the 200-day
moving average.

Stalling at the
50-day moving
average.

Big-volume
gap-down
and neckline
breakout.

Gap-down off the
peak of the
second head
sends stock lower.

Undercut
& rally.

Voodoo
rally into
200-day
line.

Volatile,
high-volume
gap-downs
off the peak.

High-volume
reversal at
the 200-day
moving
average.

Heavy selling.

Volume Window, 50 DMA Line

Notes: LED-lighting manufacturer Cree (CREE) is a very unusual example of an extended H&S formation that has two heads—a sort of "hydra and shoulders" formation. By the end of September 2013, CREE looked very much like a textbook H&S top that was merely setting up for lower lows. The big price break off of the peak occurred on a huge gap-down following a disappointing earnings report to form the right side of head, and this was followed by a rally into the 10-week moving average that looked to be forming a vulnerable right shoulder. But the stock fooled would-be short-sellers and rocketed back up to its prior highs in early October, only to gap-down and give up all of those gains in the latter part of the month. That gap-down did in fact lead to lower lows as the stock broke below the 200-day moving average in early November, eventually finding a bottom along the prior lows in what became a hydra and shoulders formation extending back to May 2013. At this point, with two massive-volume gap-downs in the pattern, the stock was somewhat "sold out" and so needed some time to work off this arguably oversold condition. That occurred over the next five months as CREE went on to build two right shoulders. Notice how the action following the late October gap-down and extending through April 2014 has the look of a fractal H&S within the right shoulder complex. A final low-volume rally into the 200-day moving average reversed on heavy volume in late March 2014, and the stock dropped down to the neckline of the hydra and shoulders formation. One last rally into the 50-day line was followed by a gap-down neckline breakout on heavy volume that moved lower over the following three days.

3D Systems (DDD) 2014

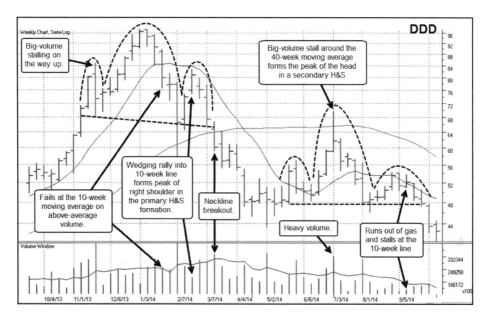

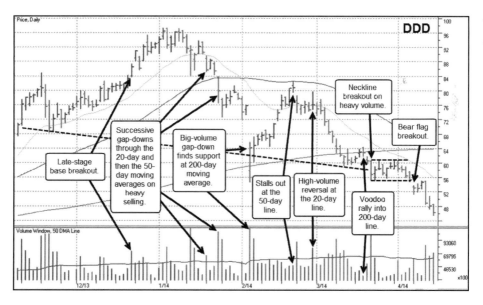

Notes: 3D Systems (DDD) is discussed in detail in the Chapter 8 Case Study.

Stratasys (SSYS) 2014

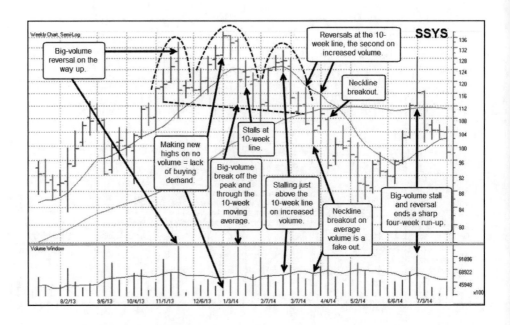

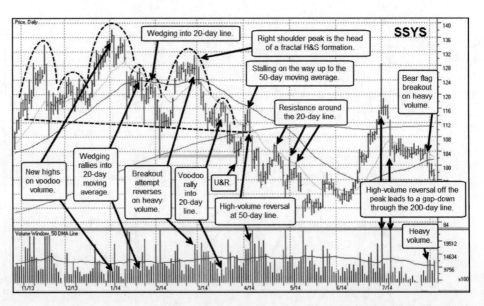

Notes: The top in 3D Systems (DDD) was part of a group top when other previously hot 3-D printing names joined the topping party in 2014, including Stratasys (SSYS). SSYS's 2014 top is discussed in detail in Chapter 4.

■ Exone Company (XONE) 2014

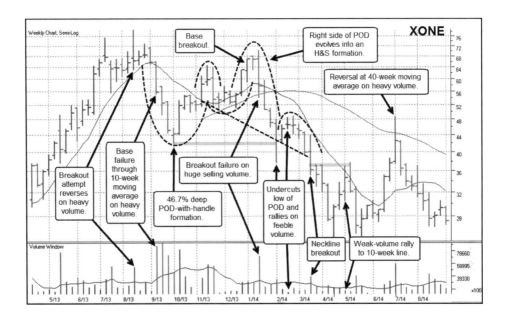

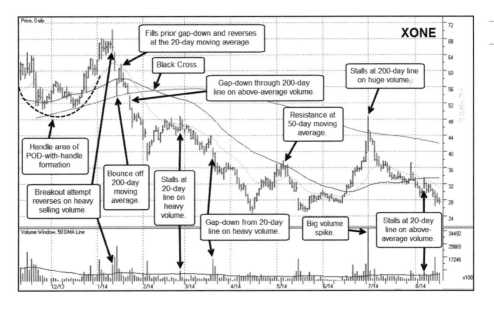

Notes: Exone Company (XONE) was another 3-D printing name that topped in January 2014 with the group. Its early 2014 top was discussed in detail in Chapter 4. Note how all three 3-D printing names shown in these three examples—DDD, SSYS, and XONE—all had big upside bounces at the beginning of July 2014 as a result of rumors at that time that one might be bought by a larger technology company like The International Business Machines Corporation (IBM) or Hewlett-Packard (HPQ). When these rumors proved to be false, the news-related rallies all provided short-sellers with the gift of a fantastic contrarian short-sale entry point!

■ Lumber Liquidators (LL) 2014

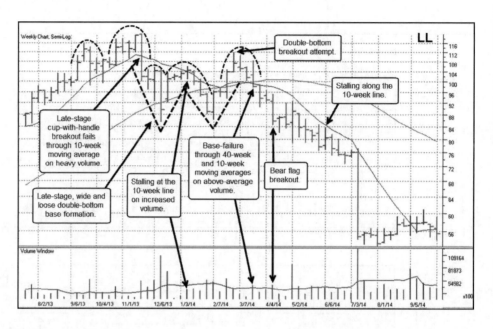

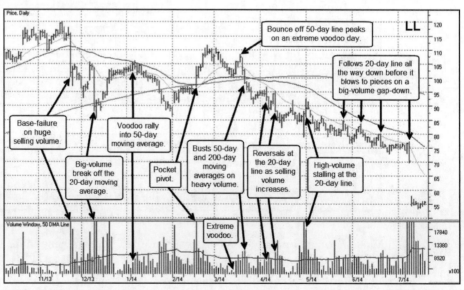

Notes: Lumber Liquidators (LL) and its 2013–2014 top are discussed in detail in Chapter 4.

■ Pandora Media (P) 2014

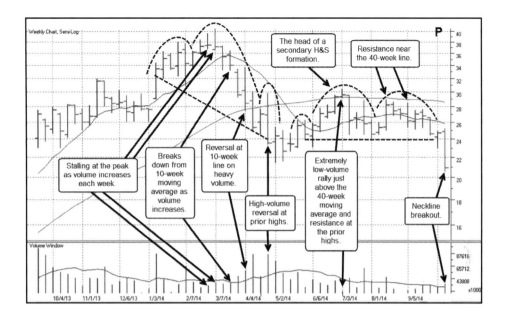

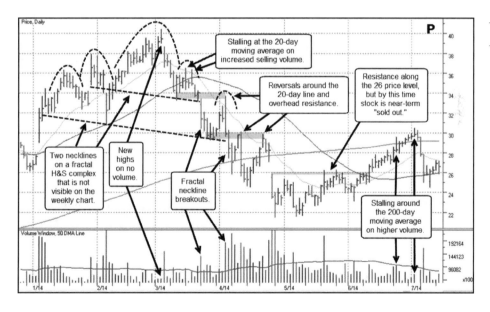

Notes: Pandora Media (P) and its 2014 top are discussed in detail in Chapter 4.

■ Amazon.com (AMZN) 2014

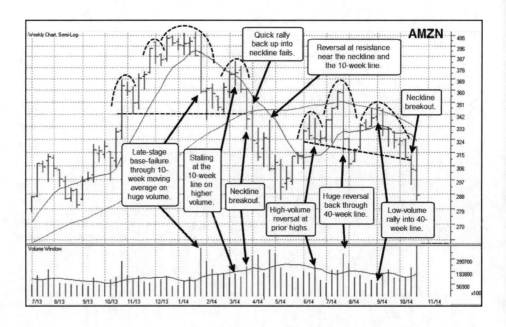

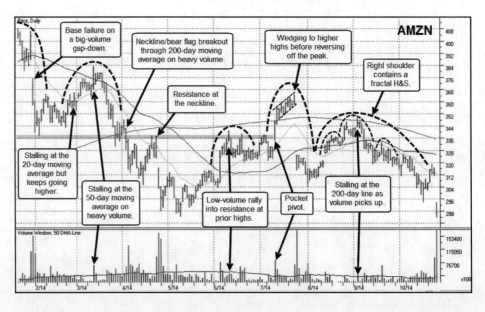

Notes: Big-stock NASDAQ name and juggernaut Internet retailer Amazon.com (AMZN) was making all-time highs in late 2013 before it broke down from a late-stage flat base in late January 2014 at the same time that a short-term general market correction began. While the general market's correction was very short, AMZN broke down hard off the peak on massive-volume gap-down through the

20-day and 50-day moving averages. This breakdown formed the right side of the head in an eventual H&S top. As the stock undercut the lows of a short three-week flag it formed in November 2013, it turned and rallied back up through the 10-week/50-day moving averages, where it began to stall on higher volume. This formed the peak of the right shoulder in the H&S formation and the ensuing decline, which occurred at the same time as a general market correction began in early March and carried down to the H&S neckline and the 200-day moving average on the daily chart. A short bear flag formed along the 200-day line before the stock broke out to the downside and through both the 200-day line and the neckline. A short rally back up into the neckline reversed on a big-volume gap-down that took the stock to lower lows and near the lows of a prior cup-with-handle base AMZN formed back in August–October of 2013. The stock found support at that level and rallied back above the 40-week and 200-day moving averages in a wedging rally that failed on a late-July 2014 gap-down break. This formed the peak of a secondary H&S formation, and the undercut of the June lows set off a rally back up into the 200-day line which failed and sent the stock back to the downside. Note that this rally forms the right shoulder of the secondary H&S while also containing a small, fractal H&S within its structure. Once the stock started to break out through the neckline of this secondary H&S, it rallied once back up into the 20-day moving average before gapping down to lower lows near the 285 price area.

■ Netflix (NFLX) 2014

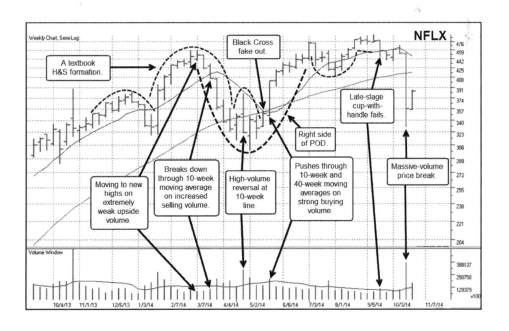

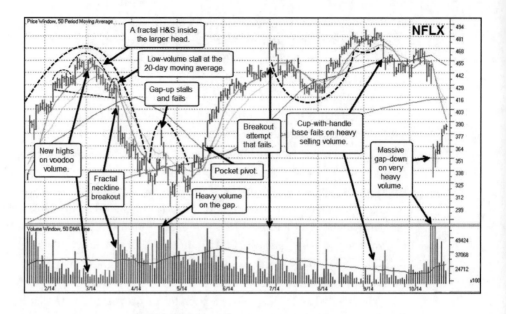

Notes: Netflix (NFLX) has often been a favorite of "valuation" shorts, most of whom shorted the stock into its rallies in 2010–2011 and again in 2013. Of course, NFLX was also a strong short-sale target stock during these periods once it began to show bona fide signs of topping, as we first saw in the example of 2011–2012 shown earlier in this chapter and in the Chapter 6 Case Study. NFLX's top and severe breakdown in 2011 was a very profitable short-sale event, and the stock had another shortable top in early 2014. This was an unusual top, however, in the sense that if one had been operating solely on the basis of what was shown on the weekly chart, one would have been pushed out as the stock rallied up and out of the right shoulder of what looked like a "textbook" H&S top in May 2014. However, using the information available on the daily chart, one could have picked off the stock as it was breaking down through the neckline of a fractal H&S it formed within the head of the larger, so-called textbook H&S formation. This would have led to a very profitable decline. As well, the big-volume stalling gap-up move that formed the peak of the right shoulder in the larger H&S was also a shortable event, and the ensuing breakdown and undercut of the prior lows might have been sufficient to cause one to cover their short position at that time. In late May, NFLX flashed a pocket pivot as it came out of the big right shoulder and moved to new all-time highs by July 2014. At this point the stock tried to break out but pulled right back in to form a 10-week cup-with-handle base from which it failed in mid-September 2014 as a general market correction took hold. Notice that the breakdown off the March peak and the subsequent rally back up to new highs in July formed a big POD topping formation. This started to look shortable, but the stock turned and made another run to new highs. After dropping back below the 50-day moving average in mid-September, it blew wide open in October on a disappointing earnings announcement.

Chris Kacher began his investment career in 1994 at Trust Company of the West where he worked as an analyst to portfolio manager Charles Larsen while launching his first website, the original www.virtueofselfishinvesting.com, in 1994. In 1996, he joined William O'Neil + Company, Inc. as an institutional sales person and in 1997 was promoted to internal portfolio manager where he was responsible for managing a portion of the firm's proprietary, internal assets. While at William O'Neil + Company, Inc. he had regular conversations on his research studies with Bill O'Neil, worked very closely with Gil Morales, and assisted in the institutional services group, where he essentially functioned as a market and stock research analyst responsible for conducting market studies and other proprietary, internal market data research in support of the institutional services and internal portfolio management group. He left William O'Neil + Company, Inc. in 2001 and pursued his own path abroad in the investment and music fields, launching a private fund in Geneva, Switzerland. In 2009 he and Gil Morales, with whom he quite successfully collaborated and worked very closely during his tenure at William O'Neil + Company, Inc., joined forces once again to form MoKa Investors, LLC and launch the stock and market information website known as www.virtueofselfishinvesting.com. Today he is a managing director of MoKa Investors, LLC and its wholly owned subsidiary, Virtue of Selfish Investing, LLC, both based in Playa del Rey, California. In 2010, both he and Gil Morales authored the top-selling book *Trade Like an O'Neil Disciple: How We Made 18,000% in the Stock Market*, and followed that up with another top-selling book, *In the Cockpit with the O'Neil Disciples: Strategies That Made Us 18,000% in the Stock Market*. Dr. Kacher received his B.S. in chemistry and Ph.D. in nuclear sciences from the University of California, Berkeley, in 1995.

Gil Morales began his career in the securities industry in 1991 as a financial consultant (otherwise known as a stockbroker) at Merrill Lynch's Beverly Hills, California office, where he achieved Executive Club status in his first year as a producing broker. In 1994, he was recruited by PaineWebber, Inc., where he moved his business in order to focus on managing O'Neil-style accounts as a senior vice president of investments. Over the next three years at PaineWebber, Inc., he rapidly achieved Chairman's Club status as one of the top producers in the firm on a global basis. In 1997, he was personally recruited by Bill O'Neil himself to join William O'Neil + Company, Inc. as a vice president and manager of the Institutional Services Division, responsible for advising more than 600 of the world's largest and most successful institutional investors, encompassing mutual fund complexes, hedge funds, pensions funds, and banks, among others. Mr. Morales was also recruited to serve as an internal portfolio manager at William O'Neil + Company, Inc., responsible for managing a portion of the firm's proprietary, internal assets. In 2004 he was named chief market strategist at William O'Neil + Company, Inc. and co-authored with Bill O'Neil the book *How to Make Money Selling Stocks Short* (John Wiley & Sons, October 2004). Mr. Morales left William O'Neil + Company, Inc. in November 2005 in order to pursue his own path; in 2007 he founded Gil Morales & Company, LLC, and he launched the investment advisory website www.GilmoReport.com in March 2008. In 2009, he and Chris Kacher, with whom he quite successfully collaborated and worked very closely during his tenure at William O'Neil + Company, Inc., joined forces once again to form MoKa Investors, LLC and launch the highly successful stock and market information website known as www.virtueofselfishinvesting.com. Today, he is a managing director of MoKa Investors, LLC and its wholly owned subsidiary, Virtue of Selfish Investing, LLC, both based in Playa del Rey, California. In 2010, both he and Dr. Kacher authored the top-selling book, *Trade Like an O'Neil Disciple: How We Made 18,000% in the Stock Market*, and followed that up with another top-selling book, *In the Cockpit with the O'Neil Disciples: Strategies That Made Us 18,000% in the Stock Market* in 2012. Mr. Morales received his B.A. degree in economics from Stanford University in 1981.

Washington Mutual, FDIC seizure, 25

Wave, term (usage), 22–23

Wedging rally, 76, 174
    action, occurrence, 77
    Pandora, 86

William O'Neil + Co., 31, 35

Workday (WDAY)
    daily chart (2014), 119f
    leading stock, 118

X

XLF. *See* Financial Select Sector SPDR

Y

Yelp (YELP)
    daily chart (2014), 119f
    leading stock, 118
    runs, 285

Youko Tuduo (YOKU)
    ascending fractal neckline, 266
    charts (2011), 265f
    50-day moving average, breakdown, 266

Z

Zippy formations, 59

Printed and bound by CPI Group (UK) Ltd, Croydon, CR0 4YY

17/04/2025

14658911-0001